- Can't analyze Christ hist

The *Doctrine* *of Jesus Christ*

By

Thomas F. Torrance

Wipf and Stock Publishers
199 West 8th Avenue, Eugene OR 97401

The Doctrine of Jesus Christ
By T. F. Torrance
Copyright 2002 by T. F. Torrance

ISBN: 1-57910-728-1

Publication Date: October, 2002

Wipf and Stock Publishers
199 West 8th Avenue, Suite 3
Eugene OR 97401

Preface

In the summer of 1939 I returned to Edinburgh from Switzerland where I had been studying at the University of Basel under the teaching of Karl Barth. There I had begun to write a doctoral dissertation on the Doctrine of Grace in the Early Patristic thought of the Second Century, and planned to return to Basel in the Autumn. But one day in Edinburgh I was approached by John Baillie who had been asked to find someone to teach Systematic Theology at Auburn Theological Seminary in Upstate New York. He had himself begun his own theological teaching there, and had greatly enjoyed it. The sudden departure of Professor John Bennet had left the Seminary with the urgent task of finding some one to take his place in the Autumn. They appealed to John Baillie, asking him to find someone as soon as possible to take over the task of lecturing on Systematic Theology there. And so John Baillie approached me, who with Professors Hugh Mackintosh and Daniel Lamont, had been my teachers in Divinity (the Philosophy of Religion), Christian Apologetics and Christian Dogmatics in the University of Edinburgh. I was looking forward very keenly to returning to Basel to continue work on my doctoral dissertation, and sitting again at the feet of the great Karl Barth. And so I was not at all keen to go to Auburn, New York, but John Baillie pressed me, and told me of his friends in Auburn and the Seminary there. I eventually agreed. But it was very short notice, and I set about getting ready: buying a typewriter, and packing several boxes with a selection of the books which I thought I would need to help me in preparing the lectures.

Eventually I embarked on the Queen Mary, spent the journey thinking and typing furiously, and eventually after four days or so arrived at New York. There I was met by Dr Harry Reed, the Emeritus President of Auburn Theological Seminary and a warm friend of John and Jewel Baillie. He arranged for me to stay that night at the Yale Club in New York, and the next day to take the train to Auburn up the Hudson valley through the beautiful State of New York to Auburn. There I was warmly welcomed, and established in comfortable rooms in the a large Building on the Seminary Campus. Soon afterwards I was introduced to the Weir Stewart family, who as their name suggests were of Scottish descent, with whom I soon became warm friends. Their home in Auburn became for me a home from home.

I quickly settled down to work, planning lectures in Systematic Theology. I found that I was the only one teaching Systematic Theology, Biblical Theology, the Philosophy of Religion and Christian Dogmatics, and so the courses I planned had to cover the whole field. In addition to Christian Dogmatics to which I gave most attention, I prepared lectures on Biblical Theology (Old Testament and New Testament), philosophy and theology, science and theology, theology and psychology, theology and art, theology and education, theology and action. It was very hard work, though I enjoyed it, and learned a great deal from it, and made good use of the Seminary Library. I was hard pressed to get the lectures ready day by day. It was often very late in the night or in the early hours of the next morning while it was still dark, that I managed to get the lectures prepared. Fortunately there was an all-night coffee stall run by an emigre Italian family just outside the Seminary

Campus which was a godsend to me, as their coffee helped me to keep awake and finish the lecture or lectures for the following day. My study was equipped with a very serviceable radio which I used in tuning into the regular broadcasts by the New Friends of Music from Boston, which were devoted almost exclusively to works by Bach, Haydn and Mozart, just what I loved. My most helpful friend in the Seminary was Harry Mason the Episcopalian Professor of Music.

I tried to get some sleep in the afternoons, and of course at the week-ends! As I now read over those lectures, hastily typed out, I realise how rough and unpolished they were, but, I hope, they served their purpose. And I enjoyed it immensely, for not only was my mind working at top gear, so to speak, but I was learning at the same time from fresh reading, the reactions of students, not least from discussion with them in class, and also from frank interchange with some of the abler students in my rooms afterwards. They helped me to find ways of thinking out and communicating to them what I intended.

When several years ago Professor Alister E. McGrath of Oxford, scientist, scholar and theologian, read the typescripts of my Auburn Lectures, he urged me to publish them, at least "the theology lectures", he said. I had not been intending to do so, but after he urged me several times to consider it, I dug them out and looked at them again to see what might be helpful to others, and eventually did agree. They had been put together in a hurry when I was twenty-five years of age and were rather rough-hewn and jejune. They were written at Auburn, New York in 1938/39, where Auburn Theological Seminary, as I was to learn, was a very modernist Presbyterian Seminary, notorious for the "Auburn Affirmation" it had promulgated 1927, intended as a bulwark against what Americans had called "Fundamentalism", a rather rationalist form of conservative Evangelicalism. It was in New York State, however, that Jonathan Edwards used to live before going to Princeton. In Edinburgh Professor Norman Kemp Smith (the renowned authority on Immanuel Kant, and the translator of his great *Critique of Pure Reason,* who published along with it *A Commentary to Kant's Critique of Pure Reason),* used to tell us that Jonathan Edwards was the greatest thinker the United States had produced. It was to his chair in Princeton that Professor Norman Kemp Smith had been appointed before coming to Edinburgh. When I was in Auburn I studied the two great volumes of Jonathan Edwards' *Collected Works,* and used to persuade my students there to read them as well. He became a Professor of philosophy in Princeton where in due course Norman Kemp Smith was to occupy his Chair before returning to Edinburgh.

Here, then, are my lectures on Christology and Soteriology. I notice that the typescript pages of the lectures were divided into "chapters". Evidently I had once thought of preparing them for publication, but never got round to doing that. In my early list of those chapters, I find that one was intended to be specifically on "The Atonement", but I seem to have dropped that idea as atoning significance of the death of Christ had been discussed in three other lectures. Unfortunately, however, only several pages of the chapter on "The Resurrection of Christ" have survived. But perhaps readers might like to read my book "Space, Time and Resurrection" (1976) written as a sequel to "Space, Time and Incarnation" (1968).   The Auburn lectures reproduced here are more or less as they were delivered, but I have tidied them up here and there, and sometimes a little rewriting had to be done. I have usually translated the Greek and Latin citations, and the German from Karl Barth's *Kirchliche Dogmatik,* I.2, which I had brought with me to Auburn and which proved a great help to me. Perhaps I may remind readers that the text of these lectures was prepared before the rise of feminism and the change demanded in the use of traditional linguistic terms like "men, "man" etc.   When I have used the word "man", "men", for example, I have used it as in the Bible, without a any intention of excluding or being derogatory of the feminine sex.

This book is dedicated to my dear friends,
Eileen and Sam Moffett in Princeton.

Thomas F. Torrance,
Edinburgh, April, 2001

THE DOCTRINE OF JESUS CHRIST

Auburn Lectures

1938-39

Contents

Contents (cont'd)

CHAPTER 1

Introduction

It is my conviction that the Person of Christ has too often been studied without close attention to his work. Cf. H. R. Mackintosh: "In point of fact it is at the Cross that the full meaning of `God in Christ' has broken on the human mind."

In any discussion of Christian Doctrines I believe that central place must be given to the doctrine of the Person and Work of Jesus Christ who has been regarded throughout the history of the Church as the supplying the actual ground for believing knowledge. That is clearly evident when one examines the doctrine of revelation and the doctrine of God which are possible only because of the Incarnation of God in Jesus of Nazareth. Moreover it is clear that the doctrine of the Holy Spirit is not at all independent of the doctrines of the Person and the Work of Jesus Christ, for the sending of the Holy Spirit was held back until the completion of Jesus' incarnate ministry in teaching and training his disciple, in Judaea and Galilee, and his saving work had been fulfilled at the Cross and the Resurrection. And of course that applies above all to the doctrine of God as the Father of Jesus Christ his Only begotten Son. As the Lord Jesus himself said: "All things have been delivered to me by my Father; and no one knows the Son except the Father, and no one knows the Father except the Son and anyone to whom the Son chooses to reveal him." That verse together with its Synoptic parallel in Luke, Professor Mackintosh used to tell us in Edinburgh was the most important in the New Testament for our knowledge of God. It is upon the Person of the Lord Jesus Christ that the whole of Christian faith and life is grounded. That is very evident when we turn our attention more exclusively to the second Person of the Holy Trinity, as being himself the immediate Object of believing knowledge and worship, and himself the essential factor or element in the world of faith. Christ is himself the content of the Christian Faith, not simply its Author and Founder; nor is he simply the Mediator of a new day or a new relation to God. He is *himself* very God of very God, the belief which forms the *centrum* of the whole of Christian faith, life, and practice.

Thus it is our duty in any discussion in Christian Dogmatics to fix carefully the place which the Person and Work of Jesus Christ occupy for the Christian Faith. The *Westminster Confession* (of great historical importance for Scottish and American Presbyterian Churches) states :

"It pleased God in his eternal purpose, to choose and ordain the Lord Jesus, his only begotten Son, to be the Mediator between God and man; the Prophet, Priest, and King; the Head and Saviour of his Church; the heir of all things; and Judge of the World: unto whom he did from all Eternity give a people to be his seed, and to be by him in time redeemed, called, justified, sanctified, and glorified. The

Son of God, the second Person in the Trinity, being very and eternal God, of the one substance, and equal with the Father, did, when the fullness of time was come, take upon him man's nature, with all the essential properties and common infirmities thereof, yet without sin; being conceived by the power of the Holy Ghost, in the Womb of the Virgin Mary, of her substance. So that the two whole, perfect, and distinct natures, the Godhead and the Manhood, were inseparably joined together in one Person, without conversion, composition, or confusion. Which Person is very God and very Man, yet one Christ, the only Mediator between God and man."

In approaching this area in Christian Dogmatics, however, we should not treat it in isolation from the rest of Christian belief. We are not here concerned to establish *de novo* the Christian approach to the Christ, but inside the Church Confession, we are concerned to state clearly and systematically the sum and substance of the Church's faith, in its relations to the other sections of its confession. Just as in careful discussion of other doctrines, we presuppose discussion of the Person and Work of Christ, so here we shall presuppose the discussion of the doctrines of God and the sin and fall of men from the grace of God. No part of Christian dogmatics can be discussed adequately or with intelligent understanding without adequate reference to the whole - that is particularly the case with this central doctrine. The doctrine of Christ which presupposes a doctrine of God, which it produces, and may be understood properly only in relation to the background of sinful humanity in need of redemption, the human state of affairs which, however, we see for the first time with clarity in the doctrine of Christ and the Redemption he came to bring mankind.

In view of the discussion and historical debate on this section of the Christian faith, particularly in more modern times, several preliminary affirmations seem called for before the way is cleared in which we may address ourselves to our task.

A. The relation of the Gospel to history

One of the first things to strike any intelligent student of Christology is the connection which it has to time and history. The central object of the Christian Faith is to be found in a *Person* who was without doubt historical; and it was his life and work carried out under Pontius Pilate that has been the pivot of the world ever since. It must be quite as evident to the serious student that this connection with time and history is absolutely vital to the Christian Faith and to the Christian Church which take their rise from that definite historical source. And yet it is just this that provides such a stumbling-block to the faith of many. How can redemption and revelation concerned with the eternal verities of God have to do with the relative world of history and contingency? The difficulty here has been brought to the surface by Hegel's philosophy of history, but in reality it goes back to the Greek view of things which regarded changing events as mere appearance. On that view the valuable element in Christianity does not lie in any person or work but rather in certain ideas that have come to be in the possession of the human race. It is one of the ruling principles of these thinkers that no fact in the time-series can have absolute value or eternal significance at all. This means of course the ultimate ruling out of the picture the Person of Christ himself. His place, it is claimed, lies in his giving birth to certain ideas which once received are seen to be necessary and eternal truths of reason. Thus the ideas divined by Jesus are the objects of their faith and not the Master himself. It places the truths of Christianity on much the same level as the truths of mathematics or of physics. It doesn't matter much now whether Euclid was a good man or whether he even existed, what does matter is the body of truth that he happened to be instrumental in mediating to the world; but his person is really irrelevant and incidental. Much the same attitude is adopted toward a merely historical approach to Christianity. Strange as this attitude may seem to be it has taken great effect upon the modern theological discussion, and stranger still at a time when the historical sense has been greatly quickened. Thus no age in all history has been so concerned with history as ours has been. The Greeks never had much sense of history, far from a philosophy of history. The inherent Orphism or Pythagoreanism in Greek thought would have ruled out such an idea; that aspect of things comes out strongly in the Platonic emphasis upon the world of forms and ideas, for example, in contradistinction to phenomena and appearance. It rested with nineteenth century thought to suggest that there might be such a thing as a philosophy of history. But even in Hegel and Lessing, the great exponents of this thought, history was in the end reduced to mere appearance, the picture book of the eternal ideas which are of absolute importance. And yet the interest in history and in historical research was quickened, and there have been repercussions in the new critical approach to all things ancient and modern with a time-coefficient attached to them. Thus we have in Christian Theology a renewed emphasis upon the actual history of thought and its development, with critical examination of Christian truths and the documents important to the historic faith. In short we have produced one of the great achievements of modern liberal thought — the so-called "Jesus of history". Here it would appear that history is given its proper place, for the whole approach is historical; the Old Testament prophets are interpreted historically, the New Testament epistles are approached as historical developments of the ideas expressed in the Gospels. The attempt has been to excavate below the accretions and accumulations of the centuries in order to capture the Spirit of the Original Jesus, and to assure people of his authentic message or Gospel. And yet this emphasis, while in many respects rewarding, has in the end meant the negation of the true historical approach to Christianity, for Jesus Christ the Son of God has been held to be made but a historical teacher, very near to God to be sure, but a teacher about God, a mediator of new truth. His importance lies not in himself but in the truths that he taught, and in the ideas of a Loving Heavenly Father and of a New Kingdom of God on earth in which peace and good-will would reign among men. Sincere and evidently earnest as these modern teachers have been, they have not advanced one step beyond Hegel; all that they have succeeded in doing is to retain for a while the historical dress with which historical Christianity had so long been draped. But even that has in modern times been exploited and exposed. It has come to be found that with the giving up of the importance of the old view of the Person of Christ the historical events which gather around the figure of Jesus go as well, and are accounted of no real or final significance; and soon they too fall victims to the critic's knife.

The situation today has been summed up well in the Words of Karl Adam of Tübingen: "We must either give our consent to the historical existence of the whole Christ, the Christ of the miracles or openly in the face of all historical evidence venture the assertion that the Christ of the Gospels never existed. To escape from the dilemma by differentiating from the Christ of faith and the Jesus of history, that is to say by accepting the historical significance of the Man Christ while denying the supernatural in his works, is in the light of our present knowledge no longer practicable." (*The Son of God*, p. 16) The question at issue is, simply put, thus: Either in Jesus Christ we are confronted by God himself and therefore by One whose Person is himself of the utmost importance, or we have in Jesus Christ a Teacher about God, albeit a religious genius, indeed the greatest genius who has ever lived, and but one whose person nevertheless is only of relative importance and who will succumb like all other persons to oblivion before the importance of timeless and eternal truth.

Against this latter view the Christian Faith must react in the strongest terms. We must assert that it is a pure unwarranted assumption that no fact in the time-series can have absolute or decisive value. The Christian Faith asserts that here in time it is confronted with a fact in the presence of which we become aware of the very presence of God; and it is this truth that is the fundamental and unalterable presupposition of the Christian Faith. The Christian faith is not simply composed of a body of timeless truth which is always in the end simply abstract idea, but we are concerned primarily with a *Person,* with God himself acting in relation in his creatures who live in time and history. Christianity is concerned, yes actually concerned, with God-in-Time, with God-in-Action in relation to men. Apart from that historical act of God with historical people, there is for us no knowledge of God, no living experience of Divine help or redemption. Christianity has to do with men, with men in a purely contingent world. Redemption, then, has to be actualised in history and must be mediated through history. No salvation would be intelligible or even accessible to us which was not thus historically conveyed. All this is true for the study of the Person of Jesus, who could not have become our Saviour except through his human life and experience. However, everything here centres on an actual Incarnation of God — an invasion of God in time bringing and working out a salvation for people not only understandable by them in their own historical and human categories but historically and concretely accessible to them here on earth and in time, in the midst of their own contingent existences and circumstances and sin. Thus it is that the Christian Faith takes its firm stand upon the belief that history is the medium in which God's redemptive purpose or plan is actualised; indeed it is through history that redemption is really mediated — in Jesus Christ, born of the Virgin Mary, who is yet God among men. That in Christ we have God in history is a fundamental dictum of the Christian Faith. If we nowhere have God actually among us, then are we of all creatures most miserable; hence Christian faith will never give up its belief in the Divinity of the historical Jesus Christ.

All this means, however, a new and important emphasis upon history. History is no longer regarded as a picture book in which we have our first and imperfect conceptions of eternal truth childishly portrayed, but history becomes the sphere of *God's* operation and the medium of *divine* Redemption. The important elements in Christianity will not ultimately be a body of ideas and principles but will be rather *the Person of God in Christ.* That Jesus is a Teacher about God, a hero and a perfect example, are thus but the very peripheral matters of the Christian faith if they belong to the Christian faith at all. The fact of overwhelming importance is the *Person* of Christ himself and his work in immediate relation to you and me and our Redemption, and thus to personal communion or fellowship with the Living God. The believer's attitude to Christ the Son of the Living God is thus the central item of the Christian stand and confession — it is to the clarification of this that the task of the theologian is addressed in Christology.

B. The Relation of the Old Testament

It is precisely this fact that God in his self-revelation invades history, that the self-revelation of God to men takes place within our human sphere and time, that we have the great importance of the Old Testament for the interpretation of Christ, and therefore for Christology. Christ cannot be understood without the Old Testament. (See Emil Brunner, *The Word and the World*) By that is not meant that the historian needs the knowledge of Israelite history and literature to be able to explain the life of Jesus — much as those are necessary — but that is rather a separate matter, and hardly concerns us now. The point is that the individual believer or the Church as a whole cannot know Jesus as Saviour, without the knowledge of the Covenant between God and Israel made known in the Old Testament. From its first beginnings the Church has held fast to that conviction by calling Jesus the Christ, the Son of David, the *Messiah* promised to Israel. Christ or Messiah means the personal fulfilment of that to which the whole Old Testament points. It is here that we have in the Old Testament prophets a strong corrective to erroneous views of history in modern times. In the Old Testament, history is not merely contingent, because God himself acts in history and through history, not merely figuratively, in order through it to make known certain truths or ideas among mankind, for the acts of God in history are themselves of primary importance.

It is thus, we learn from the Old Testament revelation, that God makes himself known in historical acts and events. God invades human society in a series of definite acts which bring knowledge of God to mankind. That means that the Old Testament does not present God as an object of abstraction or knowledge of him in terms of necessary truths of reason. God is always a 'historical' Being, that is to say, a Living God who comes into living contact and actual fellowship with his historical people. That is the basic meaning of the covenant. God has come among men and established a bond of communion between them and himself within which his revealing and saving acts take place.

The whole of the Old Testament has a twofold relevance. There is first the relevance, often tacitly assumed, that man is in dire need of Redemption due to sin and evil. That situation we learn came about through the defection of the race from God in the Fall of man, in which man placed himself at enmity to God, in rebellion against his Will and Grace. To meet this situation God instituted a Covenant of Grace with people in which he promised deliverance in a Personal Redemption — to that end the Old Testament is altogether a *preparatio evangelica*. Thus the second and most important relevance of the Old Testament lies in the promise of Redemption. The Old Testament is essentially Messianic; its centre of gravity lies in the future, and with that colour or slant it is to be understood. But at the same time it is this covenant relation of God to mankind initiated and revealed in the Old Testament and promised by God through his interaction with the people of Israel that supplies the categories for the interpretation of the *Christ* or the anointed Messiah. Even should God reveal himself in human form, and even should he send his Son to Redeem men and restore them through reconciliation to the divine fellowship and likeness, we need, in the event of the coming Redeemer, categories with which to interpret and understand him. We need to understand the whole situation into which the Christ had projected himself as Deliverer. That is what we are given in the Old Testament, and thus it was to the Old Testament that the early Christians turned to interpret the Incarnation of God in Jesus Christ. Jesus was the Christ, the anointed Messiah, the Lamb of God, who had come to bear away the sins of the World. In the Old Testament we have the anticipation of the New in the establishing of categories and figures which were to supply the language and the forms of interpretation for the Messiah when he came. No doubt that took a long time of preparation and education in which the Law and the Prophets played a great part. The three main categories or conceptions which are employed in the Old Testament have been called by Reformed theology, the *triplex munus* — the conceptions of *Prophet, Priest*, and *King*. The Prophet represented the Mouth of God, the Word of *Jahweh*; the Priest represented the Mediator who offered up in himself the atonement for the sins of the people on which basis forgiveness and reconciliation alone were possible; while the King represented the Personal rule of God. All these three ought to be combined in one, and were all Messianically conceived in the Old Testament. Their specific gravity lay in the future as well as the full understanding of their import. They were fulfilled in Christ just as they supplied the basic conceptions for the interpretation of Christology for the early Church and still do for us today. However, this Person as such did not lie within the range of the Old Testament history itself, but in the fullness of time, at the end of the *preparatio evangelica*, when the Word became flesh, our High-Priest and Mediator, the Christ-King and Sovereign Ruler in the Kingdom of God. He was himself the Word, himself the Priest and the Atonement, himself the Personal Sovereign, "God in Christ reconciling the world unto himself". This is how the Christian community related itself to the Old Testament, and this is how the Christian Church and her theologians should also understand the Person and work of the Christ of God, if they are not to allow Christology to degenerate into Greek rationalism or mysticism. It is only in relation to the historical people of Israel, in relation to the Old Testament, or the Old Covenant, that the New Testament or New Covenant may be understood - thus in relation to the continuous activity of God in the history of mankind in which he had been preparing a special people and preparing for us a specific revelation of himself which in the saving purpose of God at the same time means our reconciliation to God the Father.

C. The dogmatic approach to Christ

All this means that we do not undertake in Christology a neutral or impartial approach to Christ. That has never been done by true followers of Christ, certainly not he authors of the Gospels. Our approach to Christ can be only from the standpoint of the sinner whose sins have been forgiven, for whom Christ is the Son of God become flesh reconciling the world unto himself. We are not to think of Jesus as the Founder of the Christian religion or merely as its Teacher but of Jesus Christ as himself the full substance and content of the Christian faith. What Karl Adam has called *Jesuanismus*, the approach of Liberal theology to Jesus Christ, has little to do with genuine Christian faith, and stands outside the orbit of the Teaching of Jesus himself. It is now admitted that even in the Synoptic presentation of Christ in the Gospels we do not have a "Jesus of history" who was later interpreted by the Church as the Christ, and turned into a theological dogma. What we have even in the Synoptic Gospels is no merely historical Jesus but a "dogmatic" Christ, that is, *Jesus Christ as seen through the eyes of sinners who have experienced in him the Redeeming presence of God, who believe in him as the God-Man who lives and works among men*. From first to last the Jesus Christ presented in all the Gospels, in the Synoptics as well as in the Fourth Gospel, and all that is written and witnessed to about Jesus the Christ in the New Testament, is based upon the certainty and seen in the light of the fact that Jesus the man who rose from the dead, and is ever present to the believer through the Holy Spirit is the incarnate Son of God. Thus in the Gospels or anywhere in the New Testament we do not have any neutral presentation of Christ but a witness to Christ as God and Saviour. That fact means that it is not simply a historical Jesus Christ that we are concerned with but with *the Christ of faith*. If Christ really confronts us as God and Saviour and brings into our midst the Salvation of God, then that fact determines not only the fundamental attitude of the inquirer in general, but also influences the act of apprehension; that is to say, the act by which you and I apprehend Christ. This point must be thought out carefully. If Jesus Christ is really the Son of God then it must be obvious that quite a different approach must be adopted toward him from that in regard to any other person however exalted. And if, further, Jesus as God confronts me, God the Self-Existing Being, the *I am that I am*, then my apprehension of him will be determined by his Spirit and made real and possible through him; and again if Lord God thus confronting me in Jesus Christ becomes my personal Saviour, then all my thought about him will take its rise from that conviction of his saving activity.

This means first, then, that my approach to Christ may not be that toward an object, even if that object be personal but, and secondly, that in the theological point of view, my Christology will not start from a bare fact as such, but from a *fact-in-meaning*, a *fact-in-interpretation*, yet not a fact in my own interpretation although it must be one that I must appropriate as my own, but a fact in the Light which God himself illuminates and gives me through the Holy Spirit.

All this means a greatly different approach from that which liberal theology has attempted since Ritschl especially. The approach of liberal theology even in its best representative, Wilhelm Herrmann, has been really a historical one. It has attempted to gather from the historical analysis of the material to hand as well as by the reconstructive aid of the imagination a true historical picture of Jesus, and then in the light of that and the impression it makes upon the mind of the observer, a judgement is passed, on the same historical level on the ground of the value-coefficient attached to the personality of the original Jesus, on his Person and Nature. Of course it need hardly be pointed out that a strict approach in that way was bound to end in the result presupposed from the beginning, namely, in the methodical abstraction which such a neutral and impartial approach necessarily involved, the abstraction from the account or presentation of Jesus of all later witnesses and of all supernatural elements which as such are neither visible to the historical eye nor amenable to scientific treatment. It was a foregone conclusion from the start that a Jesus thus stripped of these elements should be interpreted as but a great human figure, a prophet, a teacher and an ideal. Hence the greatest difficulty faced by these more modern theologians and churchmen is to maintain their faith in the deity of Christ in accordance with the Church tradition. The best that could be done was to argue with Ritschl that such a man had for us the value of God, and therefore was divine - with varying degrees of emphasis put on the word "divine", and varying shades of intensity as well. That is quite unsatisfactory.

There can be no question of denying the historical significance and importance of the Life and Person of Jesus Christ, as some modern champions of the *Formgeschichtliche Schule* (Formcritical School) are prone to do. The act of God in his self-revelation takes the form of an historical event, even when regarded from the point of view of the most orthodox Christology. The historical element is absolutely essential and necessary. But the question at issue is whether something regarded purely on the historical level can possibly yield something that is superhistorical or divine: or whether the case to be construed in the opposite way, namely, whether the object of faith, while being historical, must be regarded as a coming down into history from above, rather than as a product of history which would mean nothing else than the evolution of humanity. As a matter of fact the Liberal view when forced out into the open to declare itself in its true colours does represent Christ as the flowering of humanity, the most perfect example in whom the ideals of the eternal verities have been actualised in history. The real question at stake, however, cutting across all such fancies, is the question as to whether the object of Christian faith can be a fact of history?

If the object of faith is merely a fact of history as such, then faith is simply a form of moral perception, or inspection. That leaves faith open to all the assaults of rational criticism; and the validity of faith will then depend on the amount of validity that the human reason can adduce for the particular section of history in question. If there is no or little possibility of historical and scientific proof, then there will be little possibility for faith. Apart from this objection, it must be clear to the genuine believer that the Christian faith does not spring out of historical observation, though of course the basic historical event which the deed of God always takes is necessary. Faith in contradistinction to all ways and procedures of the natural reason working in historical, psychological, or some other science, means *the apprehension of its object in a unique way in accordance with its nature.* Admittedly that apprehension involves the historical picture of Jesus of Nazareth but it does not merely arise out of that. Faith arises from the impact of the Word of God, and faith in Christ arises when that Word in and about Christ evokes a corresponding trust in him. Ordinarily faith does not arise out of the study of history but out of hearing the word proclaimed or preached or out of listening to the Word when reading the Bible — that is, in both cases out of a definite witness borne to the fact of God's revelation in Christ, a witness which becomes at the same time the actual vehicle of power and is the means of producing faith. It is this power which confronts us and arises in us through the historical facts, that creates faith. That power is the Working of the Holy Spirit. It is the Spirit who gives reality and meaning to the historical facts. The facts of the life and death and resurrection of Jesus may and do supply the worldly form which the Word of God takes toward us, but it is the supernatural working of the Creative Spirit who through the mediation of these vehicles that conveys to us the Living Christ and begets faith in us. The plain facts of history as such have no real significance by themselves for faith. The divine meaning of the life of Jesus is not the same as its historical meaning and significance. Historically, the death of Jesus means an act of human heroism and sacrifice. The Divine deed is the Divine purpose accomplished by Christ in and through those actual historical events — the work of salvation. Thus the divine deed is for us the meaning, evangel, message, promise, revelation, interpretation, not the bare or sheer objective matter of historical fact. It is this *divine* character or nature of the historical Jesus that is of religious significance and not the other as such. It is this divine revelation or evangel that comes through the saving acts of the Christ that awakens and constitutes the reality of faith. Thus "A meaning and a message break out from the historical event which are other than its historical meaning and significance. The divine Word is no mere verbal message from outside of or alongside of the historical event; it is the divine meaning, sense, content of the event reaching man's consciousness and eliciting there—from the response of faith. It is the spirit of the dead." (F. W. Camfield, *Revelation and the Holy Spirit*, p.51)

Now when we examine the New Testament and see what it has to say about Christ Jesus our Saviour and Lord we do not find any attempt to give a purely historical picture such as the liberal theologians have tried to find or even to construct. What we do find is the witness of a living faith in Jesus who is always pointed out as Christ the Lord and Saviour. There is never in all the writings of the New Testament any disagreement or even hesitation in the matter of Christology. There is complete agreement on the fact that he is the Christ, the Son of the Living God, the Saviour or Redeemer. Thus this problematic issue we have noted never arose in the primitive Church, for with one accord the purpose, intent or business of all the writers of the New Testament has been to testify in the witness of faith that this Man Jesus whom the Jews took and crucified was the Christ of God. There was no attempt there to describe what Jesus looked like or to portray the figure of Jesus of Nazareth — as far as the Apostles were concerned, those facts in themselves mattered little. What they were concerned with was *the Christ of faith,* Jesus viewed and known in the light of the Resurrection, an anticipation of which three of them had seen on the Mount of Transfiguration. Thus we have in the New Testament inextricably woven together the Jesus of history and the Christ of faith, the Christ set forth under two aspects and with stress sometimes one more on one than the other, but never the one without the other. The Only Jesus we see is the Jesus who died and who rose from the dead. It is this "transcendental" Christ, this glorified Christ who illumines the Jesus of history and casts over him the halo of revelation light. We do not see the Jesus of Nazareth apart from that light anywhere in the whole of the New Testament. The only place where we get such a report about Jesus is in the writings of Tacitus or Josephus or Suetonius, but not in the Bible.

It is only from the actual encounter of people with the risen Jesus Christ that we have him presented to us; and so we do not begin in the New Testament with a historical fact that is later made the basis of a value-judgement, but we begin with a fact *IN* an interpretation, an interpretation given in the Apostolic witness to Christ. In other words we begin right away in the New Testament with a fact which is presented in faith, and which has become a divine *WORD*. Our starting-point is that there is a fact, "a fact *in* an interpretation given in the apostolic witness", the fact of Christ, which is a Word of God to man, the Word of God to man (F.W. Camfield, *op.cit.*, p 268 f.). The Word of God of course takes historical form in Jesus — we cannot be too strong in emphasising that. It takes form in our language and human categories, but it is all that, human language about the historical Jesus permeated with the Evangel, with the Message of divine Salvation. It is of that nature and character, that we find the New Testament writings to be composed.

Corresponding to this aspect or character of the New Testament is the way in which we discern the Nature of Christ. It is not Christ after the flesh that is presented, but though a Christ in the flesh, yet that Christ *after* the Spirit. And it is precisely this Christ *after* the Spirit that is the object of faith for the New Testament believer. The importance of this New Testament distinction lies in the fact that while Christ is in the flesh he cannot be known after the flesh. Thus Brunner writes: "The 'Christ in the flesh', offers a common point of interest both to the chronicler and to the believer. The believer believes in the Christ of whom the chronicler also must have something to report. But the Christ who is set forth by the Chronicler, by the author of a report, or by the historian who is profoundly prepared by all his previous training to understand the great and truly human in history, or by the man who in all reverence watches and listens for the voice of God within history, is the 'Christ after the flesh'. The believer alone sees more than 'the Christ *after* the flesh', in the 'Christ *in* the flesh' ".

What we have in the New Testament is not thus the report of a chronicler or of trained historians but the witness of men of faith who look at the Christ in faith and testify that this Man is the Son of the Living God. Thus to repeat, there is here no disparagement of the actual Jesus Christ of history, far from there being any indifference to historical facts, for the only Jesus Christ who is spoken of is the Jesus Christ who suffered crucifixion in the year of the governorship of Pontius Pilate in Judaea. The important difference is that the believer knows this same Christ in a way that the other does not; the man of faith thus knows Christ as someone quite different, and it is this knowledge which really matters: "Yea", writes St. Paul, "though we have known Christ after the flesh, yet now henceforth know we him no more." (2 Cor. 5:16) This significant knowledge is the knowledge of Christ after the Spirit, the confession of faith in the Power of the Holy Spirit, for no man can say that Jesus is Lord except by the Holy Spirit.

Thus to approach Christ as the Jesus of history, however ably done, can never lead us beyond the ethico-religious, historical personality. It is not the historical personality; it is not the historical or human personality that saves men; there is no principle or power in the human Jesus as such by virtue of which he survived death and passed to a higher abode. The Manhood of Jesus as such is not divine, nor the revelation of God. The human Jesus is never as such the "locale" of revelation in the New Testament. The New Testament is astonishingly indifferent to that aspect of things. The modern conception of a great dynamic personality radiating spiritual vitality and power is not the New Testament emphasis. The modern, or modernist, approach is entirely on a naturalistic level, and is mainly psychological or idealistic. All that it does in the end is to convey an idea; it approaches Jesus in the spirit of an undertaker!

It is often asserted that while it may be granted that this is the believing approach to Christ that we find in the writings of St. Paul and even of St. John, but it is not the approach we find in the Synoptic Gospels! This has long been a bone of exegetical and theological contention, but it cannot be consistently maintained, and it is now admitted even by those who would decline to have the dogmatic Christ that fundamentally there is very little or no difference in the presentation of Jesus as we have it in the Synoptics from that in the Gospel of John or in the Epistles Paul. The Synoptic Gospels are evidently written by men who discerned, like St. John and St. Paul, revelation not in the historical Jesus as such, but in the historical Jesus interpreted in terms drawn from the conception of a transcendent mode of life. (See F.W. Camfield, *op.cit.*, p. 62f.) It might even be said that, far from the interest being biographical, it was apologetic, it was dogmatic. This transcendental mode of existence was the Christ after the Spirit. It was the Spirit who gave the interpretation of the Christ to the Evangelists and Apostles. He was not recognised as divine from the impact or influence of his human personality upon men — such conceptions belong only to the field of modern historico-psychological speculation. It was no natural devotion to Jesus that constituted the faith of his followers. The disciples were not men who had been swept off their feet by the friendship and impact or spell of the man Jesus. They encountered in him the power of God's Spirit, and it was this that enabled them to call him "the Christ", "the Son of the Living God". It was only in surrender to this supernatural working of God in their hearts that such confessions might be made. Thus we do not find men attributing a value to Jesus merely because of his influence upon them; how they came to believe in him as the Christ, the Son of God, was a sheer miracle; they did it because they had received a supernatural endowment of the Holy Spirit. In the power of this endowment they recognised that in Jesus Christ there is God's immediacy among men.

The persistent fact which is conveyed throughout the New Testament is that at last the time of intermediaries between God and man is at an end; man now stands in immediate relation to God in Christ. In Christ God has come as his own Mediator. It is precisely in this light that all the Gospels were written. They are not secular histories, but *Gospels*, that is Christian messages; they constitute the apostolic evangel, the apostolic interpretation of Christ made under the power of the Holy Spirit; and it is assumed that it was the special office of the Apostles to made this witness and give to men this interpretation vouchsafed to them through the Holy Spirit working on the facts of Christ. This is the same case whether we take the Synoptic or the Johannine writings, or Paul's epistles, though the interpretative side is much more pronounced in St. Paul; but even he asserts with emphasis that what he has to offer is the common faith of the whole Church. He but passes on what he had received. But he too was constituted a Special Apostle, though one born out of due time; for he also had been allowed to see the Christ, and the Spirit had given him the Gospel which he preached in common with the other Apostles. Thus what we have in all the New Testament is Jesus Christ presented in the light of the *Mind* of Christ, who now indwells the believer. "Thus in all the attempts of the theologians to formulate a Christology we must remember that one does and may not begin with the historical Jesus as such, and proceed thence to the Apostolic Christ, but contrariwise. We must not seek to show how the Jesus discoverable by historical investigation, psychological insight and religious intuition developed, as it were, into the Christ of Paul or John. Rather do we take the latter for our starting point and from thence seek to interpret the Jesus of history." (F.W. Camfield, *op.cit.,* p. 264) It is only thus that the Jesus of history becomes intelligible; it is only thus that we can understand the proper form and message of the Synoptics and of the whole Apostolic witness in the Christ.

"There was that hidden in Jesus of Nazareth which does not yield its secret to historical or rational inquiry, nor even to that sense of subjective sympathy and kinship with him, which is produced by the historical influence which flows forth from his human life and personality. This secret which does not so yield itself is p recisely that which makes him the revelation of God, the Word of God directed upon those discontinuities of our life where the need for revelation arises. The significance of Christ's life and work is not comprehensible to man on his natural levels, it is in its true nature comprehensible to God alone, and to the men to whom God discloses it through his Holy Spirit. How is it possible for man on his natural levels to see in Christ's death an atonement for sin? What natural, rational connection is there between a man's death and a radical dealing with the world's sin? How also is it possible for a man on such lines to see in the story of the resurrection, which is so vulnerable on the side of historical criticism, and which from the merely historical point of view can never be completely assured, the overcoming of death for the world, and the beginning of a new and eternal mode of existence? How is it possible from the historical episode of Jesus of Nazareth to discern one, who in his own experience and mission gathered up the contradictions and discontinuities of life, death and life, sin and righteousness, chance and choice and made the one side of the antithesis to have the promise and assurance of the other? How, in a word, is it possible for mere natural, rational man to discover in Jesus an actual coming of God into the midst of the contradictions of our life, into the midst of our death, our sin, our human contingency and chance?

"It is no wonder that the historical critic is driven to drive a wedge between the Jesus of history and the Christ of Paul and John and the Christian Church, to declare that the latter is entirely different from the former, and to attribute the latter to the myth-making activity of man's mind? How can he do otherwise from the standpoint of history alone? To the ordinary reason and understanding what can the Christ of revelation be, but a problem and offence? How can he ever become the Christ of *revelation*? To meet the Christ of revelation, one must in some way come to share his risen life, the life in which the discontinuities of our human life are transcended and reconciled, one must know him, that is, after his transcendent mode of existence. But that is not a rational possibility. The possibility lies in God not in anything in us. Only if that movement from God to the world whose sign is Jesus Christ, be involved in a movement from God to the sphere of human consciousness, reason, and understanding, is it possible to see in Christ the revelation of God. There must be a divine movement towards and within the soul of man, answering to the divine movement in human history. In other words revelation demands the Holy Spirit for its receiving and understanding. What takes place outwardly on the plane of history, must take place inwardly within the sphere of consciousness; but take place not in a rational-causal way, as if history as such produced this inward result, it must take place from God. It is for that reason the Holy Spirit becomes in the New Testament the principle of revelation. Christ cannot be known as the revelation of God save in and through the Holy Spirit. And it is in pointing to the Holy Spirit as the principle of revelation that the New Testament witness reaches its crown and climax." (F.W. Camfield, *Revelation and the Holy Spirit*, p. 77 f.)

And now to sum up this chapter: the data for Christology will not be the facts of the historical events as such but the facts witnessed to by those who have seen Christ as the immediate presence of God, the Christ of faith. There is here no disparagement of the facts of history and it is not that there is no revelation in these historical facts; but that these facts do not shine merely in their own light. We must look at them from above and beyond if we are to discover their true significance. On the historical plain there is an inscrutable secret about Jesus; he is an insoluble problem. No, if Christ is to be interpreted, it cannot come from the mere record of him, it must come from the witness of faith to him — and that as a matter of fact is what we have in all the Gospels. But when we stand at the point of view of the witness we stand above the facts as such in the region of the interpretation, and when through the Holy Spirit their interpretation becomes real light and understanding, then the facts of the historical life become full of revelationary meaning and significance. The historical Jesus only can be theologically explained and understood, never just historically or psychologically. What concerns us here is thus the Christ after the Spirit — *the dogmatic Christ.*

Addenda: The Dogmatic Christ

"The Christian religion is theological or nothing. We are but vaguely and partially right in saying that Christ is the Gospel. The Gospel is a certain interpretation of Christ which is given in the New Testament, a mystic interpretation of historic fact. It is the loving, redeeming grace of a holy God in Christ and his salvation alone. Theology, it is true, does not deal with thoughts but with facts. That is the great note of modern theology. But the Christian faith is not an historical fact or figure simply; it is a superhistorical fact living on in the new experience which it creates. The fact on which the Christian theology works is the Christ of faith and not of history only, of inspiration and not of mere record, of experience and not of memory. It is the Christ of the Church's saving, justifying faith." (P.T. Forsyth: *The Person and Place of Jesus Christ,* p. 3 f.)

"Theologically, faith in Christ means that the person of Christ must be interpreted by what that saving action of God in him requires, that Christ's work is the master key to His Person, that His benefits interpret his nature. It means, when theologically put, that Christology is the corollary of Soteriology; for a Christology vanishes with the reduction of faith to a mere religion. It means that the deity of Christ is at the centre of Christian truth for us because it is the postulate of redemption which *is* Christianity, because it alone makes the classic experience possible for thought... The Christian experience is the evangelical experience, the new creation in atoning forgiveness. It is not mere love and admiration of Jesus, however passionate. It is not simply a hearty conviction of the Christian principle. Nor is it a temper of Christian charity. When Paul said he had the mind of Christ he did not mean the temper of Christ; he meant the theology of Christ. And by that he meant not the theology held by the earthly Christ, but that taught him by Christ in heaven. A Reference to 1 Cor. ii.16 will show this at once. "Who hath known (by a gnosis) the mind of the Lord that he may instruct him? But we have (by faith) the mind of Christ. That is, of the Lord, the Spirit." (P.T. Forsyth, *The Person and the Place of Jesus Christ.* p. 6f.)

CHAPTER 2

The Encounter with Christ

In the introduction we considered some general principles about how one is to approach or which one may adopt in Christology. It became evident that we cannot adopt any purely natural or historical approach to Christ, without at the same time eliminating every possibility of regarding him in any other way than as mere man; and that is of course an arbitrary assumption which begs the whole question at issue. If then we are to approach a study of the Person of Christ it can be only with the witness to Christ which we have in the New Testament. There, we discover, that what we have is not just a historical presentation of Jesus, but a faith presentation of a Redeemer. Thus the data with which the theologian is first confronted is a presentation of Christ as Saviour and God, that is a view of Christ that is already dogmatic. It is a presentation of Christ from within the belief in the Resurrection. This means that it is impossible to write an "objective history" of Jesus Christ, because we do not have the materials for it — apart from some four or five references in pagan literature and one in Josephus and another in the Talmud. Thus our business is to examine the New Testament witness to Christ as divine Saviour and as the very presence of God to men. If we do that there are two possible results: 1) Either we will agree with the witness of the Apostolic testimony and come ourselves to confess belief in the Deity of Christ and our Redemption through Christ; or 2) We shall fail to find any such Christ, and thereafter discredit the whole affair. Once again in the potent words of Karl Adam: "We must either give our consent to the historical existence of the whole Christ, the Christ of the miracles, or openly in the face of all the historical evidence venture the assertion that the Christ of the Gospels never existed."

Our task therefore is to examine the New Testament witness to Christ as Lord and as Saviour, and indeed as the very presence of God to men. We may formulate the difference in another way: that is the difference between the historical picture of Jesus as reconstructed out of the Gospels, and the witness of the Apostles and the Church who follow in the wake and faith of their witness. It is the difference between that which can be known of Jesus Christ outside and inside the knowledge of the resurrection. (See Emil Brunner, *The Mediator*, p. 407)

What we shall do here in our study of the faith and theology of the Christian Church, is to follow the Apostolic witness, for it is assumed that as members of the Church deriving from these Apostles we too have come within the same bounds precisely because we have found their witness to be true: and because in examining their witness, already dogmatic as to Christ, we too have encountered the same Christ, and have come to know him as our Saviour and Lord. Our task in the study of Christology, then, is to make explicit and clear this faith in Christ and what it entails.

The approach we adopt here is thus based upon the fact that faith has already been engendered in us through a real encounter with the Living Christ. It is not an impartial approach therefore, though it may have been with impartial eyes that we first examined the witness. Our business here is not to preach, not to bear witness, but to examine our confession and set its content in order. To do this, however, we have to think of the way in which this faith arose, in order to make ourselves clear as to what Ritschl called in this connection the "epistemology" of theological thought. As we have already noted and discussed in the introduction we do not make here any historical or natural judgment, and therefore, we can say right away, that we are not concerned with any kind of epistemological issue which we have first to clarify for ourselves. Faith in Christ which is the presupposition of Christology arises under the creative and illuminating impact upon us by the Word of God in the Gospels and Epistles of the New Testament. As we read the testimony of the earliest witnesses to Christ, which in divine providence has been given and handed down to us as the divinely inspired vehicle of mediation of that divine Word, we too are constrained to cry with Peter. "Thou art the Christ, the Son of the Living God", and with Thomas, "My Lord and my God." As we read the pages of the New Testament or listen to a modern witness of Christ, a witness based on those pages, we are convicted of our sin before the Holy Presence of the Christ, and cry: "Depart from me, O Lord, for I am a sinful man"; and like the people afflicted in body and soul of whom we read in the Gospel testimony, we too cry : "Thou Son of David have mercy on me"; and like the paralysed man we hear from the lips of Christ the Redeemer, the words of divine absolution: "Son be of good cheer, thy sins are forgiven thee". Then, like the impotent man long bound in sin and disease, we hear the words of divine forgiveness and healing, and casting away the crutches or evidence of our impotence and bondage we walk in new power and new life, and confess that "This man is none other than God himself among men, for who but God can forgive sins and Redeem his people?" In this Man, Jesus, who steps out of the pages of the New Testament, as it were, and encounters us all personally, we find the immediate presence of God. There is here no mere Teacher about another God beyond and behind the dark clouds; there is here no intermediary between man and God; there is here no elder brother travelling the same upward road with the saints of God. *There is no God behind the back of Jesus*, for there is here none other than God himself, and this Man is the Temple of the Living God. In Jesus God has become his own Mediator, the Eternal Word has come among men and we behold his glory full of grace and truth; and to as many of us as believe in him there is given power to become sons of the living God.

This is the way that the Christian Gospel has ever taken and still takes, the way of joyful evangelical faith in Jesus Christ. And it is within this experience and belief that Christology takes its rise. There is here no special "epistemology" for us to worry about, but we may well examine a little more closely the way of people's encounter with Christ when they come to know and believe in him.

Once again we may return to our old dictum that God is known only in and through his own action upon us. This is a fundamental feature of the whole Christian faith: that God is known through his saving action. By this action is meant not his activity in general but a special act in which his Person is identical with his Act; it is an act of his incarnate revelation in which the Lord God comes himself in Jesus to redeem men. And the most important thing in the action is precisely God's own personal presence — his own presence to and action on men and women in redemption. When we come later to discuss the Person of Christ we must bear all that in mind. The important elements have been summed up in a famous sentence of Philip Melanchthon in the first edition of his *Loci,* namely, *Hoc est Christum cognoscere, beneficia ejus cognoscere.* "This is to know Christ, to know his benefits." In other words, knowledge of Christ is essentially knowledge of his saving activity or his mighty work of redemption. It is through the saving and redeeming activity of Christ on and in us that we come to know him and know who he is. In the New Testament Christ encounters us as *Saviour.*

This sentence of Melanchthon has been the centre of a great deal of theological discussion especially in the days of later Lutheranism when Ritschlianism held the field in the camp of theology. The danger here lies in making this a pragmatic approach to Christ, in which man and not Christ holds the immediate focus of attention, where the centre of gravity is not upon Christ himself so much as upon the thinking of the Christian believer or thinker. Thus the statement came to be construed to mean that we come to believe in Christ and come to know him, come to attribute divinity to him so far as he has value for us in our practical lives, so far as he redeems us. From this Albrecht Ritschl built up his epistemology of value-judgments which were the fundamental tools of Ritschlian theology. The judgment made there is essentially an ethico-historical judgment, and becomes little more than a moral pronouncement on the Christ. The root of the mischief lies in the fact that if I make a value-judgement the basis of my belief in Christ, then my judgment hinges ultimately if not entirely on my human situation and its values and categories of thought. It becomes essentially anthropocentric in character. Value judgements we make have as their criterion human-values. Thus to make a value judgement on anything external like the influence of Christ is to have resort to a previous store of human principles and worths or values and so to measure out of these or in this coin, so to speak, the market value of Christ. True Christian faith will have nothing to do with these thirty pieces of silver, for they mean the betrayal of the Son of God in handing him over to self-righteous humanity.

The tendency is here after all to reduce the decision of faith to something like adopting a *Weltanschauung,* and to bring Christianity within a certain philosophical world view or metaphysical outlook. Much as Albrecht Ritschl tried to repudiate metaphysics there is no doubt that he had some real metaphysical presuppositions in his theology derived mostly from a Kantian philosophy. And that is what always happens when we try to make a value judgement out of the immediate decision of faith. It means a rationalising of faith, that is, an understanding of faith in terms of rational categories and values; the issue in question is broken up and related to worldly values already to hand, and judged accordingly. Thus man and his self are set up as the critics of the Christ when one's value-judgment naturally varies with the times and the scale of values one possesses.

Now to say the least this imports a real danger for our understanding of the Christian faith. It is impossible to crush an understanding of Christ and his work, as it were, into some kind of weighing machine, and to value him accordingly. In the first place it presupposes that man is the measure of all things, that he is already in possession of values capable of judging the Christ and estimating the worth of his Person. This is little less than the self-assertion of man and the subordination of Christ, not to the individual man to be sure, but to humanity at large and at its morally best. But what if there are no categories in human experience that may be used in such a value-judgement, what if there are no rubrics under which we may bring Jesus? What sort of estimation are we to pass upon him? That question cannot be entertained here. For it is presupposed that we may be able to pass judgement on the Christ. Thus what happens in the end is what happens in the purely historical approach. There is no provision for a Christ greater than what is man-made; there is no possibility there for people to pass a judgement on a Christ which will take more than mere human valuations to assess. This very approach in a value-judgement means that it is *eo ipso* impossible to see in Christ any more than human values. The whole question is a sheer presumption from the start. It is quite impossible to meet any other than a human Jesus in this way; and that is evidenced by the result which the Ritschlian theology has brought within the Church in the last generation. While there are elements of truth here we must affirm that this approach to Christ cannot be seriously undertaken by the believer who in genuine humility partakes of forgiveness of sins at the Cross. It is inconceivable that the self-assertion of man and humanity involved in the value-judgement theory is compatible with the humility evoked by the presence of Christ in Holy Love; it is further inconceivable that any estimate of his Person could be crushed within the meagre limits of human estimation or valuation. What value may we sinners set upon the Christ issuing out of our own estimation? No, the opposite is the case; it is not any judgement or examination that we make of Christ that gives birth to faith in his Person as Redeemer, but the examination that *he* makes of us. Here we are confronted with a Person who is utterly unique, and who cannot be brought under the rubrics of human estimation. The best of our language used to speak of him falls far, far short of the Christ. It is an insult to call him "good Master", as someone once addressed Christ. If we are to approach Christ in the right light we have to approach him *in his own Light* and in the categories that his person creates for himself in our relations with him. Christ's person is his own self-authentication; he never appealed to external authority, and refused to be brought under the judgement of men, though of course he was ever willing to be confessed by men. He asserted that judgment concerning his person was a supernatural act; for nobody knew the Son except the Father, and only those who shared the Holy Spirit might partake of the same knowledge or revelation.

See here *The Fact of Christ*, by P. Carnegie Simpson, p. 51 f. "We had thought intellectually to examine him; we find he is spiritually examining us. The roles are reversed between us. Not that historical and intellectual questions on our part about Jesus end, but far more pressing and immediate are these moral questions about ourselves that have arisen out of them. All this is found true by many and many an one who simply reads the Gospels. It is a very singular phenomenon. We study Aristotle and are intellectually edified thereby; we study Jesus and are, in the profoundest way, spiritually disturbed. The question — apparently so innocently and morally non-committal — of `What think ye of Christ?' passes into the most morally practical and personal of questions: `What shall I do then with him?' And this presses for an answer." (Note, however, that Simpson was still under the Ritschlian tendency.)

Thus to return to the words of Melanchthon: *Hoc est Christum cognoscere, beneficia ejus cognoscere*, we must assert that the saving acts of Christ cannot be construed in any merely rational way as the theologians of Ritschlian Luthertum tried. The theologians of later Lutheranism reversed the dictum of the Reformer. Whereas they made central the judgement of man on Christ, for Melanchthon what was central and important was the fact that *Christ* acts and addresses us, not what we think of him. In the theology of the Reformation the whole emphasis was on the glory of God. It is not because Christ brings us *beneficia* that he is the Son of God but it is because he reveals God himself to us that we know ourselves to be sheltered and healed in him, and saved by him. The primary object of God, it might well be said, is not salvation but the glory of God, for God as God does not seek an end less than his own Being, else he were not God. But the Glory of God *includes* our salvation, and we must learn always to think of God as at the Centre. In Ritschl's theology man's self-end is placed in the first-rank, and in the last resort Christ is simply the one who guarantees this self-end, much like the God of Kant which he had to postulate in order to ensure that the end of man which he discovered in the human consciousness of a categorical imperative and a desire for happiness, should not be lost.

The right emphasis in the interpretation of Melanchthon's dictum lies in acknowledging that it is Christ himself who speaks to us, and speaks savingly; *he* speaks to us, *he* encounters us in his presence to us and on the Cross, and there we humbly and believingly say "Truly this was the Son of God." That cannot be called a value-judgement, for the judgement is not ours but one generated in us under the impact by the Holy Spirit.

Christ cannot, will not be brought under any human rubric. He speaks, he encounters us as Subject, as our Lord. He saves us, and we know in his Presence that we are before God himself, and break out into confession. "Confession", I say; for there is a world of difference between "confession" and "value-judgement". It is not primarily a matter here of an intellectual decision, but of a moral or spiritual decision, not primarily an act of knowledge but of acknowledgement, not of grasping but of being grasped and apprehended in the power of the Spirit. Our knowledge, or our decision, or our confession is something that is not independently grounded, not our judgement, but what is evoked from us by Christ himself and generated in us by his Spirit - it is an act of humble submission and grateful obedience to him. We are here confronted in Christ with an Authority to whom we only can surrender and give our full allegiance and loyalty. Christian knowledge is primarily a matter of obedience, not of judgement; and obedience in knowledge takes the form simply of acknowledgement. It is thus that we are forced to pit faith over against value-judgement in Christian theology. Faith is not something which *we* may work up, and which we may gain independently at will when we like. Faith is, thus, an act of obedience; it arises only at the point of encounter by the Word; it is engendered in us by the Word and is the correlative of the Word. Thus faith is a gift, it is not of ourselves, as St. Paul puts it. Faith is our surrender to the examination which the Word of God makes of us, and as such is ultimately a supernatural act wrought out in the power of the Spirit.

Thus the central thing in faith, in acknowledgement of the Person of Christ is *Christ's own action*, his encounter with us, he who has come to save us. To know Christ is to be encountered by his saving action, by his presence confronting us in his Word with absolute authority. What the believer does in his believing is to let himself be told by the Word, let himself be determined by the Christ who confronts him in the Word. It is thus through the action of Christ himself that we know him, through Christ's determination of our lives by his Person and saving activity. The believer is what he is as a believer through this determination by Christ. But we must be clear that this determination by Christ in our faith and acknowledgement is not confused with a self-determination of our own. "If a man lets himself be told by the Word of God that he has a Lord, that he is his creature, a lost sinner in receipt of *his* grace, a candidate for eternal redemption and, therefore, a poor stranger in this sphere of time, then this particular content of the experienced Word will forbid him to ascribe to himself, wholly or in part, the possibility of such experience or even to equate dialectically with a possibility proper to himself the divine possibility which is realised in such experience." (Karl Barth, *Church Dogmatics*, I.1, p. 227).

Of course looked at merely humanly or rationally we cannot say anything else than that this man chose Christ as his Saviour, that he decided Christ was divine, and so that people determine themselves in these decisions. Such a view is the view of the onlooker, the view of the observer-attitude, not the view of faith itself, not the view or confession of the man standing within the actual experience of being overwhelmed by Christ in his saving love and acknowledging him in the power of the Holy Spirit. Certainly there is here a human act and a human determination, but the observer attitude or that of the man making a value-judgement (they are the same), but it would be wrong to think that the act of God and the act of man are on the same level; man's self-determination is quite subordinate to the determination by God, it is, I repeat, a matter of joyful acknowledgment and humble obedience. Our very self-determination needs this determination by God in order to be a genuine act of faith and a saving experience of God's Word. "In this relation of utter subordination and need over against determination by God it cannot possibly, as Pelagius wished, co-operate with it, or, as Augustine wished, be secretly identical with it." (Karl Barth, *op.cit. p.* 228)

However, it would be quite misleading to insist that there was no human self-determination is this act of faith in Christ. A man is encountered by the Christ as a sinner; that is, precisely as a man who has taken his own way and is determining his own life. It is as he is completely within this action of determining his own life that he is encountered by Christ or the Word. To this man the Word of God comes as a summons, and the hearing which he gives it is the right hearing of obedience or the wrong hearing of disobedience. As the man gives to the Gospel message the right hearing, the Word itself determines it in obedience, and as the man gives the wrong hearing the same Word determines it in his or her disobedience. But at the same time it is the man's hearing that is his action, decision, self-determination. The relation between these two cannot be solved from the side of rational observation or psychological analysis; for regarded in this way, it would be determinism or paradox. There takes place, however, what Karl Barth helpfully spoke of as an "overlapping determination which befalls his self-determination. But that makes no difference to the fact that his hearing is self-determination, action and decision". (Op.cit.,p.229). "Our very self-determination is here subordinate to determination by God, and, our self-determination requires this determination by God in order to be experience of his Word. Were it not precisely human self-determination that is here indicated as, so to speak, the raw material, the subordinate factor, the thing in need, when we speak of the determination of human existence by the Word of God, how then would we speak of the determination by the Word of God? If the Word of God is not spoken to beasts, plants, or stones, but to men, and if determination by the Word of God is really determination of human existence, of what else then should it consist save in this, that the self-determination by God and Above what is absolutely superior to it, that as self-determination and without in the least being infringed upon or destroyed as such, it is given a direction, is put under a judgement, has a character stamped upon it, in short, is determined exactly as a self-determining being is determined by a word, and as man in this case is determined by the Word of God. The fact that this befalls it and the nature of what thereby befalls it are not the work of man's self-determination. But conversely it is the work of man's self-determination which this befalls, to determine what may therewith befall it." (*op. cit.* p. 229f) This divine determination means the determination of the whole self-determining man. (p. 233)

To return to the special case, in the examination of the New Testament witness we are encountered by Christ, and through his action upon us we acknowledge that he is the Son of the Living God. This faith is evoked from us, and is not a matter of our independent value-judgement; as such it is not ours, though it is a definite human experience; our action in it is that of a subordinate determination under the determination of Christ our Lord and Saviour who encounters us; he summons us and we obey. He authenticates himself to us as the immediate Presence of God and our faith confesses the truth of it.

The problem here is much the same as that which we discussed in the relation of faith to the know-ability of the Word of God, or the knowability of God. We cannot speak of God being knowable apart from the actual event of his being known. God cannot be known before he is known. Consequently in the event of man's knowing God it is not a possibility contributed by the man himself, by the knower but by God the Object known who gives himself to be known. Thus faith takes its absolute and unconditioned rise in the Word of God, independently of inborn characteristics and possibilities in man. Only in actually hearing the Word of God do we have the possibility of hearing it generated in us, namely, faith. By really apprehending the Word of God man is made fit to apprehend it. The possibility of knowing the word of God is a self-grounded possibility wholly in itself. Man has capacity and possibility for knowing the Word as a reflex of that self-grounded possibility. Thus in the last analysis man's believing is wholly dependent on the Object known, God himself, whose reality and therefore possibility of being known, is grounded in himself alone. Thus when man believes or makes a decision of faith that is one based on and created by the Word, or the object known. Man does not reach faith himself; he passes no value-judgement! The Word has creatively evoked his faith and his decision.

Nevertheless, we must say all that without in the least causing prejudice to the fact that in the event of faith it is *man* himself who believes, not God; it is certainly a decision of man himself. He is not a block of stone or wood, but in his believing he is actually a self-determining man. The point is, however, that in faith and in surrender to the confronting Christ, man must regard his very self in its activity, his own self-determination which is by no means diminished, as itself through grace evoked by and determined by the living Word of God. In his very freedom in the full sense of his freedom as a man, he must regard himself as someone who has also no power of himself or in himself to be, who he is not free to become or to be, who he can be only by being himself! Man acts by believing, but the fact that he believes by acting is due to God's act upholding and undergirding his act of belief. Man is, of course, the subject of faith. As Barth writes "It is not God but man who believes. But the very fact of a man thus being subject in faith is bracketed as the predicate of the subject, God, bracketed exactly as the Creator embraces his creature, the merciful God sinful man, i.e. so that there is no departure from man's being a subject, and this very thing, the *Ego* of man as such, is still only derivable from the *Thou* of the Subject, God." (Karl Barth, *Church Dogmatics* 1.1, p.280f)

Thus the fact that man knows God is an event *in* man's freedom, not a product of it, and yet not the result of an intuition, of a value-judgement. Recall the incident of Peter sinking in the waves, but walking on the water under the power of Christ; and that of Christ knocking at the door, which man must open, but in which event even that fact is *quoad actum* and *quoad potentiam* the work of Christ who stands alone. This faith-act of ours which is a real human act is an act of humble obedience in decision and surrender. But even in an act of disobedience there is acknowledgement, a disavowal not of Authority as such, but a disavowal of the rule of that Authority over the sinner. In either case the central act is God's, the determination by the higher power without which and apart from which not only would the whole situation not arise, but there would not be within the situation the possibility for obedience or disobedience. It is through this action, this act of determination by Christ, in which he confronts us in our sinful self-determination, that we acknowledge him, and confess him in the humble obedience and faith. That is the basis of our Christology. *Hoc est Christum cognoscere, beneficia ejus cognoscere.*

Ultimately the knowledge and faith we have in Christ do not arise from any judgement we ourselves pass upon him but from the examination to which we are subjected before the eyes of the Man upon the Cross, he whose eyes are as a flame of fire, and upon whose lips there are the words of pardon that can issue only from God himself. And precisely because this Christ encounters us in our sin, precisely because obedience means a reversal of our disobedience, is the decision we take against our own wills, contrary to own natures which have affected by sin. It is thus that Christ comes to bring a sword; it is thus that his Person throws down the gauntlet of mortal combat, as it were. It is thus that it becomes the most difficult thing in the world to acknowledge the Deity of Christ, his Lordship, and to surrender ourselves to him in humble obedience to *his* summons and determination of our lives. It is most difficult because it involves death, death to ourselves, mental and moral crucifixion. For there is nothing nearer to death in human life that the relationship of absolute surrender that Christ demands from those whom he encounters. It is nothing less than an utter denial of self, and a crucifixion, for we cannot follow him without taking up our cross. The way to the Deity of Christ is through the Cross, and it is so dreadful because it is we who must in humiliation there surrender the sword of self-determination and existence.

We have now reached a stage where we must be clear about a particular point: The encounter by Christ means immediately encounter by God. If in this immediate confrontation with Jesus Christ we do not see that we are immediately confronted with nothing less that the very Person of God the Father Almighty, then we cannot reach belief or faith in Christ otherwise or later. The confession of the Deity of Christ arises out of the immediate confrontation by the Word, by God the Word. It is not reached afterwards by a process of reflection or argument. It is all very well to admit the Fact of Christ to be central in the Christian faith, but we cannot think of the Deity of his Person as a kind of addendum reached or not reached, as the circumstances may be, by later thought. If Christ is not found and acknowledged to be God, very God, in the immediate contact of faith, then there is no other way to believe in and assert his divinity which will be satisfactory. This is evident in much of modern theology which seems only to advance to the belief in the deity of Christ after much reflection, and then states it in such a guarded way and couched in such hesitating words that it appears evident that they have not really seen the Lord of Glory. Now I admit there have been people who have arrived at a belief in the divinity of Christ this way, but it is extremely shaky and dubious, and certainly the reasons they adduce for their faith do not coincide with the way in which their faith arose. Thus while their faith may be recognised, their theology which is a later concern is rather ambiguous, to say the least.

This does not mean that the confession in the Divinity of Christ's Person is not *a posteriori.* That I have asserted all along. We cannot know Christ *a priori*, but only after and only in his action, but in *his* action. Thus to assert that we know the deity of Christ *a posteriori* is not to say that it is an *arrière-pensée!* The Divinity of Christ can be no after-thought for faith but is its immediate asseveration in the holy Presence of the Son of God. After-thoughts as such are bound to degenerate into value-judgements, and thence into doubt and even disbelief.

Faith will not have it that what we meet in Christ is something divine; but that he is the bearer of the divine Word in a unique way, and that therefore we must call him divine. There can be only one denotation to the world "divine", and that is *God himself.* What the Christian believer finds in Christ is not simply a word about the Word, or teaching about God, but is a life and a power that are of God himself. Christ was no prophet, no bearer of the Word; he was the Word himself. All that faith finds in God it finds in Christ, and "he finds God not beyond Christ, but in him." (Carnegie Simpson, *op.cit.* p. 130) "There is no reality in your assertion of the dogma of the divinity of Jesus unless you mean that for you Jesus is that which only God himself can be." (*Ibid*, p.131) The Word of God comes to us in Jesus Christ in such a way, and so personally or immediately, that we know Jesus Christ and God are one, for such a self-revelation of God can be only when the Revealer and the Revealed are one. Nothing short of God himself can so reveal God.

Difficulty, of course, will arrive here when the attempt is made to view this from the point of view of the spectator; that is to say, from the outside. The difficulty will always remain because the outsider's questions can never be answered unless he ceases to be an outsider! If God speaks to me, I hear him only by letting him speak to me and speak to me as God. Revelation means that what is said is truth recognised as being true only by him who permits it to be told to him. It is truth carrying its trustworthiness within itself. It is, as Calvin expresses it, *autopistic.* "Looking at it from the human angle, what manner of faith is the faith that must be propped up by proof? It would be something like a suitor who, on the point of asking the lady of his choice for her heart and hand, were to employ a detective to spy out her character. Faith is the venture by which one trusts the truth of a word, not because one is courageous and tries it out for once, but because one cannot do otherwise under the constraint of the word." (Emil Brunner, *The Theology of Crisis and the Crisis of Theology.* p.38 f.) If Christ is God himself speaking, God himself coming from the beyond to this world, then all we can do is to halt and listen, and receive him. Whatever comes directly from the Beyond must be simply accepted or simply rejected. To argue about it is to presume that it is not from the Beyond of God and thus to signify that we have not heard it as the Word of God (Cf. Daniel Lamont, *Christ and the World of Thought*, p. 153.)

To conclude this chapter, it must be further observed, that faith used in relation to Christ can have only one sense. "Faith is an attitude we can take only to God." (P.T. Forsyth, *The Person and Place of Jesus Christ*, p. 6) God is the only correlate of faith, if we use the words with any conscience. Faith in Christ involves the Godhead of Christ. "Christian faith stands or falls once and for all with the fact that God and God alone is its object. If one rejects the Biblical doctrine that Jesus Christ is God's Son, and indeed God's only Son, and that therefore the whole revelation of God and all reconciliation between God and man is contained in him — and if one then, in spite of that, speaks of "faith" in Jesus Christ, then one believes in an intermediate being, and *then* consequently one is really pursuing metaphysics and has already secretly lapsed from the Christian faith into a polytheism which will forthwith mature into further fruits in the setting up of a special God-Father faith, and a special Creator faith, and in the assertion of special spiritual revelations. The proclamation of this polytheism can most certainly be a brilliant and pleasant affair, and can win continuous and widespread approbation. But real consolation and real instruction, the Gospel of God and the Law and Love of God, will find a small and ever diminishing place in the proclamation. The Church of Jesus Christ as the assembly of lost and rescued sinners will come less and less to be built by this proclamation. How could it be otherwise than that error at a crucial point makes it utterly impotent? It is just here that a circumspect Dogmatics will give warning. It will have to ask the whole Church to consider that the ground out of which it has sprung and out of which it alone is able to live, is the admittedly rigid and uncompromising recognition that no one knows the Son, but the Father, and no one knows the Father, save the Son, and he to whom the Son will reveal Him." (Matt. 11. 27 - Karl Barth, *Credo*, p. 49 f.)

CHAPTER 3

The Gospel Testimony to Christ

The witness of the Gospels is fundamentally the same as the Apostolical witness. We do not have in the Gospels what I have called a dogmatic presentation of Jesus Christ but a narrative that is written from the point of view of faith in the resurrection, from the point of view of those who believed in Christ as the Son of God and who witnessed to him as the Messiah. That is to say, what we have in the Gospels is not the report of historians but the work of Christian believers, preachers and evangelists; the presentation made in them of the Christ is one calculated to confirm their witness by pointing to the person of Jesus Christ himself and the directions which he indicated faith should take while even prior to the passion and resurrection.

There is no doubt about it, the Christian religion begins not with the self-consciousness of Jesus, but with the faith of the disciples. They were the first Christians. Jesus was never regarded as a Christian, and he never conveyed the impression that his followers were simply to tread in his steps; he never asked them to take up a religion which was his. He had no religion, and the religion he founded, if we may say so, was the religion in which he himself was the Object of worship and devotion, the unique Figure of divine manifestation on earth. "The religion of Jesus was the religion in which Jesus was the Subject and not the object." (P. T. Forsyth, *op.cit.* p.59) If in our Christology we start with any other Christ than that, then we start with a Christ that is foreign to our sources and start with one of our imaginations and fanciful constructions; for the Jesus Christ whom we have in our first material is already the Christ who is Lord and Redeemer. That is the same in both the Gospels and the Epistles. We start right away with a presentation of Christ as Lord and Saviour. Certainly there is a difference of emphasis in the two strata of our New Testament literature, the Gospels and the Epistles, but no difference in principle or point of view. In the Epistles we have given us the specific doctrinal content of the Christian faith; here in the Evangelical documents we have the witness of faith in the form of narrative written especially to corroborate the witness in the Apostolic preaching and mission to indicate the more formal rather than the doctrinal substance or material content side of the Christian faith. Here we have the finger pointing to the fact that Jesus Christ came not to show us how to take up a right attitude to God; he came not as an exemplary saint whom we are all to follow, and through him are to obey God the Father. The witness and testimony of the Gospels is a bold one, as bold as that of Jesus himself to whom they point, for it means that Jesus Christ came to point people to himself; he came to reveal himself to them; he came to confront people with his own person and declared that he was sent from God and indeed as the beloved Son of God, and apart from himself there was no way to knowledge of God or to salvation.

What we have in the Synoptic Gospels is essentially and materially the same as what we have in the Fourth Gospel: the interpenetration of the enunciations of faith about Jesus the Christ with the teaching of Jesus Christ himself, and both converge in pointing to Christ as the Supreme Object of the Christian faith.

That was precisely the great point of difference between Judaism and early Christianity. If Jesus had been no more than a prophet then there would have been little, or much less controversy and no persecution of him by the Jews. But just because in the Gospels there was in Jesus Christ the very focus of the manifestation of God, and therefore the supreme object of worship, the Son of God with God the Father, there broke forth from the recalcitrant Jews the fierce denunciation and intolerance of the Priests, Pharisees and Scribes who refused to recognise God in Christ. It is only thus that the religious vehemence of the Jews can be understood in their opposition to the admittedly holy sect of Nazarenes. Against this Man they could point no sin; but that he made himself equal with God, that he declared himself to be the Son of God, and that his followers worshipped him as such, was for the Jews the greatest of blasphemies, and called forth the utmost zeal in persecution. And that, above all, the one whom they claimed to be Messiah and God should be one hung on the tree and cursed was an insurmountable offence against their beliefs. This antagonism to Jesus and Christianity we see very clearly in Saul of Tarsus and the persecution of the new sect associated with the name of Jesus.

It was against such a background that the faith of the early Christians was formulated, and it was to this situation that the Gospels were addressed, addressed to Jews for the most part but likewise also to Gentiles or Jews of the Diaspora. The whole aim of the Evangelists was to bear testimony to Jesus as the Christ, the Son of God. And this we have in the Gospels. There are apologetic elements running throughout the narratives, appeals to the Old Testament witness to Christ particularly which he came to fulfil and not to destroy. Thus in this light we have presented an approach to what I have called the dogmatic Christ, a Christ within the Christian faith as One to whom the believers had taken up a definite relation of absolute obedience and worship. The Gospels were written in order so to present this Christ as Divine Redeemer among men that others might be confronted by him as "the *Lord*", and be brought to share the same faith which he had called forth from the disciples.

In the Gospels then we have in its simplest terms the facts of the Christian faith in regard to the Lord Jesus Christ presented with clear indications as to the way faith should take. It moreover constituted a clear statement of the *paradosis* or tradition of the early Apostolic Church essential for the rise of faith after these facts about Jesus according to the flesh, and his earthly presence, were no longer directly or personally accessible. Thus the whole message of the Evangelists is simply about the life, teaching and proclamation (*kerugma* and *didache*) of Jesus Christ determined by his consciousness of unique Sonship. It is from this point of view that we must therefore examine the Gospel witness; and it is from this point of view that we must approach Christ's teaching which cannot be separated from his Person, and which he never failed to press through his teaching and action upon the decision of the observer and follower. What the Gospels present is the Messianic action of Christ taking its cue from his Person. Everything converges toward that point: and it is that point which lends religious significance to the whole story, a significance which constitutes the evangel of the new faith.

It will be convenient in this chapter to break up our discussion into two parts: A) a discussion of the place which Christ occupies in the faith of the Evangelists and the Apostolic Testimony in general, and B) the corroboration of this by a delineation of the action of Jesus as such in warranting and demanding such a position in relation to faith, an action which already before Pentecost indicated the way that faith must take in regard to his Person and teaching.

A. The Place of Christ as the Divine Object of Faith

It seems quite clear even upon the face of the Gospel narrative that the Christian Gospel *is* the Christ - God with us, Immanuel. That is the Good News announced to the parents of Jesus; a message which contains the message of reconciliation or peace on earth and good-will toward men. These latter words are to be understood in that sense, and not in the sense of a general command to kindliness all round. For the Evangelists, then, the Person of Christ has central place in their thought and faith. Everything they write takes its cue from that thought.

This is in direct opposition to those who talk about "the religion of Jesus" as the essence of Christianity and the message of the evangelists, and who thereby wish to separate the religion of Jesus from the Gospel of Paul. The truth is, the evangelists know no such thing as a religion of Jesus. That expression is a modern invention, and its idea an exotic fetish. The tendency has long been with us, at least in Protestant Churches, to see in the Christian message the tenets of the Fatherhood of God corresponding to a brotherhood of all men based on the infinite value of the soul of each man, the way of love which calls for relations of true neighbourliness to all men, which at the same time is the only true and concrete way of serving and obeying God the Father who made all his dear creatures and would have us love them too. Once again it must be asserted that this is nowhere presented as the Gospel though there are elements therein which characterise the ways of the Kingdom of God. In contradistinction to all this the Gospels call for a devotion directly to Christ himself which, as P.T. Forsyth puts it, "calls for the spikenard of our secrete souls at the cost even of some oblivion to the obvious poor." (*op.cit.* p.39) The Gospel of devotion to the poor in this way is thus the Gospel of Judas (cf. John 12.4f), and not the teaching of Christ or the witness of the evangelists. As far back as we can go we find that Christianity does not consist primarily in devotion to his humanity but in devotion to the Person of Christ himself, to belief and worship of him as the Divine Christ. Every other relationship and *duty* must be given up in face of this supreme duty, devotion to Christ.

Thus Christianity is not presented as faith in God like the faith of Jesus — it is a faith in Christ as true God. That certainly is the evident message of the Gospels. The relation between Jesus and his Father was never thought of as one that we may and are to imitate; he set no standards in that sense. The doctrine of Jesus as the great example and idea, as the Master or Teacher or Rabbi, was never the teaching or practice of the Apostolic or early Church. As a matter of fact it is generally only the unbeliever that is represented as calling Christ Master or Teacher or Rabbi — it is the mark of the Christian believer to leave these behind for his proper name which connoted Deity. The modern revival of these appellations of Jesus puts them thus into very undesirable company, with the Scribes and unbelieving Pharisees, the hypocritical Lawyers and the crafty Herodians!! The evangelists distinctly part company from these outsiders and worship their Christ as *Lord.* They did not presume to thrust themselves into the private relations which he had with the Father. His relation to God was unique, and not one that we can understand, certainly not one that we can imitate. To imitate Christ in that respect would be the height of blasphemy, for it would mean making ourselves equal to God. It was thus that Christ claimed a relationship with God which was in the eyes of the Jews so very intolerable because he made himself out to be the Son of God. Let us beware of being led by modern adventurers into paths of such irreverence, for it either attributes some form of divinity to the actual humanity of all men irrespective of who they are, or it means the denial of the divinity of Christ who comes to be reckoned as the hero-saint who by his perfect life and example leads us into the way of right relations with God the Father.

This is all strangely counter to the obvious witness of the Evangelists who give Christ the absolutely central place in their account of him in the Gospel narratives. It is his *Person* that is important, for that is nothing else than the Gospel or the Kingdom of God among men. This does not mean that for the Evangelists Jesus came between men and God. On the contrary God was in Christ, and his Person meant the immediate confrontation of people by the actual and immediate presence of the Holy God himself. This means that the Deity of Christ is of central significance for these writers and constituted the essence of their Christian faith. Any other Jesus than this must be sought in spite of the Gospels and not through them. We must be aware of digging into the Gospels to reconstruct out of them what we would like to think Christianity to be — for after all that is what constitutes the religion of many today at its best, a mere *imitatio Christi*. "To imitate the religion of Jesus is to cultivate an order of piety absolutely different from the entire tradition of the Christendom created by the Gospel of Christ, a tradition which became most explicit in evangelical Protestantism...And the declaration now that Christianity consists in imitating at a reverent distance the religion of Jesus only shows that we are in the midst of a movement and an apostasy more serious than anything that has occurred in the Church's history since Gnosticism was overcome." (P.T. Forsyth, *op. cit.* p.51 f.)

It is central to the Christian faith that in the Lord Jesus Christ we have someone unique, absolutely unique, and not merely unique by even infinite degree! He was and is what we can never be, or hope even to approximate in the very least in relation to God. In fact Jesus never even associated himself with men on the same level. By this I do not mean to assert any haughty aloofness on his part towards men, nor on the other hand to deny his personal identification with the race of men whom he came to seek and to save, and with whom he identified himself in humble solidarity since the days of his baptism. What I mean will be clear later in the second part of this section, but let it be said just now that Jesus never associated himself with men in their relations to the Father, as though both they and he stood on the same footing before the Holy God. The amazing thing about Jesus of Nazareth as the Evangelists portray him is that he preached one thing and practised another himself, and was not for a moment in so doing guilty of any false exaltation or hypocrisy. This has always been an insuperable problem for the historian who views Jesus as the Founder of a new movement; for he fails to find the inner all-important connection between the self-consciousness of Christ and the Church which so suddenly grew up and resolved itself round his Person. The outside historian is forced to put the rise of the Church with its theology down to the inventive genius of Paul or some such similar cause. But for the Christian's faith there is no problem here, for faith sees the self-consciousness and personal practice of Jesus Christ and the faith and practice he urged on others in two distinct and different categories. Jesus' relations with God the Father were absolutely unique and private and there could be NO comparison between them and those between the disciples and God. It is everywhere the witness of the Gospels that Jesus Christ is the only-begotten Son of God and enjoys a unique relation to the Father which was private to him alone as the divine Messiah. This comes out very clearly in the matter of repentance. Jesus ever preached repentance but never for a moment suggested any aligning of himself with men in that respect. In his own soul there was no state of repentance and absolutely no conviction of sin. "Which of you convinceth me of sin?" He asked. His relation to the Father was perfect, whereas he recognised that ours could be only on the basis of repentance from sin, and consequently he urged on people a different relation to the Father from that which he himself enjoyed. There is a very vital distinction here, and there can be no true Christianity until it is recognised and acknowledged.

It is sheer presumption on our part to assume that ours is the so-called religion of Jesus. P.T. Forsyth asks: "Has there ever been any influential man in the Catholic Church who could say that his type of religion has more in common with that of Christ than with that of Peter, Paul and John?" (*op. cit.* p.52) The type of religion which is repudiated here is the Judaising, moralising, religion that is everywhere countered in the New Testament, for in the end it makes Jesus into a Prophet within the old order and not a Saviour from sin. Jesus' contact with the Father knew no barrier; ours knows the barrier of sin, and there is only one way to the Father and that is through the forgiveness of Christ the Mediator. It is this central place given to the Person of Christ that constitutes the difference between the two points of view. For the Evangelists regard Jesus from the point of view of those whom he came to seek and save the publicans and sinners. Theirs is the view of the sinner who has found in Christ remission of sins and has been transported by his power from death to life. It is upon this act which they see consummated in the resurrection that they base their faith which gives the Person of Christ the central place. Thus "The Gospel of Jesus made the `Religion of Jesus' impossible." (P.T.Forsyth, *op. cit.* p.55) We cannot be sons of God as Jesus was. We may come to our communion with God only through Christ as the Mediator; and the Gospel is thus primarily his Person not his teaching about God, though this latter is included in the former. *We do not believe with Jesus Christ but believe in him* — that is the way the Evangelists looked at it. He is the supreme object of faith. "Deep as the thirst for God lies within the soul, nowhere but in Christ do we have the communion that stills it." (*ibid.*) "To whom shall we go? Thou has the words of Eternal life." "The possession of God is sure for every age and soul only IN Jesus Christ as its living ground, and not merely BY Christ as its historical medium." (P.T. Forsyth, *op. cit.* p. 56)

To sum up: The Evangelists put the Person of Christ in the very place of God himself. Christ is the actual and unique ground of faith and salvation and as such is himself the object of faith, that is, faith in God. The Godhead of the Redeemer is a fundamental conviction. Thus the essence of Christianity is nothing else than Christ Jesus, the historic Redeemer and Lord God dwelling among men. The faith of the early Church in Jesus Christ is a faith co-centric with faith in God. Christ is absolutely central — his very centrality is the meaning of the Christian faith.

B. The corroboration of the centrality of Christ

This was already indicated by the action of Jesus Christ himself prior to the Passion and Resurrection. It must be emphasisedhere that we are still working within the witness and approach of faith. We are not examining the self-consciousness of Jesus impartially in order then to see if his claims for himself are consistent with his life and then perhaps accord him place in our faith as Lord and God. The point of view of the Evangelists is one in which they are already convinced that Christ is Divine. They point out indications in the action and consciousness of Jesus in regard to himself which can and may be seen only by the eye of faith. There is no attempt at any kind of apologetic here, but rather a review of the life of Christ reached after faith in his Divinity has fully dawned upon the Church, a review which goes back to indications which Jesus himself gave as to the way faith should take in regard to his Person with the descent of the Holy Spirit. It indicates that Jesus did not reveal himself openly but rather kept the significance of his Person a secret, and only allowed it to be revealed to *faith*. Thus the Synoptic Gospels trace the life and teaching of Christ in its significant phases with regard to this action of his which is seen now to be determined by his consciousness of Sonship; and their faith is corroborated by the indications or hints that Jesus gave even before the passion and the coming of the Spirit as to how people should regard his Person. In this regard, then, we review the life and teaching of Jesus Christ, and through it faith discerns his divine self-authentication. That realisation was not properly appreciated by the disciples at first, for the firm revelation of the divine nature of Jesus' Person was held back until, with the coming of the Holy Spirit promised by Jesus, it would become clear to them what he meant by those frequent cryptic words about himself. In this way the teaching Jesus' teaching is understood properly for the first time; that is to say, his teaching falls into line with the place faith accords to his Person, and the elements of his teaching are seen in their true perspective and significance. This is the only way that we too can adopt a Christian approach to the teachings of Jesus. We may not approach them in the way of an eastern Sage who utters words of wisdom, or iterates teaching on God, but in the light of his *Person and work* as faith sees them in the acts of redemption and salvation he brought to sinners through the Cross and Resurrection and in the founding of the church through the promised descent of the Spirit. That way of understanding Christ and his redeeming activity is simply not amenable to rational integration outside faith, and presents an insoluble and permanent problem for all other historical or psychological approaches from the outside.

It is worthwhile noting here a difference in emphasis between John and the other evangelists without going into the problem of the Synoptic-Johannine traditions. The Gospels present everywhere the Jesus of action, in all its aspects, and everywhere those events in word and deed which throw into clear relief his coming as the Messiah-Redeemer from God. Thus the parables point to him, as we shall see, and his teaching is given so far as it indicates the revelation of his Person. This comes out most clearly in the Gospel according to Mark where there is a comparative sparsity of teaching and where the words of Jesus are generally thrown into paradigm form to illustrate some point in the action of Jesus as the Divine Son of Man among men. The other Gospels take up the same point of view with more or less varying emphases: in Matthew the Jewish apologetic element comes out strongly, while in Luke we have combined a historical interest and an attempt to give the Person of Christ its place of centrality especially in the light of the parables he taught in which his own Person always plays central place. In the Fourth Gospel, however, we start out with a clear theological approach, and the Gospel is not written with the object of corroborating faith like the other two, but having settled the matter of his Person as the eternal Word of God dwelling among men, it gives us an account of his life and the inner significances of his Person in immediate relation to the Word which he was and taught — culled largely from the inner relations of Jesus with his believing disciples. Here a definite attempt is made to formulate the teaching of Jesus in respect of its theological interest; not as in the Synoptic Gospels, where the object of the teaching is presented very close to Jesus' presentation of himself before men as the central figure in the Kingdom of God now come among men. This is rather the reversal of the modern point of view, but it is so because it is the point of view of faith and not of the historian which has dominated our thinking too long in this connection. And until that relation can be thoroughly rethought there will not come a solving of the relations between the Fourth Gospel and the so-called Synoptics. However, whatever the motive and the method of presentation in the Synoptics or the Fourth Gospel, the message of both is essentially the same and it is agreed that both represent truly in their own way the mind of Christ. *Hic cadit quaestio*!

The point of importance for us to remember in dealing with this aspect of the Gospel testimony to which we address ourselves is how the whole is interpreted in the light of faith in the coming of the Son of God; the revelation of God himself among men. And the very fact that this is shown later after the Resurrection and Pentecost indicates the approach of the Evangelists was of people to whom the full revelation of the Person of Christ did not come before the passion. It indicates the truth that the Church saw later and that in fact Jesus already taught, namely, that Jesus Christ was present in the form of a servant to seek and save the lost. He did not come to shout out his identity from the roof-tops of Judaea and Galilee, but to carry out a self-affirmation that could not be directly perceived and at the same time by a life on earth to accomplish not only an objective revelation of God but to carry out his work of atonement and Redemption. Think what would have happened if Jesus had authenticated himself to all and sundry as God on earth, to those not in faith as well as to the true disciples! The purpose of his life seems to have been largely to conceal his Divinity until the accomplishment of his work on earth, and not to lay himself open to the rude gaze of unbelievers but to reveal himself to faith, albeit through an actual historical manifestation. Thus the features in the life of Jesus which are historical and human are rather signs and hints which faith alone can interpret. The Word came in human flesh, veiled among men. Jesus Christ was God *incognito* on earth. Men were never intended in Jesus of Nazareth to see God, that is, in any natural or open way, but to believe in him, that is, to see him in faith. Thus our approach to the Gospel testimony must be in this light which faith in him indicates through the Evangelists; and his teaching and the place of his Person are to be understood and interpreted accordingly, that is to say, from the point of view of the whole message of Salvation and Redemption through Christ.

The Gospels present Jesus Christ first as a Preacher of the Kingdom of God, and it was within this framework that his gradual self-revelation and his teaching took place and are therefore to be interpreted by faith. One of the first things that struck the people of those days was the note of authority that attached itself to his teaching. He was certainly no Rabbi, this man; no scribe, for his inherent authority evidenced him as quite in another category. It was moreover an authority that he quite consciously assumed. "But I say unto you." This position was not one accorded to him merely because of the strikingly and startlingly high note and truth of his teaching but was one that characterised his whole Person and activity, and as well his deliberate intention. He was a preacher of a new order, different from the prophets of old, different from the Baptist. It was different in this respect that some put it down to the fact that it was the Baptist but the Baptist risen from the dead: "Therefore mighty works do shew forth themselves in him." With this authority, then, and one of which he was quite conscious, Jesus preached the Kingdom of God. It is the tragedy of much modern thought that its representation of the Kingdom of God has often been such a parody of the reality, and has missed the main point of Jesus' Teaching — simply because, as I have asserted, it approached the question from the wrong angle altogether.

Modern thought has turned the Gospel of the Kingdom into an ethic, whereas in the intention of Christ it meant the very subversion of the traditional ethical approach altogether. I have already indicated this in a previous lecture in regard to the actual position of the believer in relation to obedience in the Kingdom of God. But note here the trend of this subversion of the ethical approach in the idea of the Kingdom of God. What Jesus preached was: Repent! For the Kingdom of heaven is at hand! This had already been the message of the Baptist, who the Evangelists tell us was sent by God to be the harbinger of the new Kingdom itself. Then Jesus came upon the scene and took up the same message and redoubled it in vigour. John the Baptist said: The Kingdom of heaven is at hand. Jesus repeated it, but also said: The Kingdom of heaven is come already. In fact, the Kingdom of God is among you now! We must understand this correctly. The message of the Voice crying in the wilderness was that God was coming, the Kingdom of God was at hand. Therefore repentance was required. There was the utmost urgency characterising John's preaching; and before he was aware of it, there came along the Messiah himself and John pointed to him as such in his witness. There you have the beginning of the Christian faith, in this witness of the Baptist. And immediately thereafter certain disciples of John left the fiery prophet and followed Jesus. The work of John was accomplished. Come and see, said these disciples. Is not this the Christ who should come? They followed Jesus and found him preaching the same message of the coming of the Kingdom; but that developed into the fact that the Kingdom had now arrived. "This day are these words fulfilled in your ears", said Jesus. John said, God is coming! Jesus taught that God had come and was among men! And it is in the light of that truth that the Gospels bear witness to the life and action of Christ.

Now note here the significance of the Kingdom. The Kingdom, as Jesus proclaimed it, is not, most emphatically not, a repromulgation of the old order of things on a new and higher level. Jesus did not come to teach a new way, or a new ethic or the old one in a new dress. Prior to his coming the emphasis had been on the law, on the ethic, on the human task before God. Now it is to misunderstand Jesus' preaching altogether to assert that he came to do the same, that he came to set up a higher code, or a new law; that he came to declare to men how they ought to live before God, and to build up a Christian social order of brotherhood and all the rest of it. The emphasis in his teaching was not on the task of man, but on the work of God. It was not on the ethic, on the law, but on the fact that *God* had come to deal with men; Jesus came to announce the will of God in the Kingdom of heaven; the personal rule and sovereign action of God toward sinners now. It is in this light that we are to understand the Sermon on the Mount. The Sermon on the Mount, in either of its forms, does not represent a new ethic and may not be treated or understood as such, though it does naturally involve a new way of life. The Sermon on the Mount on the very face of it represents an obvious subversion of all ethics. It says that in the presence of God man can have no claims at all. Who shall inherit the Kingdom of God? The poor and meek, the humble and the outcast, the publicans and sinners — all these shall flock into the kingdom before the ethically righteous, the Pharisees and Priests. The whole intelligible scale of ethics is undermined and destroyed in the Kingdom. Wages and rewards are not to count any more, and the man who does his "duty" is an unprofitable servant. In the presence of God, in the Kingdom of God, man can have no claims at all. We must all turn round and become as little children. (See Brunner, *The Mediator*, p. 421 for above; and see also Bultmann, *Jesus and the Word*.)

What is the Kingdom of God, then? It is like the coming of a shepherd who seeks his lost sheep until he finds it. It is like the woman who seeks a lost coin and gets all excited over it; it is like the Father running to welcome home the lost prodigal and spends more joy over him than the other who never ran away or did wrong. This reversal of the ethical standards, this rejoicing over the "ninety-and-nine", over the lost coin, over the prodigal, means that the message is wholly on the mercy of God; on the divine saving action; and at the same time the devaluation of the accepted ethical religion as such. What is the significance of this teaching, what is the meaning and purport of these parables, and the preaching of the Kingdom of God? It is simply that the Kingdom of God has arrived and is now taking place in Jesus Christ's own presence. *God has come in Christ* — that is what he is saying — and in him is seeking the sinners; in him is subverting the moralistic approach; in him is forgiving the publican and justifying the ungodly! This teaching in the Sermon on the Mount, this preaching of the Kingdom as coming and as indeed now come, these parables on the nature of the Kingdom of God — what are they, but commentaries on Christ's own Person and his own coming? His own coming is the coming of the Kingdom; he is the coming King; he is the One who says with authority, "son be of good cheer, your sins be forgiven", "woman your daughter is healed"! Thus the significant thing about Jesus for the Evangelists is not that Jesus preaches the Kingdom of God — for after all, all the prophets did that until John the Baptist — but that Jesus dares to say (albeit generally in a hidden way) that the Kingdom *has* come — and he is not thinking of a national-ethical kingdom as the Jews did, nor of an international-ethical kingdom as modern people do, which is the same mistake as the Jews made, only on a larger scale! Nor is he thinking merely of a realm of inwardness which shall dawn on all hearts, but he is thinking of the transcendent Kingdom of God which breaks into history in his own Person. It is not too much to say that *Jesus Christ is himself the Kingdom of God*. It was of him that the prophets spoke, and this is why now everything hangs on people's attitude to his Person — and therefore why it would be more tolerable for Sodom and Gomorrah than for those who spurned him! His whole message, his teaching and all the signs of the Kingdom, have one import — and that is, *Jesus Christ* himself. Therefore he speaks with authority, and not as the Scribes!

Here let me cite Emil Brunner again: "His whole message is simply his action determined by His consciousness of Sonship, understanding the word in the definite eschatological, transcendent sense. Only from this point of view can we understand his whole behaviour. His message cannot be separated from His Person at any point; by `person' we mean here not the historical personality but the mystery, the divinely authoritative Person. Since He thus proclaims the Will of God, the Kingdom of God, forgiveness, repentance, in so doing He is at the same time proclaiming Himself. His whole message is an act of authority, in the eschatological sense, a Messianic act, a self-authentication of His authority. The view that His language about forgiveness is meaningless, or indeed false, if it be severed from connection with His Person, applies equally to the whole of His work as a teacher.

He is not merely the herald of something which is to come, like all the prophets, but, since He proclaims nothing different from that which the prophets foretold, save with this difference that in Him what is proclaimed is already present, He is herald of Himself as the One in whom the dominion of God, the 'other-worldly' element, the wholly Other, is actually present. Hence He does not point to a greater one who is to come; this is why He does not divert attention from Himself but towards Himself, that is why He does not turn men away from His Person, but binds them precisely to Himself and regards the decision which is made in His presence as one which is made in the presence of God Himself." (*The Mediator*, p. 425 f.)

A question arises again at this point to which we must give closer attention. (See *The Mediator*, p. 542) If this is the intention and the work of Jesus why is it that he does not proclaim himself more explicitly in his self-testimony? Why is it that the explicit witness to his Person is left always to others, to the Baptist, to Peter and then to the others later? This question is not one that we can really answer in any full way, for we cannot pretend to enter into the secret counsel of God and his Christ. But we may at least give certain indications as to reason which we gather *a posteriori* from the fact that the self-revelation of Christ was actually carried out in this way, and then we can go on to look at instances in which this was done through his actions and words.

In the first place, it must be clear that the testimony to Christ and his Person cannot be the same as the historical self-testimony and picture of Jesus. With the descent of the Holy Spirit it became the business of the believer to witness to Christ, to proclaim him, and that precisely in virtue of the indwelling of the Spirit who came not to bring a separate revelation but to reveal what had already taken place in the acts and teaching of Christ Jesus. This is therefore a different task from that of Jesus himself whose mission it was to carry out in the hiddenness of his historical life, the divine work of revelation, and precisely in so doing to reveal himself. The accomplishment of the objective revelation was necessary before the subjective illumination should supervene upon it. As a matter of fact as Jesus accomplishes his purpose we do see *pari passu* with it an increasing tendency to speak about himself, especially towards the close of his earthly life, a tendency which culminates in the institution of the Lord's Supper. His revelation thus kept step with the actual historical circumstances in his life — it was thus strictly historical and did not violate the intention of his true historical humanity. It may be said that any other way would have destroyed the full significance of his humanity which was essential to his self-revelation as much as to his work of Atonement which he was to accomplish on the Cross.

Thus we find Jesus concealing his Messiahship except to those who knew him and even to them his speech was always by way of an indirect communication. There is no other honest construction of the words of Jesus on many occasions than that which indicates that he deliberately meant to hold back his unveiling or self-revelation, at least in part, and conceal himself. Difficult as it may be to see the full significance in this act of his wisdom, as we cannot doubt it to be, it seems evident that the double behaviour, the explicit concealment, and the explicit unveiling of his Person, has to do directly with his position as the Mediator, as the God-Man who as such is both hidden and manifest.

The interpretation we shall have to give here can be only a theological interpretation, that is to say, in the light of the whole significance of Jesus' Person and work. We shall have to recall the fact that the veiling of God is necessary to his very unveiling and only because there is an unveiling and a veiling of God is there also a self-impartation of God. The proclamation by Jesus of his own personal identity from the house-tops would at once have destroyed the veiling and unveiling of God in Christ, destroyed that without which there may be no actual revelation, and therefore any revelation in the true sense would have been precluded. Jesus as such was not God — by that I mean, his human personality as such was not put forward as divine, though it was only through the medium of that human Person that the Divine could be revealed to man. Still that revelation could not be made in such a way that the humanity as such and in itself was given out as or taken to be divine.

We must be careful here, for Jesus was indeed divine. But it does seem that it is along this line, at least in part, that we are to look for a reason for Christ's definite mode of concealment, the veiling/unveiling, of his real Person. We can perhaps approach nearer the problem when we assert that the self-revelation of Christ did not lie in the expression of his humanity. Jesus never discussed himself in that way, nor did he ever indicate that his humanity was something to be expressed. On the contrary, it seems that his revelation of himself took place step by step with his surrender of himself, with his progress towards the Cross. Thus it may even be said that his self-revelation took place as he renounced his humanity in the action of self-sacrifice; it is in his suffering already apparent long before the day of Calvary that we find the Divine breaking through the Human Jesus. And of course the greatest example of this passion experience is the Transfiguration on the Mount when Elijah and Moses appeared to discuss with him the "desease" that he should accomplish at Jerusalem (Luke 9.31), which Jesus had told the three disciples with him, to hush up. In the suffering and passion there already apparent he was transfigured before the disciples — but they were forbidden to tell any one until these things had actually been accomplished. Thus the life of Christ so far as his self-revelation is concerned must be thought of as a continual passion growing, as proceeding *pari passu* with it, in suffering and intensity as he pressed towards the Cross — and all this time, as the writer to the Hebrews puts it, the Captain of our Salvation was being made perfect through Suffering. The whole of his self-revelation is finally brought to a great climax on the Cross which breaks through the darkness into the light of the resurrection and we have revealed in all his glory and majesty the Only begotten Son of God. It is the Cross and the Resurrection that shadow and light up the whole life of Jesus, and his self-concealment and self-manifestation are to be understood in this shadow and light. In this way we can understand the whole historical life of the Lord Jesus as a kind of *kenosis*, a self-emptying, a humiliation, a yielding of itself up in suffering to God. But with that *kenosis*, Camfield points out, there is an ever-increasing *plerosis* through which the fullness of God in Christ breaks forth culminating in the Resurrection Glory.

Now we must be careful again here. There is something else involved in this surrender by Jesus of himself to God which we find in the Life and Passion of our Lord. It was not the surrender of humanity as such merely, but the surrender of a humanity which had identified itself with our sin. "He who knew no sin was made sin for us that we might be made the righteousness of God in him", as St Paul expressed it. The humanity Christ surrendered was in a vicarious sense our humanity, laden with our guilt and sin; and this had to be surrendered if true humanity is to be revealed, the new creation that arises out of the Cross and Resurrection. Let me cite F.W. Camfield here. "In and through the self-emptying of the actual empirical humanity, the true humanity which is after the original creation of God finds continual expression until it rises up revealed and complete in the resurrection. The works of God are manifested all along the line of his earthly life because the works of man as such are renounced. Therefore on the part of the earthly historical Jesus we have on the one hand, a continual dependence upon and subordination to God, a striving and struggling and waiting upon his will, a looking from himself outward to the leading of God, a perpetual activity of prayer, a declaration that God alone is good and that he himself must not be called good; and on the other hand, we have an abiding sense of possessing divine authority, the feeling of a unique relation to God, the consciousness that God's kingdom is present in him and that he exercises the power of that Kingdom. These two attitudes are not contradictory; they are the inevitable expressions of a divine-human life, the inevitable results of that deathward movement in him which in virtue of being such is in its deepest reality a life-ward movement. So we say that Christ was wholly human, and wholly divine. Not wholly divine because wholly human, as if the full expression of humanity is divinity; and not wholly divine in addition to being wholly human, as if a perfect humanity and a perfect divinity stood in him side by side with one another: but wholly divine because in him occurred a deed of God in which the human nature which the divinity had assumed was wholly turned round, negated in its empiric actuality and restored to its divine definition." (*Revelation and the Holy Spirit*, p. 271 f.)

Thus there is here no disparaging of the historical and human Christ nor an emptying him of meaning and significance as such. On the contrary such a self-revelation as some demand from Christ if he were the Son of God would destroy his humanity and so destroy not only his revelation but his redemption in and through which alone can a revelation be made to sinful men. "If Thou be the Son of God, come down from the Cross", that is in effect the words that are hurled in the teeth of Christ today by the demand for another self-revelation than that which he gave. The self-revelation could be so accomplished only as he went towards the Cross in his divine mission of suffering and atonement. Is it too much to say that Jesus as such, as bearing our guilt, as the One, in St Paul's words, "made sin for us", could not give us a revelation of himself, at least no more than an indication until he had ascended to the Father on the Resurrection Morning? That seems to be one very important element we must not overlook here in discussing the self-revelation of Christ. What we have in the Christ before the Cross is the Christ "made sin for us", suffering under the load of our guilt (recall Jesus' identification with us in the prayer, "Our Father, forgive us *our* trespasses"). It is with the self-sacrifice that this all involved, with the surrender and passion of the Lord Jesus culminating in the Cross, that we have the indications of his own Person I have been speaking of. As the vicarious sin-burdened humanity of Christ is surrendered, and surrendered by a divine act in Christ, there comes in the full revelation, fulfilment, or *plerosis* of his divinity. Not by any means, that it was through this passion that Christ became Divine for the first time — certainly not that — but that his Divine glory concealed in his Person and kept concealed until the bearing of the world's sin was accomplished, only now breaks out to view in its fullness and power. (See Phil. 2:9)

This takes us on a further step. It was not flesh and blood that revealed Christ and the true significance of his Person, not even the flesh and blood of Christ himself. What constitutes the revelation is not his personality in the historical and psychological sense or at that level, but the Divine within Christ — *God* in Christ. Thus the revelation of Christ as the Son of God is a matter for the Spirit, for the Spirit of Christ. That revelation came fully at Pentecost, but there were anticipations of it, such as we find in Peter's confession: "Thou are the Christ, the Son of the

Living God!" Such a revelation was on no natural level, and Jesus made it clear that it was not even a matter of his telling. It was only after such light dawned upon the disciples, albeit imperfectly, that Jesus began to speak to them of his Person. The real self-revelation was an activity of the Holy Spirit who dwelt in Christ bodily. Thus the witness to Christ was not primarily the actual word of Christ though it came through his words as part of his historical life; the primary witness to Christ is the Father in heaven through the Spirit. And it is quite evident that Jesus let his manifestation take that course in every case. He explicitly refused to speak about himself in a point-blank way, or to give any open sign of his Person which amounted to the same thing. The manifestation of the Son of God was an act of the Spirit to faith and could not be carried out on any other level or ground. This is the express teaching of Jesus in John's Gospel, for example. There Jesus declares plainly the situation with regard to the manifestation of his Person: "I can of myself do nothing: as I hear, I judge: and my judgement is righteous, because I seek not my own will, but the will of him that sent me." (5.30) "He that speaketh from himself, seeketh his non glory: but he that seeketh the glory of him that sent him, the same is true, and no righteousness is in him." (7.18) "I am come not for myself." (7.28) "If I glorify myself, my glory is nothing." (8.54) "As the Father hath life in himself even so gave he to the Son to have life in himself." (5.26)

Now we must be careful here also. That Christ does not so testify of himself, does not mean that he does not manifest himself. This divine attestation of Christ is not something that is of itself unconnected with the historical Jesus as such, and only comes to view with the crucifixion or submergence of the historical Jesus. Not at all. The whole point is that this divine manifestation or attestation of Christ involves the actual historical Jesus and is made only in and through him and his words — though therefore in a direct/indirect way. The historical Jesus as such and therewith the teaching of Jesus are the media through which the Holy Spirit supervenes in witness to Christ and thus to reveal to us the Father. But apart from Jesus Christ, apart from this worldly form there could be no revelation. Apart from the Christ who in humiliation took upon himself the form of a servant, that is, came among men humbly *incognito*, there could be no revelation to us men. Hence there can be no thought of disparaging the teaching of Jesus Christ as such: though there is necessarily a disparaging of the idea that history as such reveals the Christ. The Teaching of Jesus Christ has its proper place within this revelation of God through Christ, and the teaching will be properly understood only when seen in that light and perspective. That is in fact the way the Evangelists look at it — it is teaching so presented that it breathes the resurrection and is lit up from that side of the Cross. The situation is of the utmost interest, for Jesus does not explicitly state who he is, at least until the end; he only hints it and enlarges on what the disciples have already seen; but at the same time all his teaching and all his actions are calculated to draw attention toward himself. What he did was to confront men with himself; it was the Holy Spirit operating in and through him and that confrontation which bore witness to his Person. At most what Jesus did was to indicate the lines that faith should take in regard to himself. And in the event of faith under the illumination the whole teaching of Jesus is seen to centre on himself; the parables all tell of him and his work in the Kingdom of God; and further, his work is equivalent to the very Word of God. Thus the Evangelists in their presentation make faith in Christ absolutely co-centric with faith in God. They give Jesus the very place that God the Father occupies for faith, and the whole narrative with its miracles and parables and teachings converges toward that specific end —

pointing to Christ as God among men in grace.

The fact that this true revelation and witness to Christ comes indirectly through the Person and words of Christ is something that we must consider in earnest. The facts of his teaching and Person shine in their own light which is the Light of the Spirit; they do not need the explicit testification of Christ himself — and, as we saw, he generally refused to give it. Thus we must see that the counterpart to faith in the Gospels is not simply teaching. "It is, be it observed, not the teaching or doctrine of Jesus that is this, but the fact of what Jesus himself is and means. Faith is not based on the ideas of even the noblest teachers, but on a fact which declares itself to mean the supreme Word. It is not that Jesus has spoken and his words are in the Gospels; it is that God has spoken and his Word is in the history and experience." (Thus Carnegie Simpson, *op. cit.*, p. 121) Not even the words of Jesus are the Word of God to us apart from the witness of the Spirit — no external authority whatsoever can demonstrate faith!

Thus we are to see that the actual Teaching of Jesus belongs, as Brunner says, to the Mystery of his Person. Or, in the words of Barth: "The possibility of faith does not go automatically with the fact that Jesus takes the stage as the revelation of the Father, or as the Person he is, namely, the Son or the Word of God." (*Op. cit.*, p. 514) Certainly the whole teaching of Jesus is saturated with the consciousness of his Sonship and it all directs attention towards his own Person as the Son — but the teaching is for those that "have ears to hear"! Not even an explicit testimony on the part of Christ, as Christ himself said (*vide supra* on John, 8.54), can be as such the revelation or witness to himself. It is here that we are to see the real significance of the method of Jesus in using parables to convey his message. They will be greatly misunderstood if the parables are thought to be dramas of the way in which the Christian ethic works out in actual life. The parables are nothing else than indirect ways which Jesus used to speak about himself and his saving and healing work in the Kingdom of God. Indirect, I say, for he only unravelled them to those about him who really knew who he was. To those who already "have", he "gives"; but "from those who have not, he takes even that which they have"! The teaching of Jesus on this subject is that he presents his mystery of the Kingdom of God purposely in parables. Now mystery is not merely something that was once hidden and is now revealed, but revelation is made in an indirect way. It is the word of God becoming manifest in a hidden way. Hence the mysteries of the Kingdom were given in the form of parables, that is, in stories which were yet not in themselves obviously the reality they were intended to convey. The whole purpose of this indirect teaching is exactly the same as the indirect witness Jesus gives of himself — because it is given only to faith; it is seen by those who accept the word sown in their hearts honestly (Luke 8.15). The Word of God thus confronts men in these parables, but to those who resist it there is not given an initiation into the real mystery; on the contrary, the light that comes to them when the Word confronts them is taken way and the word of grace turns through their own action into criticism. Thus, while they see, they do not see, and while they hear they do not hear, so that they cannot be converted and their sins are not forgiven them. The whole assumption of Jesus is that the unbelief is due to definite resistance against the light. And because that light did actually come there could be no cloak for their sin. Hence it is more tolerable for Sodom and Gomorrah in the day of Judgement than for these people such as in Capernaum and Sidon or Chorazin because they deliberately refused the light when it came to them. The word of Christ is everywhere presented with a moral challenge; it is because it hurts and causes pain, it is because the word brings a sword that men refuse it, and in their refusing of it, the very word which came to them as a word of grace became a word of judgement. There is no doubt about it but that Jesus assumed that this unbelief was a due to disobedience — and surely he is the best judge on the matter who sees right into the heart. It was not his intention, then, that those who refused to accept the word honestly should know the purport of the parables in regard to the Mystery of the Kingdom and in respect of his own Person. He refused to give that which was holy to dogs and to cast his pearls before swine. "Then Herod questioned with Jesus in many words, but he answered him nothing!"

To return then to the point in question, this teaching of Jesus in regard to the method used in the parables means that his teaching is subjected to his own Person, even while the parables are in themselves indirectly speaking of his very Person. The teaching with or without the parables may not be understood except in direct relation to himself and with faith in his Person, so that the relation of faith to the actual teaching of Jesus is parallel to the relation of faith and the witness of the Spirit to the Person of Christ, the former depending on the latter, though the latter is made in and through the former. In the words of Brunner: "As Jesus then (objectively) bears witness to himself, even when he does not speak about himself (historically, in the sense of an actual record), so also his (historical) self-testimony is not the Gospel about Jesus Christ, but the prophetic indirect indication pointing towards his own Word, which he does not pronounce, but which he *is*, which therefore he only 'says' to him who knows who he is." (*Op. cit.* p. 429) "Thus we may finally conclude that even in the most explicit speech of Jesus (that is, of that which could actually be recorded) he concealed himself quite as much as he manifested himself, and that in so doing, through the suggestions contained in his teaching, he expressed the essential meaning of the whole matter which is contained in the Word of God." (*op. cit.* p. 431) Thus Karl Barth wrote: *"His entrance into our world was not violent in character, such that no one could see without believing. There would have been no necessity for any words, for any dialectic further. He chose rather to approach infinitely near, whence he could be seen in faith and believed." (The Word of God and the Word of Man,* p.f.)

This problem being faced, it is quite evident that whether Jesus Christ directly spoke of himself as the Son of God in public or not, it is certainly the case that his whole method of preaching and self-presentation was to draw attention to himself as the One in whom the Kingdom of God was actually being realised — in other words, that he himself was his Gospel: Jesus himself was the Shepherd come in search for the Sheep, the Father in him was welcoming home the lost prodigals; he himself was the heir and the Son, the Saviour and Redeemer of Israel. To this presentation in word and deed we must now turn more explicitly in the Gospel records. But all the time we are to remember what we have just noted, namely, that "The self-revelation of Jesus grows organically out of his teaching. It does not stand by itself as an isolated message in an historical vacuum, but is part and parcel of his Gospel of the Kingdom of God." (Karl Adam, *The Son of God,* p. 158)

What is generally irrelevant in other teachers, the person of the teacher, Jesus makes absolutely central in his message. It does not matter a whit now who or what Pythagoras was, but not so with Christ — for the striking thing to all historians even about Jesus of Nazareth is that he obtruded his own Person always into the field of his teaching, and all was calculated to concentrate attention on himself. In him was to be found the data of Christianity.

Carnegie Simpson puts the matter well: "That, according to the records, the strikingly distinctive thing about the way Jesus taught and trained his followers is that he so persistently and energetically presented himself to them is a thesis that is now almost a common-place in any trustworthy discussion of the subject. It strikes the casual reader of the Gospels; all the more will it do so if he compares with the manner and method of Jesus as a Teacher, the manner and method of Moses or Isaiah or John the Baptist, or if he opens his Plato or Koran. All other great teachers are profoundly conscious that they are but pointing to a realm of truth, and — all the more if they are truly great teachers — they efface themselves before its eternal principles. Alone, absolutely alone, among leaders of the soul, Jesus absorbs the highest principles into his own Personality. To the seeker after eternal life he said, 'Follow Me'; of one who would see the Father, he asked, 'Hast thou not known Me?' No other teacher has ever dared to speak and act like that. Who else said of truth not that he teaches it, but that it is he; of the vision of God, not that he has found it, but that it is in the sight of himself; of that which supplies all man's need of rest, spiritual food, of strength, of pardon, not that he can point to it, but that it is all in him? Not Moses so spake nor the prophets; not Plato nor the Buddha nor Mahomet. But Jesus spoke thus. He did so habitually, deliberately, pronouncedly. There is no doubt about all this, and it differentiates him as a teacher from all other teachers. Others know they are but messengers of truth; but he also is the message. They are but torchbearers; he called himself 'the Light of the world'. They point to truth; he said, 'Come unto Me.' All this is the unique note of Jesus' teaching. In his training of his disciples we see it carried on systematically and step by step so distinctly that an intelligent reader perceives that the conversation at Caesarea Philippi was not incidental, but a carefully planned climax, and therefore its result so gladly welcomed a consummation." (*Op. cit.* p. 15 ff)

At the same time we must note that Jesus' method was never the egoist's way of doing things. He never made his self-assertion cheap and blatant, nor did he hawk it about among men as a salesman his wares. He was ever in the form of a servant, was ever humble and lowly. At the same time this humility cannot be offered as an explanation of his silence or refusal for open avowal, for such open avowal would not have been undue self-exaltation. Jesus was never humble in the sense that we are (or should be), for no humble man would have even dared to say the things that he actually did. His humility is rather to be understood as a humiliation, as we have already seen, a self-emptying or self-humiliation for our salvation. Nevertheless, although not bluntly naive as egoists are, Jesus made it quite clear who *he the Son of Man* was, and made it moreover an irresistible belief in the disciples. He had his own way of carrying out the instillation of these convictions and always refused a point-blank demand to declare himself, or to give a visible demonstration in some sign or miracle. There would be given no other sign than that of prophet Jonah — that is to say the sign of his death and resurrection. That we saw to be in line with his whole life of humiliation and self-renunciation for us within which passion there broke out the glory of his transcendent Person finally culminating in the resurrection. At all events we can heartily agree with the statement of Wilhelm Herrmann in the words: "He knew no more sacred task than to point men to his own Person." (*The Communion of the Christian with God*, p. 76) To the candid and honest reader of the Gospels there can be nothing more patent than that. "Whom say ye that I am?" he asked. "What think ye of Christ?" "I am the Truth", he said. "I am he." "Come unto me." The crux of everything was the attitude of people toward *him*. That attitude was equivalent to attitude toward *God*.

It might now be well to enumerate some of the main points in which the Gospels indicate this attitude of the Christ towards himself in his life and work.

1. It is very evident in the teaching of Jesus that the central point of reference was ever himself. It is quite a mistaken notion that his central message lies in the teaching of the Fatherhood of God — if it was, it was attained only through an immediate relation to the Person of Christ himself first as the Son of the Father. Who else was the Shepherd in search of the lost sheep than the Christ now welcoming publicans and sinners into the Kingdom? Who else was the physician of lost and sick souls than Christ, and who else the Saviour and Messiah than he? Examine the parables and you will find that they are pointed towards Christ's own Person; they are calculated to place himself on the stage: and decision must be taken accordingly, decision directly in relation to his own Person and place in the Work of God. In him has occurred the final act of God in which he had long intended and which he purposed for the salvation of the World. The Householder who has gone into the far country now sends his only son; the heir of the husbandman is sent; the bridegroom comes, and the marriage feast is prepared: in Christ God has come to deal finally with the world and once-for-all with sin and evil. In Christ are the purposes of God in the Old Testament fulfilled. Thus we find Jesus in his teaching consciously aligning himself up with the teachings of the Old Testament and all its prophecies which were loaded toward a future day. Those events are now fulfilled in his Person: and he dares to take to himself the sublime Old Testament passages referring to the Messiah and the Personal act of God as referring to himself. Where and when the Prophets see God at Work — there Jesus sees himself and places his own ego in the very place of God. (cf. Karl Adam, *op.cit.*, p.190) (See Matt. 11.10 f; Luke 7.f;. Mal. 3.1; Matt. 11.5; cf. Is. 35.4 ff, Is. 4011; Ez. 34.11; Matt. 16.16; Jer. 3.14; Ex. 16.8; Mark 2.20 etc.) It is quite evident that in relation to the Old Testament Jesus takes a stand in act and in being where only *Jahweh* stands in the Old Testament: he is even Lord of the Sabbath and of the Law. We never hear from his lips: "Thus saith the Lord", for he is conscious that his words are the words of the Lord. He speaks in his own right, in his own knowledge even in regard to the sacred institutions such as the Temple — and it was because he took this relation to the Temple and made himself out to be the "I am", to be *Jahweh*, both in word and deed, that the Jews took up stones to stone him and eventually crucified him on the charge that he made himself equal with God.

2. This same relation Jesus took in regard to his disciples. As in his teaching he was not one of the labourers in the vineyard that God appointed to be his messenger, nor one of those to whom God had bestowed a talent and who had perfectly fulfilled his obligation, but the Only begotten Son, the Son plucked from the bosom of the Father who had to travel from the far country to come to the vineyard or the householding, so Jesus in relation to his disciples never associated himself with them as one of the hired servants, but as the Lord and Master, as the Heir, as the Only Son of God the Father. His relations are therefore quite unique, and he evinces a union with the Father that is private to him alone. He alone says "My Father" — it is this very consciousness of being an *only*-begotten Son that is the primary fact in his Coming and Presence and his Work. For the disciples God is "Your Father", "Their Father". These words we must take seriously in the context of his consciousness. He presented himself as ever above and in a different category from the prophets of the Old Covenant and the angels in heaven; he was the Messiah; and Jesus explicitly argued that the Messiah was God (Matt. 22.41.) As such he was conscious of not being on the same level with men, with the

disciples, and he refused to allow himself to be so regarded — on the contrary he was to be regarded only as the Unique Son in unique relation to the Father (See Luke 10.f; Matt. 11.f; 13.f.) This comes out very clearly in John's Gospel (John 16.15; 17.2,10,15.f).

Jesus certainly came as a Mediator, but never as an intermediary. That is, as Mediator he was from the side of God not from and on the side of men. His Person was the very presence of God and when he entered the house of Zaccheus, salvation entered that day. The Mediator was himself divine; in him God was his own Mediator coming in direct contact with men, and saving them thereby. This consciousness of his unique relation comes out very strongly in the private scenes of our Lord's life in which he departs to a desert place alone, and always returns in the fullness of Divine power and might. On the Mount of Transfiguration he is transfigured in such a way that he is unmistakably evidenced as God: and when the blundering Peter dares to associate the Christ in the same breath with Moses and Elijah for the three of whom he suggests the building of three tabernacles, the voice of the Father intervenes from heaven and says: "This is my beloved Son, hear him"; and when their eyes are opened the disciples see none save Jesus only. Likewise in the passion scenes Jesus removes himself a stone's throw away from the disciples — his work is one for him alone, one in which the disciples may not share; it is FOR them as for all others.

3. All this is very clear in Jesus' demand for an absolute relation toward himself. That is only something that may be given to God himself. With true insight Kierkegaard formulated the principle: "Relate yourself absolutely to the Absolute, and relatively to the relative." To all other than the absolute we may only relate ourselves relatively. But here in Jesus of Nazareth we are confronted with One who actually dares to demand from men a relation of absoluteness. No other in the whole of history in the Old Testament or New Testament has made such a demand sanely and with such seriousness. Paul in the profound consciousness of his divinely-appointed apostleship may go so far as to ask his converts to walk as they have him for an example, but no other has come to confront men with his own Person as Jesus had, and to demand that they relate themselves to him in a relation of absolute submission or surrender. In this Jesus sets his work absolutely above all of the Old Testament, (cf. Karl Adam again, *op.cit.* p. 187), and claims that in his Person has come the immediate Presence of God such that men must yield up all before it. It was no mere imitation that Jesus demanded from his disciples; there were things in which, as we have just seen, he could not be imitated. What he demanded from men was a relation that men may adopt only toward the Absolute God — a relation of unconditional attachment and even worship — one without any limit. If you like, it was a totalitarian relation. Jesus consciously issued totalitarian demands; he was Lord of life and death, body and soul; everything was to be submitted to his absolute disposal. The words which Jesus used in issuing such totalitarian claims are very strong. "If any man will come after me, let him deny himself and take up his cross and follow me." To be a disciple of Christ means nothing less than absolute self-negation, or self-abdication; it means a relation of death, of self-crucifixion. Anything short of this is not worthy of Christ. The true followers of Jesus must be willing to forsake father and mother, wife and children, property and country and absolutely everything for his sake — without such a complete surrender no one can be his disciple. In other words, Jesus confronts people as the Absolute Lord God; for he demands an absolute relation to him from them in everything. "He who does not take up his cross, and follow me, is not

worthy of me." Any man who demands his rights before Jesus Christ, does not know what it is to be a Christian; be those rights rational or human in any way whatsoever. Blessed are those who shall not be scandalised in me, says Jesus. We believe in God, says Jesus; then we are to believe in him in the same way. He who does not so believe is judged already (John 38.18). When Jesus enunciates as the greatest commandment the love of God with heart and might and soul, absolutely, he says in the same breath: "He that loveth father or mother more than me is not worthy of me; and he that loveth son or daughter more than me, is not worthy of me." (Luke 14.26; Matt. 10.37) These claims of Jesus must be seriously considered. Either he is a megalomaniac like Hitler or any other totalitarian dictator, or he is none other than God himself. If he is God he has a right to make these claims; if he is not, these claims make him out to be anti-God. There is no false alternative here: and Jesus demands from every man an either/or decision in regard to the matter, in regard to the absolute claims of his own Person.

Thus in Jesus' own teaching and action his own Person is the central point of reference in the Universe. His coming brings a subversion of the world; an upturning of all standards, ethical and other. Everything must be decided and done in relation to him — he is the Centre and Sovereign God of the world. What he asks is unconditional attachment to his own Person, and absolute obedience to his will. "For my sake", "in my name", those are key words to the Life and Message of Christ and his Person and Place in the world. Everything is to be subordinated to him — and in this he assumes a right that belongs only to God. Thus we find that in his preaching of the Kingdom, membership in it depends entirely on relation to his Person. It is not kindness or goodness to the poor or to the outcast that earns his approval, but all that done in his name, for his sake. Either men were against him or for him: they that were not against him were for him; they that did not scatter with him scattered against him — both mean the same, precisely because the emphasis is on the Person of Christ himself.

4. This assumption of the very place of the Absolute God comes out clearly in Jesus' assumption of the place in judgement and forgiveness. In the whole region of life Jesus carries himself in a sovereign and final way: he claims that all judgement has been committed to him. He was aware that he was the future Judge of the world — and he held the fate of the world in the balance; he is Lord and God of kingdom-come. It is in this sense that he generally called himself "Son of Man" with the theological-eschatological significance of the One coming on the clouds of heaven to judge the world. (Dan.7:13) "In his Person eternity breaks through into time, the supernatural onto the level of history, the divine into the human. Thus the claim of Jesus to be the Son of Man runs parallel with St. John's phrase: 'The Word was made flesh.' We have in him an epiphany of the right hand of the power of God, an apparition of the divine in the garment of the human. Only this epiphany is seen here in its sociological operation within the framework of Daniel's prophecy of the Kingdom of God, in reference, that is to say, not to the present but to the future, as a manifestation of the kingdom of God descended to earth in the Person of the Son of Man. Hence it is not an epiphany of God's Word simply, but of God's Word of Judgement. In the Son of man the eternal judgement of God and his eternal kingdom have appeared. Therefore he is the judgement of mankind, 'set for the fall, and for the resurrection of many.' (Luke 2.34) He is the stone which the builders rejected and which is become the head of the corner. (Matt. 21.42) People's attitude towards his Person in time is decisive for all eternity. Therefore he can say, 'Everyone that shall confess me before men, I will also confess him before my Father who is in

heaven. But he that shall deny me before men, I will also deny him before my Father who is in heaven' (Matt. 10.f); and `Blessed shall you be when men shall hate you...for the Son of man's sake.'" (Karl Adam)

Closely connected with his self-affirming as Son of Man is the prerogative of Christ to forgive sins. Jesus Christ not only demands absolute relation to himself in faith and trustful surrender, he not only claims to have the final authority of judgement, but he dares to pronounce an unconditional word of forgiveness, which only the Moral Order may do, which only the Lord God himself may do. He does not simply teach forgiveness as a fact or as a truth with God, he *grants* forgiveness as a fact — and his parables of the prodigal, of the lost sheep and coin are but commentaries on his own behaviour — it is of himself that he speaks there, and yet of none other than God. Here his claims reach their very apex — that the Son of man has power on earth to forgive sins. It places Jesus in the very place of God himself. "If it be said that forgiveness for Christ's sake is not in the Gospels but only a direct forgiveness from God, it must be answered that is not so. It is true that forgiveness for the sake of Christ crucified is not expressed in the Gospels; but, apart from all disputes about the meaning of 'Thy sins are forgiven thee', it is not disputable that it is always forgiveness conditioned by faith in Jesus himself, and repentance before his great and condescending personality, whose mighty humility the Cross did but gather up and consummate. It was a forgiveness he knew to be guaranteed by something peculiar to himself. The kingdom, moreover, is promised only to those who attach themselves to his Person. If it is not expressly forgiveness for the Cross's sake, it is forgiveness for Christ's sake. But in the light of after events and experience we see what that meant. We see the whole Christ. It meant for the sake of one who had the cross latent in his very nature, and that not only as his fate but as his consummation (for the cross did not simply befall Christ). It was for the sake of one whose Person never came to its full self, or took full effect, but in the cross — even as he came to earth altogether by a supramundane sacrifice, that in the exercise of a cross assumed before the foundation of the world." (P.T. Forsyth, *op. cit.* p. 107 f.) To this consciousness of having the final and supreme right to forgive we must therefore connect his words about his passion. He emphasised that the Son of Man must suffer (Mk. 8.31; 9.11; Mk. 10.45; Matt.16.21; Lk.9,22; Matt. 20.28; Mk. 10.45 -cf. Is 53.11 f, etc.) Jesus was well aware that he came to bear the sins of the world, and in suffering, to forgive. Here we have the assertion in word and deed by Jesus Christ that "He was and is a personal and eternal pole in Godhead." (P.T. Forsyth. *op.cit.*, p. 109)

5. "In Jesus of Nazareth, then, we have a completely new thing in religious history: We have a Man in whom dwells the Consciousness of God that must have its roots in an ego which was God." (Karl Adam, *op.cit.* p.189) Here we have Eternity entering time, a redemption that is at hand, the coming of the "acceptable year of the Lord." To quote Karl Adam again: "Hence we cannot eliminate from the teaching of Jesus his supernatural, Divine claims without destroying the teaching itself. Whoever overlooks this or denies it has no historical right to warm himself at the glow of the philanthropy and sinlessness of Jesus. All his noble human characteristics derive directly from his superterrestrial nature and destiny. Historically they are only intelligible as radiations and revelations of a man who in the heart of his being and consciousness belongs to humanity but to Deity." (Karl Adam, 182 f.) "It is quite evident in a reading of the Gospels that we have in Christ something absolutely unique which evidences itself as coming from God. He knows that in his person here and now there is spanned the hereafter and the

present, the end of time and the generation in which he is living. (Karl Adam, *op. cit.*, 168) The Kingdom is yet to come in the teaching of Jesus, and it is nevertheless here — precisely because that is nothing else than his own Person. The Kingdom has come, come in the coming of Jesus Christ himself and present with his presence, now manifest to men. And he knows that in his Person, words and acts, the forces of the new Transcendent order are breaking forth upon the world in defeat of the kingdom of evil. The Kingdom of God is among the Jews, Jesus announces; he is standing among them with the whole power of heaven, and the works that he does they are works done by "the finger of God". (Luke 11.20) The Kingdom of God or Heaven is Christ's Kingdom. (Matt. 13.41; 16.28; 20.21; Lk. 23.42; Lk. 22.29 f.) True the outward majesty and ultimate victory of the Kingdom is yet to come, but the whole reality and power of it all has come with his Person — and the consciousness and assertion of that are absolutely fundamental to Christ's message and work. In him now the Divine has come. Consequently a word spoken against him is like a word spoken against the very Spirit of God; rejection of him means rejection of God.

Thus when the Pharisees spoke against the miracles of Jesus and called them sorcery they were resisting the very power of God to his face. They were not just miraculous displays of power, but were natural operations of the very Being and Nature of the Christ who is thus conscious that in him time and eternity meet together. Note the words of magisterial command with which Jesus works his miracles. "I say unto these, arise"; "I will, be thou clean." etc. Here we have Omnipotence in Person among men healing and saving. The miracles are to be understood as the friction that arises when God comes into conflict with a fallen world of evil, when God himself makes bare his mighty arm to smite and to heal, and to defeat the powers of darkness and evil. It is thus that Jesus is aware of it — in his own sovereignty as God over all other powers and contrary forces: "Peace. Be still."

6. Finally, we must take cognisance again of the words of Jesus' direct self-revelation and self-assertion of his Person. These we may find epitomised in the verse of Matthew 11: "No man knoweth the Son but the Father, neither knoweth any man the Father but the Son, and he to whom the Son willeth to reveal him." Here we have the fourth Gospel *in nuce*. These words are prefaced by the others "All things are delivered to me by my Father." "There is literally nothing which is held by the Father alone, nothing which does not also belong also to Jesus." (Karl Adam, *op.cit.* p. 199) (Cf. John 16.15; 17.10; 5.f; 17.2 etc.) Of these words Karl Adam writes: "The Son is a reality to which, in its ultimate depths, no one has access save the Father alone. Conversely, the reality of the Father is revealed to the Son alone. Thus Father and Son stand in a wholly unique, exclusive communion, in which no one else has any part. And the uniqueness of their communion lies in the fact that they are Father and Son." (*op. cit.* p. 200) "They alone know and possess and permeate one another down to the very depths of their being, because they alone stand in relation of Father and Son to one another." (*Ibid.*) (See John 14.10; 14.9; 8.19; 10.f; 10.38.) "Jesus asserts here that he is a correlative of the Father as no other is." (P.T. Forsyth, *op.cit.* p. 112) The fact is that in these words Jesus asserts that he, the Christ, is the Consciousness of God; that he knows the Father with a knowledge that is not transferable; that in the depths he and the Father are one. "No one knows the Father but the Son"; "I and the Father are one"; "Before Abraham was, I am". Christ is God manifest, and as such is the Only way to God hidden, the Father. He is co-eternal with the Father, the eternal Son of the Eternal Father; but that Eternal Son now come among men that we may behold him and see him, and in seeing him know God. These are staggering words of Jesus to all who

would look at him and observe him. But to the ears of faith they are the right words — the words that we expect to hear from one in the face of whose confrontation we see and know our Lord and God. In calling Jesus Christ Lord and God we but give him his proper name.

CHAPTER 4

The Apostolic Testimony to Christ

In a previous discussion we noted that there was actually no other approach to Christ in the New Testament than the one we are about to consider. The Witness of the Gospels must therefore, in a strict division, come under the Apostolic Testimony to Christ: for even there we do not have a historical account of Christ but a dogmatic account written from the point of view of faith in Christ in the new experience made possible by the Holy Spirit. However what we did consider in the Gospel testimony was more the factual or formal side of faith which included the objective facts of revelation. Here in the Apostolic Testimony we are to consider the content or material side of the Apostolic testimony as we find it in the preaching and epistolary documents of the Apostles. At the risk of repeating points already enunciated in this connection we may find it worthwhile to remind ourselves of several things.

1. The Apostolic faith and testimony to Christ were not founded on an investigation of the self-consciousness of Christ. Where we do have that self-consciousness indicated in the Gospels, it must be pointed out that it was written after the full development of faith, and with a view to corroborating it as faith examines the facts, formally considered, with which faith has to do. The attempt to build up a Christology upon a psychological analysis of Christ's self-consciousness — for what else is the approach of much modern Christology than that? — cannot stand, and was not one used until modern times. Faith in Christ does not arise through any examination we may make of Christ as he is presented to us, but through an examination *he* makes of us — it arises in the divine encounter with which we are aware as we are faced with the Person of Christ when he meets us as the Eternal Word from heaven. In the light of that encounter we take a way in faith which is not amenable to any kind of observation — the Kingdom God does not come by observation! Faith in Christ may be understood and interpreted only *theologically*. The writers of the Gospels do not present us with data for any other approach — and any data that may be used for such a purpose is simply given by the way. What we have in the Apostolic Testimony is a faith which stakes itself on Christ as God, upon his Person and his Cross as appropriated in the experience of the Holy Spirit and the new life and revelation in the Apostolic Church. Confronted with Christ, yielding to him in the submission of faith, the Apostles experienced a death and resurrection in and with Christ in which *faith* was the operative principle of their understanding and trust. In the supervention of the Holy Spirit which created their faith in its understanding of Christ their faith formulated a confession as to the Person and work of Christ.

2. Dr. P.T. Forsyth asks this question in relation to the Apostolic testimony: "Was Christ valuable for the sake of certain spiritual ideas, or were the ideas valuable as expositions of Christ?" This distinction must be seen clearly. We must naturally repudiate the view that the value of Christ lies in certain ideas to which he gave birth, for that subordinates the Person of Christ to certain ideas which later become detachable from Christ, as today in the secularisation of the Christian ethic. On the other hand we cannot know or believe in Christ without having certain ideas about him. While these ideas are valuable for the sake of knowledge about him and the exposition of his teaching, Christ himself, on the other hand, is not to be understood apart from or without these ideas or categories of thought. This we have already discussed under the head of the Dogmatic Approach to Christ. What we need to note here, however, is that we cannot think of having Christ, of having him in any real sense in which rational beings may know and have him, apart from some such set of ideas about him which are absolutely crucial in their importance. To do away with the set of ideas which we have in the Apostolic testimony means that we only wish to set up another set of ideas with which to interpret Christ and through which we hope to be able to appropriate him. It is impossible to talk about having the fact of Christ without having some interpretation of the Christ himself, which of course derives from Christ. There is a lot of sheer nonsense talked about today when people urge us to go back to the Jesus of the Gospels — why, they ask, is that not enough? Why bother about St. Paul and the Apostles anyway? Far from being Christian such talk is confusion itself confounded. When you think of it, it is impossible to know and assess the fact of Christ without having a real interpretation of the facts about him which have been handed down to us from the Apostles in regard to him. I cannot do better than quote some wise words of James Denney here which he uses in writing *The Death of Christ* (p. 199 ff.): "A fact like the one with which we are here concerned, a fact in which the character of God is revealed, and in which an appeal is made to the reason, the conscience, the heart, the whole moral being of man, is a fact which must be, and must be seen to be, full of rational, ethical, and emotional content. If instead of `theory' we use an equivalent word, say `meaning', we discover that the absolute distinction disappears. The fact is not known to us at all unless it is known in its meaning, in that which constitutes it a revelation of God and an appeal to man; and to say that we know it in its meaning is to say that we know it theoretically, or in an through a theory of it. A fact of which there is no theory is a fact in which we can see no meaning; and though we can apply this distinction so far when we are speaking of physical acts, and argue that it is fire which burns and not the theory of heat, we cannot apply it at all when we are speaking of a fact which has to tell on us in other than physical ways: through conscience, through the heart, through the intelligence, and therefore in a manner to which the mind can really respond. St. Paul's own words in Romans 5.11 enable us to illustrate this. We have received, he says, or taken, the reconciliation. If we could take it physically, as we take a doctor's prescription, which would tell on us all the same whatever our spiritual attitude to it might be, then we might distinguish clearly between the fact and theory of it, and argue that as long as we accepted the fact, the theory was neither here nor there; but if the fact with which we are dealing cannot be physically accepted at all — if it addresses itself to a nature which is higher than physical, a nature of which reason, imagination, emotion, conscience, are the elements, then the fact itself must be seen to be one in which there is that which appeals to all these elements; that is, to repeat the truth, *it must be an interpreted fact*, something in which fact and

theory are indissolubly one. The Cross must be exhibited in ὁ λόγος τοῦ σταυροῦ, the Reconciliation in ὁ λόγος τῆς καταλλαγῆς; and λόγος is always a rational, theoretical word. It is much easier to say there is a distinction of fact and theory, a distinction between the testimony and theory of St. Paul than to prove it; it is much easier to imagine that one can preach the Gospel without any theory of the death of Christ than, knowing what these words mean, to do so. The simplest preacher, and the most effective, is always the most absolutely theoretical. It is a theory, a tremendous theory, that *Christ's death is a death for sin.* But unless a preacher can put some interpretation on the death — unless he can find a meaning in it which is full of appeal — why should he speak of it at all? Is it the want of a theory which deprives it of its place in preaching?"

Thus you cannot have a Christ who is intelligible, who has meaning for rational men, without having at the same time some interpretation or "theory" of him. Without having a definite theology the fact of Christ means nothing. *You cannot have Christ without a Christology.* But we must be careful here — recalling our foregoing discussion on value-judgements. The fact of Christ which we only possess as we interpret him, as he comes to have meaning for us, is most certainly not a fact which we later interpret, a fact upon which we impose an interpretation, however good or true that interpretation may be. Christ is not even in regard to his Person a fact upon which we pass a value-judgement before accepting it — that is still to deal in the realm of mere ideas only. The interpretation that we must have if we are to know or have Christ is not the interpretation that *we* put upon Christ, but the interpretation that *he puts upon himself,* one which we have to answer or acknowledge. In other words, the truths we must have concerning Christ in order to know him and have him are not our truths nor the truths of a St Paul or St. Peter but independent, eternal, divine truths which have their ground and authority in themselves and not on any value-category that we may bring to them. This matter, too, we have already discussed in the question of the divine encounter in Christ. That is the way that the Apostles grasped Christ, in being grasped by Christ. They are truths of faith, therefore, and not, strictly speaking, truths of theory, though they do involve a theoretical character, where "theoretical" means "noetic". We cannot go into this character of faith-truth any more here, but let us look into the way in which this truth was actually mediated to the Church.

3. In this truth about Christ, without which we cannot have Christ and which we cannot work up ourselves, *Christ himself must be his own Interpreter.* By this we mean, in effect, the activity and enlightenment of the Holy Spirit, who comes after the Ascension of Christ, as the Spirit of Christ, the Spirit of Truth, sent by Christ, in order to interpret Christ to the Church. Now, be it noted here again, we are not thinking of another knowledge or of other convictions about Christ than those we have already seen in the Gospels. And that for two reasons: First, the disciples had already an anticipation of the Spirit's coming and presence in virtue of which they were able imperfectly as they did prior to Pentecost to understand and interpret Christ; and Second, because the Gospels were written precisely from this very standpoint of Pentecost in which they look back and see the earlier days and experiences of Christ illuminated in this way.

The Gospels which we have considered first are actually second in order as testimonies — we had to consider them first, in order there to see the objective revelation of Christ upon which alone the subjective illumination or revelation could supervene, creating faith. Certainly the revelation in the Person and work of Christ was complete and final itself — he came to accomplish a particular work of

Revelation and Atonement and he did it, ending with the words: "It is finished". There the whole objective reconciliation was wrought out, and in his Person the objective revelation was carried out — what I have called for the moment the formal side of Christology. But that does not constitute revelation unless there is given along with those acts their proper significance and meaning. And in regard to this we have now seen two things: First, that Jesus hesitated to give this interpretation, and only did it very meagrely though with increasing readiness as he neared the Cross; and Secondly, that nevertheless such significance and meaning are absolutely essential to the fact of Christ himself as the Object of Christian experience and worship, as the Saviour. From this we must conclude two things: First, that unless you have the Christ and along with him the interpretation you have not really got the fact of Christ which is the fact of faith; and secondly, this whole fact is the Christ not only of objective revelation but the Christ of the illumination of the Holy Spirit. Thus the whole Christ who becomes the object of faith is the Christ of history who died and rose again, but that Christ as brought home and made real and interpreted by the supervention of the Holy Spirit, the Spirit of Christ, in the Apostolic witness and faith. The Christ who is the whole fact of faith is thus the Christ of the Gospel period extended into a further period through the Holy Spirit. The whole Christ is thus not the bodily Christ but the Christ of actual event carried out into the actual experience and faith of the Church by the indwelling mind of Christ, the Holy Spirit, who indwells the believer. The Christ had thus to depart in his mode of being before Pentecost in order that he might be present in the mode of being in and through which he could be interpreted and experienced. We must not delude ourselves here. The Christ whom we believers experience is precisely this Christ who may be called the transcendent Christ, the mind of Christ as Paul calls him, and that is essentially a theological Christ, the Christ dwelling in us as personal truth — and that must not be thought of in any abstract way as simply idea or teaching, but literally as the very *Mind of Christ* dwelling in the believer through the Word and the Spirit.

We must take this earnestly, that the revelation of Christ for faith was not accomplished at the Ascension; the ground material was laid; the work was done; materially the revelation was carried out, but formally it was not. Or to put it theologically, formally the basis was laid for a Christology, but materially, that is so far as conceptual content was concerned, the meaning of Christ, the eternal truth and word about him, which was nevertheless himself in transcendental form, was not conveyed until the descent of the Holy Spirit promised and sent by Christ to lead the Apostles into all truth. And as we have seen, the Holy Spirit did not come to bring a special revelation; the doctrine of the Holy Spirit has not a special content of its own; its content is the Person of Christ, Christ clothed with his own Truth. Thus the Holy Spirit, if I may say so without being misunderstood, is Jesus' other Self! And until this other Self of Christ came, until this deposit of Revelation was made, Christ himself was not really revealed, nor could he be properly appropriated, as *Christ clothed with his own Truth.*

The important point for us to notice here, is that this further existence and self-communication of Christ which constitutes the full revelation, was Christ's own act, "And *we* will come and make our abode with him", an act on the part of the Son and the Father, from whom the Spirit who thus conveys the Christ proceeds. Thus we are not to think of the revelation of Christ as ending with the Cross or with the Ascension: it was only then beginning in its fullness; it was only then that the Spirit was able to lead the disciples into all truth about Christ. Then Christ began to disclose himself through his Apostles chosen by him for this purpose, as he had deliberately not done before the Cross and Ascension. Christ living on, actually living on through his Spirit, te Spirit of Truth, in the Church: that we must take into earnest account. And it is that Christ, who gathers up in his Person the Christ of the Gospel ministry, who becomes the divine Object of Christian faith and experience that we must take to heart and consider.

There is an important thing we are to note here. Such a revelation of Christ must be the revelation within the mind of the Church, an unfolding within an intelligence, within the corporate understanding of the Church. It is not just an objective unfolding now, but a subjective unfolding as well. It has to do primarily with the *MIND* of Christ. Now this, as noted before, is not a datum to be interpreted, but an unfolding of the Mind of Christ which is to be acknowledged, which is to be answered to. And that had to occur in a definite medium, in definite minds. The facts objectively presented had to take under the indwelling Christ theological meaning in the minds of the believers. It was the mind of Christ creating in the believers the truth about himself; the mind of Christ unfolding itself, for example in the mind of Peter or Paul. Now this work of unfolding his own Mind Christ carried out through the Apostles in the New Testament, through the Holy Spirit sent by Christ to dwell in them. Thus we have in them the Apostolate the specially ordained medium in which the Christ determined to unfold himself to the world after the completion of his whole work on the earth; after that the accomplished work had to be explained — explained in a Self-interpretation. But that Self-interpretation had to be done still to and within human minds, through a specific human medium, and in human terms and categories.

Thus it is that we find Christ ordaining Apostles who as specially inspired should be the appointed media through which the further self-interpretation of Christ should be carried out — through whom the crucified and risen Christ should complete the work of his self-bestowal to the Church and the world. In the Holy Apostles Jesus Christ completed the final revelation of himself to mankind in such a way that people can appropriate him and even now have faith in him, believe in the fact of Christ and know whom they believe in. Thus we cannot say, let us go to the words of Christ in order to get faith, for there Christ does not reveal himself as he intends fully to do. We must perforce go to the *whole Christ*, the Christ as he unfolds himself in the minds of the Apostles through the Holy Spirit — and that means the *whole New Testament Christ.* You cannot therefore speak even of Christ in the Gospels and the interpretation of him in the Epistles — no! the whole New Testament Christ is the Christ; and neither the Christ of the Gospels nor the Christ of the Epistles can be understood or appropriated without the other. The Christ of the Epistles is not the by-product of revelation but part of it, an essential part of it, I say. And indeed it is in the Epistles that we have the full Christ as we do not have him in the Gospels, for there we have the Christ who is at the same time the Christ who lived and died and rose again. There we have the consummated Christ, the Christ ready for faith. Paul did not have merely an impression of Christ, but a special endowment of the mind of Christ, which was Christ's own *self*-unfolding through the Holy Spirit — it was an eternal act, independent of Paul or Peter or the Apostles, the final act of the great revelation of God to mankind through Jesus Christ.

Now in one sense all believers have the mind of Christ; we are all indwelt by the Spirit who conveys the Christ to us. But be it noted, that conveyance of the Christ to us through the Spirit is only through the Word of the New Testament, through the witness of Paul and Peter and John and the other Apostles. Thus we must distinguish between our having of the mind of Christ and that of the Apostles. There is no doubt but that the Apostleship was a special divinely endowed appointment to give final and full interpretation of the Christ, a specially ordained vessel through which Christ should pour himself out to the world for faith, an act for all time in order to act on time. (Cf. P.T. Forsyth, *op. cit.* p. 152: and consider also foregoing in Forsyth for the above.) Christ has chosen certain inspired documents into which he has poured his self-revelation, and evidently once and for all. These Apostolic documents are the specially inspired documents of the New Testament which by reason of their power as God's own Word have imposed themselves, as no others have done, on the mind and conscience of the Church to be the special vessels of the Living Christ. In other words the New Testament is a specially inspired book through which Christ conveys himself today to men and women — and the Bible, mark you, is not as such the product of the Church, for both the Church and the Bible are the products of the Gospel, of Christ himself at the springtime of the Christian era — and into both, the Church and the Bible, God in his self-revelation has communicatd himself, and through both he now conveys himself to people everywhere; through both, Jesus Christ is believed in; and through both is his salvation conveyed. It is part of the Christian faith now that the Apostleship, and the New Testament, are the special means or instruments appointed by Christ in a final way to convey and bring to a consummation the self-revelation to men and women of God in Christ Jesus, the crucified, risen and ascended Lord. It is there that we must go to seek Christ; and go not to the Gospels only, but to go to the Epistles and Apostolic preaching along with the Gospels. While in the Gospels we get the factual, and what I have called the formal side, of Christology, though not of course only the factual ann formal side, it is thus mainly in the Apostolic witness and writings inspired through his Spirit by the Mind of Christ, that we go to get the content of our Christology, the true interpretation of Christ which is but the self-interpretation of Christ now carried out in a way he did not see right to do earlier.

This point cannot be overemphasised. No doubt even in the Gospels we get all the elements of the revelation of Christ that we have in the Epistles, but it is in the Epistles especially that we get clearly and fully what Christ often only hinted at, and it is especially in Saint Paul (not neglecting of course St John and St Peter) that we get the full Christology the lines of which Christ only indicated while on earth. Thus there can be no question of any sort of wedge between the Christ of the Gospels and the Christ of Paul, nor of any appeal to the Gospels against the Epistles of Paul. Both altogether in the light of each of each other are our guide to Christ.

Hence, as we approach the Apostolic testimony, we approach it as one in which we find the full meaning of Christ for faith, and the full unfolding of the Mind of Christ himself in regard to his Person and work — that unfolding is here possible because it is not a purely objective revelation in himself alone, but a revelation in which the Christ who has completed the objective revelation now acts on people personally and subjectively in Salvation. Thus the point of view of the Apostles is the point of view of those who have come into saving contact with Christ and God through him. In them, therefore, we have the Christian view of God and of Christ, a view given in a fullness and in a way that Christ himself could not or did not yet give; for this was given not only in the light of the finished work of Christ in death and resurrection, but in the light of the revelation of the Holy Spirit who came with the act of Salvation wrought by Christ in those who believed and believe in him. Here then in the Epistles especially we have the theological essence of Christianity, the Person of Christ clothed with his own Truth in the actual work of Salvation. Here we have the sinners' view of Christ, the views of the publicans and the Gentiles arrested by the Grace of God, the view or understanding that the Lord Jesus Christ through the sending of his Holy Spirit meant us sinners and believers to have of himself. It is here then in the actual operation of Christ that we discern his full significance and reality for faith — and as we have seen already it is not simply an interpretation put upon Christ, but the actual self-interpretation of the Living Jesus himself, the Lord of Glory. As God the Father is seen and known only in his act in Christ, so Christ himself is seen truly and known truly only when realised through his act of salvation in the believer.

Schultz has written of the Old Testament thought of Salvation in these words: "The salvation of the future, like that of the past, can be brought about only by an act of God himself. However many the instruments of his Salvation, God himself is the really efficient cause of deliverance; and what he has been in the past, he will be in the future." (*Old Testament Theology*, 2, 354). This remains true for the Apostles as it was for the Prophets. Thus it is that in their experience of salvation at the hands of Christ, in the indwelling of the Holy Spirit who came to bring to them Christ in the fullness of his reality, the Apostles came to realise fully the proper nature and character of the Person of Christ and of his saving work. The whole of the New Testament is unanimous in its witness here to the Person of Christ — there never was in the primitive Church any disagreement as to the place and exalted position of Christ Jesus as Lord and God. In any theological discussion, however, it will be natural for us to turn to St. Paul, the Apostle to the Gentiles, as in him we have the issues brought out more clearly and with a greater degree of theological precision.

Whatever may have been the dubiety of the Disciples and Apostles as to the Nature and Person of Christ prior to the Cross, and whatever may have been their dismay at the events of the condemnation of Jesus and the verdict that may have been cast on his claims as Messiah, and Son of God, nay as very *Jehovah incarnate*, it is quite certain that with the resurrection of Christ all these thoughts were dispelled and all hasty verdicts were reversed. Here at the resurrection the Apostles realised themselves to be confronted with none other than the Supreme power of heaven and earth, with the very Son of God who is God. At first it confirmed their faith in Christ as the Messiah. He who had evidently died on the Cross and suffered as they had never dreamed the Messiah should suffer now evinced himself without dubiety to be the Sent One of God. This we see clearly in the language of Peter who immediately started preaching to crowded audiences in Jerusalem that Jesus of Nazareth whom the Jews took and Crucified was none other than the Messiah. We see it too clearly in the experience of St. Paul on the Damascus road. No doubt before he had only looked with horror on the sect that claimed to follow a crucified Messiah, but now when he is confronted with that same Jesus risen from the dead and declaring himself to him with power and salvation, Paul burst forth into exalted faith in Jesus the Crucified as the Anointed of God to redeem mankind, indeed all mankind, Jews and Gentiles alike. It is significant, however, that no sooner is the "Messiahship" of Christ affirmed in he New Testament, than it is dropped — "the reality of the personal Jesus has absorbed the Messianic functions." (H.A.A. Kennedy, *The Theology of the Epistles*, p. 76.)

The crucified Christ is risen from the dead and becomes an ever present saving reality transcending and bursting through all the older categories of thought; his Person confronted them with such salvation and power and with such blessing that they were forced to give to him the name that is above every name — *the Lord of Glory*. The crucifixion meant the full unfolding of the divinity of Christ, and at the resurrection that became manifest in transcendent fashion. All New Testament faith and witness start here — from the Resurrection and the Cross. The two events are seen to be correlatives, and to be understandable through each other in a work of salvation from sin, in a work of salvation that was nothing else than the very act of God himself.

The astounding thing to St Paul was that God, God who had made such stern and exacting demands on him through the law, the God of inexorable justice and who was unapproachable in the Light of his Holiness, now actually approached him in Jesus of Nazareth, with blinding light, but with the word of forgiveness. This actual initiative of God in grace and forgiveness which Paul recognised in Christ was so astounding a revelation that it changed *toto caelo* his conception of God. That was all due to Christ, for he was exalted to the very right hand of God. That Paul's thought of God should be so thoroughly transformed by and only through Christ meant that Christ had for Paul the very Place of God. What is true of Paul is true of every other witness in the New Testament. *In Christ God comes to view. In Christ the salvation that only God can could bring had been brought.* In Christ the defeat of the power of evil, the triumph over death, the forgiveness of sins only possible by the Lord God, are mow for ever possible to people everywhere: indeed they are accomplished realities: *Jesus is the Lord.*

There can be little doubt even to the ordinary historian that Christianity strictly speaking is pre-eminently the worship of Christ. It has been said that nothing has been more characteristic of Christianity from the beginning that just this central divine place which is given to Christ. The central faith in the New Testament is that everything that is connected with God in salvation and blessing present and future is to be gained and possessed precisely in and through the death and resurrection of Christ. "He that hath the Son hath Life." Christ is the divine Saviour, and is worshipped as God; he is One to whom we pray, the One who lavishes all the riches of the divine glory upon the believer. After his ascension Christ became the Object of worship and adoration in the primitive Church in a way that was really indistinguishable from that paid to God. There can be no denial of this patent fact without violence to our sources. Indeed, so evident is it that Jesus Christ is now regarded and worshipped as very God, that a notable historian like A. C. McGiffert can find the courage (and, he thinks, the evidence) to advance the thesis that Jesus was the God of the early Christians to the exclusion of the Father (*The God of the Early Christians*)! The witness of the Apostolic faith in Christian experience and in the whole round of devotional utterance and feeling focuses the attention on Christ in a way that only can mean for them that in him dwells the fullness of the Godhead. The Christian experience and faith of the Apostles and their company meant simply faith in Christ as divine Saviour, pre-existent and eternal. (Remember that the Messiah of the Jewish faith was always regarded as pre-existent and eternal. The real problem in Jesus was his humanity from this point of view. Thus an adoptionist theory cannot appeal for support to Messianic instances in the New Testament.)

The whole teaching of the Apostles in their witness is that Christ Jesus has absolute religious significance for them — be that considered in the Petrine speeches in the Acts of the Apostles or the Epistles of Paul or the Epistle to the Hebrews, or the Johannine writings. They cannot make too much of Jesus in this connection and are always reaching out after words and analogies to express their exalted faith in him. The word which they generally employ, however, to express this absolute significance of Jesus for faith and salvation is the word "Lord" - *Kyrios*. The designation of Christ by "Jesus" is quite overshadowed after the Resurrection while the application to him of the word *Lord*, which was the name of *Jahweh* in the Old Testament is very prominent, coming in St. Paul, for example, more than two hundred times. It was not a matter of formal respect which led them to apply this title to the Christ, but it was an act in which they ascribed to him the place of One with universal and absolute dominion. (Phil. 2.11; Rom. 10.12) At first, it may have been used as a synonym for the Messiah, and certainly had to do closely with the exaltation of Christ. However, in its fullorbed use it came to have the complete sense indicated above — where it is really equivalent to the Lord or *Jahweh* of the Old Testament Revelation. Take thus a word like that in Ps. 116:17 in its LXX dress: "O Lord (*Kyrios*), I am thy bond-servant (*doulos*)" - here in relation to the service and worship of men God is *the Lord*. In this relation Lordship simply expressed the Godhead of God. God is absolute Lord as the "*I am that I am*", the One whose Being is grounded in himself alone, who is completely Master of himself and all else. God is the ground without grounds, his Word is the word which needs no outside substantiation and which may only be obeyed. Thus the Lordship of God in the Old Testament means not only that God is unconditioned and infinite being but that he has perfect and complete freedom in which he has his being in and for himself. The Lordship of God expresses the Aseity of God. God as Lord is free to be Redeemer, Saviour, Creator, transcendent in his Will and unconditional in his demands. It is this concept of Lordship which the New Testament applies to Christ Jesus and with it they apply avowedly the fullness, or *Pleroma*, of the Godhead. To him shall every knee bow and every tongue confess that he is the Lord. Thus in the New Testament Christians are those "who call upon the name of the Lord". Paul makes it one of the chief marks of his ministry that he preaches Jesus Christ *as Lord*. (2 Cor. 4:5) This becomes the fundamental fact in the confession of the whole Church (1 Cor. 12.3; Rom. 10.9) for whom Christ occupies the absolutely central place, the place of very God himself. Consequently the Old Testament language which is used there of *Jahweh* is freely applied to Jesus Christ (1 Cor. 10.22; Rom. 10.13 etc.). He is regarded and referred to by Titus in terms of "the Great God"; or in the words of Paul, as the One "who is over all, God blessed for ever." (Rom. 9:5 (see the Greek text here: ὁ ὢν ἐπὶ πάντων θεὸς εὐλογητὸς εἰς τοὺς αἰῶνας, ἀμήν.) To Christ as Lord the Apostles ascribe the lofty attributes and prerogatives of God in creation and dominion and government over the universe as well as over men. Indeed Paul ascribes to him the full plenitude of the Deity: ἐν αὐτῷ κατοικεῖ πᾶν τὸ πλήρωμα τῆς θεότητος σωματικῶς (Col. 2.9).

We must note, however, that this full ascription to Christ's exercising the full power of his Godhead is attributed to Christ only after the Resurrection who as such is exalted and seen in his own Glory — therefore he is called the "Lord of Glory". It is thus generally the exalted Christ to whom the Apostles apply the word "Lord", for in his resurrection all the limitations of his self-assumed humiliation are transcended: he is not now in the form of a servant, but in the Form of the Master and Lord of all. Nevertheless, there is here no depreciation of Jesus before the resurrection, of the historical Christ, for it is precisely to the Christ of history who died and rose again that Lordship is ascribed— "the Lord of Glory who was crucified", says Paul. (1 Cor. 2:8) The whole point is that the Apostles did not so much remember Christ as believe in him — to use a phrase of H. R. Mackintosh. Paul "seldom dwells on the details of Jesus' earthly life, for his interest centres in Christ's death and resurrection; besides, for St. Paul, human life is a form inadequate to Christ's real being, so that for a full picture of the historic Jesus he substitutes the great act of the Incarnation, and is preoccupied with the risen Lord of Glory. Christ's present majesty is greater than the earthly life, now past. (2 Cor. 5:16) Yet there is continuity between the present and that past: `Jesus is Lord'."

The significant thing about the Lordship of Christ, the Deity of Christ, is that it may be confessed by people only in the power of the Holy Spirit. It is only through the Spirit of God that Christ may be recognised as belonging to the divine side of reality. It takes a supernatural act to recognise the supernatural Person of Christ — precisely because Christ is supernatural, and may not be apprehended as natural persons or things are. Thus the apprehension and confession of Christ as Lord is equivalent to *Salvation* and is of the very essence of Christianity — for it expresses the whole Majesty of Christ in all his eternal and saving acts. (Rom. 10.9; 2 Cor. 4.5; 1 Cor. 12.3; Phil. 2.11) In fact it may be that this formula that "Jesus is Lord" is taken to be almost liturgical or credal as summing up the whole Christian faith (2 Cor. 4.5; Rom. 10.9; Col. 3.24; 1 Cor. 12.3). Paul makes this confession of Lordship required of a would-be Christian. (See Anderson Scott, *Christianity According to St. Paul*, p. 249 f.) Christianity is equivalent to the confession of the Lordship of Christ, the Lordship of the crucified and risen Jesus, along with that of the Father and of the Holy Spirit. Thus St Paul characteristically ended one of his Epistles: "The Grace of the Lord Jesus Christ, and the Love of God, and the Communion of the Holy Spirit, be with you all." (2 Cor. 13.13).

One further point must be made. The title "Lord" is evidently the special title applied to Christ as divine but yet as distinct from God the Father. Johannes Weiss asserts that Paul welcomed the possibility of using the term "Lord", which for him expressed Christ's position of equality with God in the eyes of men, and his right to universal adoration, while at the same time, the word "God" is reserved for the Father — though there are passages which do apply "God" to Christ. The general trend of the whole New Testament is to link the Lord Jesus Christ with God the Father as the co-source of the Grace and Peace of Salvation — see, for instance, the prayers and benedictions of the Epistles, as well as that cited above. Both God and the Lord are regarded as distinct and yet one as the Sole object of Christian faith. Christ the Lord is one pole in the Eternal Godhead from whom proceeds the Holy Spirit. Thus while not the Father, Christ as Lord is in the form of God and equal to God, and is thought of as coming from that Eternal position to our world in a form of humiliation. There is no dogmatic formulation of the Trinity in the New Testament — though there are distinct asseverations of the Deity of the Spirit as well as of the Christ; thus forming a very definite Trinitarian background, especially as all three, Father, Son, and Holy Spirit are linked together as the One Object of Worship and the One Co-Source of all the divine blessings of salvation. Thus St Paul ended an epistle with the words: "The Grace of the Lord Jesus Christ, and the Love of God, and the Communion of the Holy Spirit, be with you all" (2.Cor.13.13) The name "Lord" is definitely the Trinitarian term for Christ along with the equivalent in the Word "Son".

We must now look shortly at the place given in the Apostolic testimony to the humanity of Christ. Upon this aspect there is little said in the New Testament outside the Gospels — it was taken for granted, and doubt as to the humanity of

Christ did not arise until the emergence of the docetic sects. The fact that the Apostles simply take the humanity of Christ for granted is perhaps a large part of the reason why they pay so little attention to the details of his life and teaching; but there is nevertheless more in it than that — for they were concerned with his death and resurrection, and so with the Incarnation from the point of view of his saving and redemptive activity. They were concerned with Jesus, the historic Jesus, so far as he was the object of faith, and so far, therefore, as they were united to him in a mystical experience of life and death, crucifixion and resurrection. But it was essential to all this that Christ Jesus be really regarded as *Man*. It must have been a difficulty for the disciples to think of Messiah as Man as even their own title for Messiah "Son of Man" was definitely recognised as of God. However, we do not find that problem coming out in St. Paul, who seems to have stuck to the truth of Christ' humanity in spite of the revelation that he was Messiah. St. Paul never doubts that he was Man in the full sense of the word; for it was a real death and a real resurrection that were Christ's. Hence we find Christ spoken of as having been born of woman, a member of the Jewish race under the Law, of the lineage and the house of David fulfilling the promise of the Messiah.

It is interesting to note that the title "Christ" which was at first so closely associated with the Messianic functions of our Lord comes to apply as often to his human Person. "Jesus" alone is seldom used by Paul or by any of the other New Testament writers, but it comes to be applied to the heavenly One at times (1 Cor. 9.1; 2 Cor. 4.11), while "Christ" is referred directly to the human figure. (Rom. 5.6; 2 Cor. 10.1) Again the combination "Jesus Christ" or "Christ Jesus" is often used of the Man Jesus Christ. (Rom. 5.15; 1 Tim. 2.5) There can be no distinctive emphasis on the use of "Jesus" for the human Christ, and on the use of "Christ" for the divine. The use of the expressions rather points to the fact that he was never thought of exclusively in one sense or the other, but that from the very start, as all along, he was always thought of as God-Man, the heavenly Man, the Second Adam who in contrast to the first Adam, was a life-giving Spirit. (Cf. Rom. 5.15 f; 1 Cor. 15.21, 45, 47f) The thought comes out with great clarity in the words of Paul in 1 Timothy (2.5): "There is one God, one Mediator also between God and Man, himself Man, Christ Jesus." It is ridiculous in the face of this to urge that the historical Christ meant nothing to St. Paul. No doubt, the historical Christ as such, as merely a figure of history, know only *kata sarka*, was of little or no significance to him, but it was of the utmost significance and importance that Jesus Christ was really *Man*, that he really died, and that he really rose again (as the Pauline Ignatius insisted with such real vehemence!). The whole Gospel was centred on the Incarnation — that is to say, on the fact that Christ who was in the bosom of the Divine came down and took our human flesh on himself. Without this fact, the Inhomination of the Son of God as he became Son of David, the substantial content of the Gospel is quite wanting, and there is no hope of salvation or of resurrection. Denney writes wisely as usual: "Paul could not in his work as an evangelist preach salvation through the death and resurrection of an unknown person; the story which was the common property of the church, and with which her catechists everywhere indoctrinated the new disciples, must have been as familiar to him in substance as it is to us." (*Two Corinthians, Expositors Bible*, p 203) A whole list of passages in his epistles cry out in corroboration. (See J. S. Stewart, *A Man in Christ*, p. 286 ff.)

This reference to the humanity of Christ comes out even more strongly in the Epistle to the Hebrews where the priestly character of Christ is largely emphasised in fulfilment to the Old Testament promises of a better day. There it is the Person of Christ which guarantees his High-priestly ministry, and real stress is laid on his human perfections and merits, even the discipline to which he submitted for our sakes. Yet there in *Hebrews* where the humanity of Christ is more strongly insisted on than in any part of the Apostolic witness, the pre-existence and eternity of Christ is also more strongly insisted on than elsewhere.

Perhaps the *Locus Classicus* in the discussion of the Humanity of Christ is the famous section of Philippians where St. Paul wrote: "Let this mind be in you which was also in Christ Jesus; who being in the form (*morphe*) of God thought it not robbery to be equal with God: But made himself of no reputation, and took upon him the form (*morphe*) of a servant, and was made in the likeness of men: and being found in fashion as a man (*en homoiomati anthropou*), he humbled himself, and became obedient unto death, even the death of the Cross. Wherefore God hath highly exalted him, and given him a name that is above every name: That at the name of Jesus every knee should bow, of things in heaven, and things in earth, and things under the earth; and that every tongue should confess that Jesus Christ is Lord, to the Glory of God the Father." (Phil.2.5-8) It is important to note that the Greek term Paul used there for the humanity of Christ in the expression "as man", *en homoiomati anthropou*, refers to "the concrete likeness of man", not to his appearance as man.

Here we have a clear statement of a belief that we can take to be uniformly Apostolic. It asserts in the strongest terms that Christ was actually, really Man, and yet was not merely Man. In fact we learn that though Man, he was eternally with God and became Man. That is equivalent with the other Apostle who spoke of Christ as the Word eternally with God and who was God, but who became flesh, who descended and tabernacled among men so that they beheld his grace and truth, the glory as of the only-begotten of God

(John.1.1f) There has been a lot of bad Greek written about this passage in Philippians two. It is evident that we cannot take the word *morphe* (μορφη) in the strict Aristotelian sense, which was a sense technical to the schools only, and which was not a current usage, especially at this time, though certain *papyri* do approximate to it, or rather to a Stoic use of the word. In other words, *morphe*, translated "form" in the English does not refer to the Eternal substance or Form in the Platonic sense, but is rather to be construed like the Latin "forma" in its usual sense where it does not mean beauty but external image, physical form, which nevertheless corresponds to an internal nature. And when we come to examine the Pauline text carefully, it is evident that what the Apostle is saying is that "The Christ who was eternally with God and in the *morphe* of God emptied himself out of that *morphe* into another *morphe*, namely the form of a servant. There is nowhere any indication in the text that Christ is spoken of as having emptied anything *out of* himself; rather that he emptied *himself* out of his divine magisterial form and came among men, the Eternal Christ *incognito* in the humble form of a servant. Nevertheless, this form of a servant was real; it was not docetic; it was a form which did really correspond to the act and reality of the inhabitant of the Form. Thus it was a true real humanity which Christ assumed concealing his dignity and divinity under the flesh; for he was made in the concrete likeness of sinful flesh, though without sin, in order that he might thereby identify himself with the sin and servitude of the world, bearing it and bearing it away in his death and crucifixion; thus slaying in his death the sinful humanity, and making atonement for our sin and bringing us deliverance from death and evil in the resurrection. Hence the Humanity of Christ is to be thought of as a definite assumption by God; the Incarnation is a movement of Eternity into time, and as such is real and historical. The Incarnation was not the manifestation of a humanity ever in the heart of God — such an idea has only been promulgated in line with some kind of Platonic or Neo-Platonic idealism. The Christ who descended into our world was in the form of God — not then in the form of man - and being in the form of God he was able at will to lay hold again of his essential equality with God. (See B.B. Warfield, *The Lord of Glory*, p. 248)

It is evident, then, that some form of the "two-natures" view of the Person of Christ is held in the New Testament. On the one side of his Being Christ is Son of God and Lord, on the other he is Son of David and Man. The two were never held in any antithetical juxtaposition in the Apostolic testimony - they were not thought of, either side, *kata sarka*, according to the flesh. Even though Christ was *en sarki*, his being *en sarki*, in the flesh, was not to be understood *kata sarka*, according to the flesh, but only according to the Spirit *kata pneuma*. There was no explanation offered, therefore, for this view of the God incarnate, God-Man; it was an apprehension granted only through the Spirit of Holiness. To say that "Jesus is Lord" is possible only under the influence of the Holy Spirit. The human side certainly has a historical beginning: that we are clearly told; but the Divine side did not. In the Words of the Epistle to the Hebrews he was eternal for ever in the heavens. In the Words of Peter he was before the foundation of the World; in the words of John, he was in the beginning.

Thus it is not surprising that outside the Gospels we do not have any emphasis on the details of our Lord's life on earth — there was all the continuity possible between the Christ of faith and the Christ of history; but the Humanity of Christ here thought of is the Humanity viewed in the light of the illumination of the Holy Spirit, the Humanity in the light of the Incarnation and the Resurrection as the climax of the passion experience of the Cross. They believed in Jesus, rather than remembered him; they experienced him, yes the Living Jesus, as indwelling their lives, rather than recalled the historical figure of a teacher.

Finally it falls to us to take some note of the eternal dimensions of Christ and of his cosmic significance as we find it in the revelation granted through the Apostolic witness. We have already referred to the eternity of Christ. For in the Apostolic testimony Christ is an eternal act of God — he is God coming out of his Eternity into time. Christ does not want to have his own Dignity as Divine for himself alone — he considered his Equality with God not something to be grasped and selfishly guarded — he wanted fellowship with us. And condescending to us in the initiative of his sovereign grace, he sought fellowship with us in he valley of humiliation that he might lift us up in his own exaltation to share with himself the glory of God in Eternity.

The Messiah in the Old Testament was always thought of as pre-existent and Eternal. Thus it must have been natural for the Disciples so to think of Christ once they recognised him as the Messiah. There is certainly no repudiation of this belief, but on the contrary an enhancement of it. In calling Christ Lord, and in dropping the term "Messiah" for that of "Lord" the Apostles came to ascribe to Christ a dominion that was absolute and reaching over all and in all. There is one Lord Jesus Christ, says St. Paul, and through him are all things and we through him. (1 Cor. 8.6) Thus St. John writes in the same vein that through Christ, the Word, were all things made that were made and without him nothing came into being. In the Apostolic faith and witness the exalted Lord is Lord of all of creation, of time and Eternity, of life and death. In him space-time limits do not count; Christ is not conditioned by them, and in this Transcendent nature he exercises a sway over things in the heaven, things in the earth, and things under the earth. The absolute centrality of Christ in Salvation and therefore even in the Godhead means that Christ is the centre of all the Divine activity. As the Word, everything that the Godhead uttered and did, was his own action; and Christ is thus regarded as central in creation as well as in salvation, in the past as well as in the future, in the present salvation as well as in the eschatological events to come. It is through the medium and activity of Christ, in fact, that the whole activity of God is now regarded. He is the pivotal point of reference in the Divine Self, the supreme Agent of all divine action, the Creator and Ruler of the Universe (cf. Colossians.1.15-19) What God alone could do according to the Prophets Christ had done, and what God alone would do, Christ will do.

In arriving at this conception the Apostles start from the work of salvation and redemption of which Christ Jesus is the sole medium. He brings the new world and new life; he is the Founder of a new humanity, the Creator of a new race in God. Hence the death and resurrection of Christ are not simply incidental to his own life but are of universal and even cosmic significance. Christ is the Sovereign power of the divine Transcendent order which even now brings to nought the things that are, defeating this present evil world. From this Paul advances to think of Christ as "the focus of the cosmic system, the constitutive principle of universal life." (H.A.A. Kennedy, *The Theology of the Epistles*, p. 153) The statement of this view comes most often in the Prison epistles of St Paul. Colossians is especially important in this respect. Moffat translates the passage thus (Col. 1:15-20; cp. Eph. 1:10, 22, 23): "He is the likeness of the unseen God born first before all creation — for it was by (better "in" - thus Kennedy) him that all things were created both in heavens and on earth, both the seen and the unseen, including thrones, angelic lords, celestial powers and rules; all things have been created by him and for him; he is prior to all, and all coheres in him." Further: "It was in him that the divine fullness willed to settle without limit, and in him it willed to reconcile in his own Person all on earth and in heaven alike, in a peace made by the blood of his Cross." (Cor. 2:15).

Here we have an insight into what it means for Christ to possess the Lordship of God. In Christ we have Ultimate Reality, if I may be allowed to use that phrase in this connection. Christ is the Ground, Centre, and Goal of all being. He is, in the words of Ephesians, "the summing up of all things, the things in heaven and the things on earth." (Eph. 1:10) Into this of course, we cannot hope to penetrate; the veil of the other side has been drawn aside only so far, and it would be folly to try to force it in any way, but it does give us a real glimpse of the exalted nature of the Person of Christ, and opens our minds in wonder at the event of the Incarnation, when the Lord of Heaven and Earth, of the Universe, came to dwell in Jesus of Nazareth that we might behold his glory and share with him the Eternal Life and the riches of his Glory. Nothing short of Eternity came down to Bethlehem and deigned to be confined to the crib of Mary and to be subject unto her discipline. But as the Child Jesus grew and waxed in favour with God and Man, he began to go about his Father's business until in the fullness of time he came forth from his solitude and shouldered in public fashion at the Baptism the burden of the sin and guilt of our fallen race. For three years as Jesus of Nazareth he lived in that humble way and exercised his public ministry, at last carrying our sinful humanity with which he identified himself to the Cross and crucifying it there, only to rise again in the fullness of his Eternity, and in the transcendent glory of his divine Majesty, now exalted as Lord of all, triumphant over evil and death which had invaded his creation and thwarted his purpose of eternal love. The same Christ, the Lord and Sovereign of all, will come again in like manner as he departed, this time as the Bridegroom for the Bride, the Christ for the Church which is his living witness and continuing incarnation, as it were, on the earth. Then there shall be a new heaven and a new earth in which all evil will be destroyed and Christ will be all in all, the Lord.

CHAPTER 5

The Significance of Christ for Faith

The significance of Christ for faith is simply that <u>Christ is the Object of faith,</u> the One in whom we believe; as such he has absolute religious significance — that is the essence of Christianity. Christ stands in the focus of true religion, and in laying hold of him we lay hold of God in a personal and immediate way. Another way of putting the same thing is to say that in Jesus Christ we are confronted with the Word of God, not a word about God, or a word that is later seen to be from God, but the Word who is God himself speaking.

A very significant fact in the New Testament witness we have just considered is the principle that the Content of what God reveals in Christ and the Manner of that revelation cannot be separated for one moment: they are One and the Same. The New Testament faith in Christ started with the conviction that he was the Son of God; that is, that Christ and the Father were correlative in relation and revelation, that there was no knowledge of the one without the other, and it is within this that faith finds in Christ as Son of God its absolute significance. It starts with this: the fact that Christ is *the Word*, that is to say, not an idea, not a logos in the Greek sense, but Word which is an actual event in history, definite reality concretely spoken in a divine act and thereby conveyed. That is Christ, the very Word of God, the term "Word" being used in a Unique sense, for here the Speaker and the Word spoken are one. What God communicates in Christ is not something separate from himself, but himself, his own Eternal Person. The Word is the Fact of Christ understood together with his Meaning; the Word is a fact-in-interpretation, self-interpretation. As such the Word it is self-authenticating, its own Authority, grounded is itself alone without external legitimisation. No apologetic theology

As we saw in our examination of the New Testament witnesses, what they bore witness to was <u>neither a man whom they saw to become God</u>, nor God somehow <u>related to man</u>. What they discerned through faith was a God-Man. Immediately these two sides become separated, and the attempt is made to go from the one to the other, disaster follows and there is brought in a dismemberment of the Christian faith in Christ as its supreme Object. The faith conveyed by Christ is no absolute truth separable from himself, for faith in God the Father is indissociable from faith in Christ the Son, the unique Truth which God actually and really is in himself. Thus we cannot approach the problem of Christology in arguing from the revelation of Fatherhood to the Sonship of Christ. In other words we may not penetrate into the motives which lead to Christology.

In some writers there are enumerated experiences in the early Church upon which follows the argument that these set them thinking, and that afterwards they came to the conclusion that the Christ on whom all these experiences seemed to centre could not but have the value of God, indeed that he must be the Son of God. That has been a <u>vice of recent Christology</u>, the attempt to penetrate into the *how* of the Christ, rather that to be concerned with the *who* of faith. Christ never asked Peter how he came to believe in him, he never asked the disciples why they followed; he asked them *Who* they thought he was, or *Who* did men say he was. That is the question of Christology: *Who is Christ*, and Faith answers immediately — else it is not faith — that he is the Son of the Living God. Faith realises that here alone we have the words of eternity: Where else can we go? In other words, here in Christ we have the very Word of God, God's own speech and action, the very Word of God who is God. The paradox of this is that this is seen by faith alone. Any other attempt which argues to Christ in his significance for faith from the impression he makes upon his followers as the Ritschilian School does (as apparently is often the case in modern Christology), or which argues from his piety or ethical values (as does the related thought following Schleiermacher and the Neo-Kantians), must face insuperable problems. They start with the humanity of Christ, and starting there cannot get beyond it, even with the aid of the best and most skilful dialectic. The perception that Jesus carried with him perfect love does not carry with it the assertion of his Deity or essential nature — it is still a value-judgement which we saw a true Christological approach has to dismiss as not amenable. It is only because faith recognises immediately that Christ is One who comes from the very bosom of the Father that the Love of Christ attests anything about his nature. It is only because the suffering of Calvary is the suffering of the Son of God that it has ultimate significance.

I have said before that the approach here is a *theological* one — in which the argument is circular, in which counter argument is a *negare per negatum!* That is so because we are dealing here with a different dimension. To pursue that analogy further, for purposes of illustration, we must say that you cannot possibly see a new dimension gradually. You either see it or you do not, you either discern it or you do not. To enter a new dimension is not like the action of a traveller who gradually enters an unknown land and subjects it to exploration. Nor in seeing Christ as the Son of God, as he who comes plumb down from above, *senkrecht von Oben,* as Barth would express it, do we proceed from any ground that we adopt before hand; faith in Christ is not an inference from anything else. It is an immediate experience of a new dimension, a new type of awareness — one we call "faith", for it involves at the same time a special mode, a new mode, of understanding and existence. Within this new mode of existence we see things in a new light, in a new perspective — but it cannot be gained gradually. We must have it, and have it wholly, or not have it at all. Thus it is that from the outside the theological approach to Christ or to any doctrine appears circular and a begging of the question. In fact in a true theological approach, a scientific-theological approach, the "whole" precedes the parts, and is presupposed by every part.

In regard to the doctrine of Christ and his place in faith, we have to take up a like attitude. To faith is given immediately the realisation that Christ is the Son of God, and faith operates *within* that new dimension. Christ is seen not in the flat as it were, in one dimension merely, but in his fullness as God-Man; he becomes the supreme object of faith, at once the sphere of faith and the very possibility of it. This is the meaning of the statement that Christ is the *Word* and that Word is a free gift! Man does not himself possess this Word; he is not naturally in this eternal dimension - that is the significance of the "fall" or of original sin. He must be forgiven and brought into this new dimension at the same time — and that happens *in Christ,* the one event in Time of absolute religious significance, the one point where the Eternal dimension come plumb down from above into our world; and therefore the one point where we may have faith, and the one point where we can discern what faith really and actually is!

Thus at the rise of faith we have to do with the truth of the oneness or unity of the Son with the Father, in other words with the divinity of Christ, or his supreme place as the object of Christian worship. It is Christ who is for us the point of entry into the new dimension, the focal pole of the Godhead, the "visibile" of the Invisible God. That is the significance of the revelation of God as Jehovah or *Jahweh* in the Old Testament, the "I am who I am". *"Jahweh"* meant the revelation of the God not known except here, the manifestation of the God who was and is himself and in himself alone. As Karl Barth has expressed it: "The name of *Jahwe*h is just *Jahweh* manifest to men." (*Church Dogmatics*, 1/1, p 458) Jesus Christ in relation to faith is precisely the same, therefore Paul ascribes to him the name that is above every name — *Jahweh, Kyrios*. He is the "Visibile" of the invisible Father, the focal point where the revelation of God the Father bears on men, the Word which is the very Person of God communicating himself through himself. The christological thought starts from this "whole" at the very commencement, in the immediate apprehension of faith — all else is but explication and orientation to the new dimension.

Where there has not been this immediate apprehension of faith in its wholeness, or where this new dimension has not been entered, that is the vision of God and the Christ in correlative unity, there have generally been adopted either one of two kinds of approach both of which were early manifest in the history of the Church, and both of which the Church saw fit to condemn as unchristian. These two approaches made their first appearance in the Church under the *Ebionite* and *Docetic* heresies, and have since persisted throughout the centuries in some form or another, and are always cropping up anew — consequently some discussion of them is called for as we think of the relation of Christ to faith.

Both of them begin because there has not been an apprehension of Christ and the Father together in an indissoluble wholeness or unity. Once that wholeness or unity fails to be grasped, one or two of these erroneous views we are about to consider are bound to crop up in some degree or another. Both start from the historical facts of Christ as the first thing, and then, proceed to ask *how* this was transmuted into faith. How could such a reversal have taken place is the question asked. The answers are: On the one hand, starting from the humanity of Christ, it was held that the Christ was thought of as adopted to be the Son of God, as the *Form-Geschichte* school of thinkers — or rather one branch of them — tends to think today. On the other hand, that Christ, the historical Christ is the exemplification of an eternal truth which we find in modern theology in varying degrees since the days of the Socinians, and the Enlightenment. These two arose early in the Church as Ebionite and Docetic views respectively. Both of these views do not start from the whole fact of Christ, but from one-sided views of Christ as human *or as divine*, as Man *or* as God, try to pass over from one to the other, and thus and develop a Christology on the ground of a dialectic, or argument from that one aspect of Christ, from his humanity to his deity or from his deity to his to his humanity, not from the whole reality of Christ. Both ask from their different starting points how Christ came to be regarded as he was, and purport to give an explanation of the problem which they set themselves.

1. *Ebionite Christology*: This view taken in its various historical manifestations consists essentially in the apotheosis of a man, Jesus of Nazareth, and ranges from the idea that Jesus was a great Man far ahead of his times, and so exalted in his teaching and Person, even sinless, that he came to be regarded as Son of God; or

as having the value of God, he came to be regarded as God. He so pleased God by a perfect life and work that he enjoyed special relations with God, who adopted him to be his only Son. Views varied as to when that took place, at his birth, as some held, at his baptism, at the transfiguration on the mount, or actually in the resurrection. Thus God exalted Jesus to a position that is above any man or prophet, and so to the eye of faith he comes to share the place and throne of God. Whatever the actual historical or factual form which this doctrine took or takes, and it is a very common one today in a subtle form. Its essential nerve is that it starts with Jesus the Man, with a human personality which is turned into God. Jesus is regarded as the peak of history soaring into superhistory (cf. Karl Barth, *Church Dogmatics*, I.1, p. 460 ff.), the flowering of humanity into divinity, the evolving of the highest in man into a divine being. Jesus is so thoroughly and so perfectly man, morally and aesthetically, that he becomes God; out of a historical form there arises a heavenly essence. Jesus starts out as a mere man, as an impressive personality, as a hero, as one in whom all the highest values of humanity have their perfect expression and fulfilment, and therefore he is raised to the level of God, either in the so-called eyes of faith, or, it is asserted that God is pleased to give Christ that status. Now what is this but the deification of man? Man at his highest point is an apotheosis of God: in other words man is made equal to God (to be sure Man at his highest), and so the step follows that the ideal man in each and all of us is to be identified with the divine, or the Christ; we are all divine in that sense, only we have not been freed from the trammels of the world of evil and sin. Christ, however, who has overcome all evil and has ascended above this present evil world will aid us also in delivering us from the empirical man which clogs the ascension of the ideal man, and as our elder brother will help us to ascend with him to the very seat of God where we too will become divine!! Such is the *hubris* of man, in making himself out to be the equal with God, in making of a man or ideal man, even if it be the personality of Jesus of Nazareth, into God; it is nothing short of sheer idolatry, and the worship of humanity. To treat even Jesus the human being in this way is to be a polytheist. If Christ is worshipped as divine in this way, then he cannot be worshipped as an historic personality, for as such that is a worship of the creature. However, Christ's own claim to worship does not lie in his humanity or personality as such, as we saw, but in the reality of his Divine nature. "Why callest thou me good? There is none good save one, even God." Those words are Jesus' answer to the apotheosis of his humanity and the sum of all high human values, for to deify the humanity of Jesus is to deify mankind! Jesus never idealised himself as God in the sense of Ebionite Christologies — for that would mean that a man could become God. This is the root error of all adoptionist ideas, for no exalted man is anything else but a creature, and his work but a creaturely work. There can be no way to divinity from man, and no way for the revelation of God which proceeds from this human side of reality. If Christ is to reveal God, he must divine, he must come *as such* from God in his coming into the world.

That view of Christ tends generally to merge at some point or other with the second vagary we are to consider. We find that, for example, in a writer like Wilhelm Herrmann who insisted that the revelation of God is through the historic personality of Jesus, but through his "inner life". This is to misconstrue revelation altogether as a revelation of the Unknown and otherwise unknowable, the revelation of the Creator God whose reality and truth are grounded in himself alone. Certainly the personality of Jesus is the *incognito* of the deity of Christ, but cannot a such be divine; and so we find the adoptionist theory in the end of its dialectic swinging the other way, for by deifying the humanity of Christ or his historic personality, it really denies the reality of his humanity! Here it merges with the docetic Christology. It is in a heretic like Paul of Samosata who has been called the first Ritschlian and modernist, that we get rather a clear view of such a transitional Christology.

The fact evidently is, that the Ebionite-adoptionist theory of Christology is the only possible account of Christ's person, when the start is made from the naturalistic-historical point of view, which has so characterised modern theology since F.D.E. Schleiermacher. The adoptionist theory has its element of truth in the fact that we have to do with two "natures" in Christ, we have to do with one who is fully man, and yet somehow become fully God. Looked at from the naturalistic or historical level all that one sees is the human personality of Jesus, and that is an essential part. But starting from this point of view, the observer can never really get out of it, for he cannot carry it over to the supernatural without supernatural aid, and that is to negate his starting point. The other way that the adoptionists have tried to get over the difficulty is to run for the help of metaphysical ideas, and that, as we shall see, means a docetic view of Christ. That is what modern adoptionists or Ebionites do if they try to give some place to the divinity of Christ — yet in the end they deny the humanity of Christ or reduce it to a mere symbol, and the Eternal in Christ becomes the eternity of timeless truth, not God among men in person. Thus these ways lead abut to a *cul-de-sac*. The only way to view the two natures of Christ is through the dimension of the exalted Christ, or through faith in which alone the two modes of the one being Jesus Christ are held together in a wholeness or unity in which neither the one or the other is impaired.

The second important method of Christological approach which falls for our consideration is that represented by the *docetic Christology* found in the early Church. This has been even more influential in modern times, strangely enough, although the humanity of Christ has been the main focus of its thinking, but that is due to the corresponding fact that here docetic Christology always tends to pass over into Ebionite views! The nerve of the docetic view is that in Christ we have the personification of an idea, of a great eternal truth, otherwise rather familiar — at least now very familiar that has been brought to our notice, and appears quite self-evident. This is generally summed up in the truth of the Fatherhood of God, the truth of kindness and love, and victory over evil by non-resistance, the way of redemption by the way of "Die and be born". (see Barth, *Dogmatics*, I.1, p. 461 f.) It is in Jesus Christ, it is held, that we have the perfect illustration or manifestation of these eternal truths. Thus because the essential point in Christ is the *divine idea* symbolised by or disclosed through the person of Christ, when his person becomes subordinated to the message in varying degrees; indeed to such an extent, as in the early Church, that the humanity of Christ might really count for nothing. That is, of course, the logical result of the teaching that Jesus is a Teacher, a part of humanity, born to convey an idea, born to be the most perfect representation or symbol of God's truth for mankind. Since Jesus is thus thought of as the symbol of the reality he may even be accorded the title Lord or son of God in a superlative sense. But whatever these titles mean, and with whatever honesty or dishonesty they are used to convey this conception of Christ, the place of Christ for faith is ultimately not that of a redeemer, but that of a midwife; it is *maieutic*, for his work what of a religious mid-wife who aid us in developing and begetting the same relations with the Father as he had so perfectly in his own life; he is here the elder brother again, and ultimately stands on the same level with all men before the Father, to be sure a great and incomparable person, so great that we may even call him divine, but nevertheless only a *Primus inter pares*!

The central doctrine in this type of Christology is that in a man, Jesus of Nazareth, we have the perfect illustration, or personification of the Divine idea or truth penetrating into history. Jesus is the most perfect symbol of the divine presence. In other words Jesus is mythologically conceived: he is the myth — not necessarily that he is not a real figure of history, though that is often denied by docetists — the myth who in his person acts out dramatically the relations of God with men. This is the opposite of Ebionite Christology where Christ was the flowering of humanity toward God; here Christ is the exemplification of the Divine in human form, but such that there is really no essential connection between the form and the reality which it conveys; the reality is not one with the symbol; the symbol represents a reality in idea, not a reality that is actually present in Jesus. As in Ebionite Christology the starting point was the human person of Jesus, here in Docetic Christology the starting point is the Christ-idea, a metaphysical timeless idea which is personified or illustrated in Jesus. As in the first man was deified, and humanity was raised to the level of God, here God is brought down within the compass of human ideas and become identified with the ideal that every man is supposed to have in his soul — a necessary truth of reason. Jesus is then just the mythologising of an idea. And his divinity can be regarded only ultimately as a misconception due to an exaggerated Jesus-enthusiasm.

Difficult as this idea may seem in the face of early Church history to accept, it has nevertheless been the most influential among modern liberal theologians since the Rationalistic formulation of it at the Enlightenment. It appears in the teaching of Jesus as an example, as a genius, as the founder of the Christian religion etc. As such Jesus represents an historical beginning in which certain truths were let loose into the world. God chose this man to be the medium to convey certain ideas to mankind, so that when they learned these truths, the truth would set them free. Such, for example, seemed at one time at any rate, the basic principle behind the teaching of a man like John MacMurray, or the idea of the Kingdom of God as a civilisation which becomes permeated with certain truths of the Fatherhood of God and the brotherhood of man etc. This view finds its highest expression in the idealistic philosophy of religion of modern times, particularly from Hegel and Schleiermacher on. The fundamental thesis is that the real is the rational. History is contingent and cannot as such be regarded as ultimately real; it only illustrates the real. The paradox of modern thought! It is now, when history becomes the centre of thought, when for the first time there has arisen a philosophy of history, when the history of Jesus and the Gospel is thoroughly investigated, that the reality of history is denied, and along with it, of course, the reality of the historical life of Jesus; it only exemplifies eternal truth; for it is part of history and history, in the phrase of Lessing, is but the picture book of reality. In consequence, a Schleiermacher is driven to conclude that the Christ of significance for the Christian faith is not the Jesus of history as such, but the Christ-idea that lives on in humanity and civilisation, in the Church. The historical has of course a place to play, but it is simply the point where the absolute truth or ideal passes into time and out again into eternity — and so docetic Christology maintains that either the person of Christ as Man was not real but apparent, or that it was of no ultimate importance. Christ is not the correlative of God, but the elder brother, the teacher; the central point in Christianity is not Christ's own Person, which has only relative significance for faith; it is the revelation of the Father — and Jesus is put aside once his work is done. That was the position of Harnack, the great scion of modern liberalism.

This teaching has certainly produced a great fund of literature in modern times, in which more has been written on the significance of Christ for faith than at any other period, and our historical knowledge of Christ has increased accordingly by leaps and bounds — but all this has been carried out in the human sphere, in an ethico-religious light. Writers speak of Christ's unbounding humanitarianism, the wealth of his personality, the depth of his fellowship, his human nature, his consciousness of God, of his piety and so on. There is no doubt about it; there has never been so much Christ-enthusiasm in all the history of the world as there has been in these latter days — but in the end *Jesus Christ himself* is ignored. He certainly had a great grasp of God and reality, but it is God that counts, the God of idealism. Brunner quotes Goethe as saying that in the Gospels we catch "The vital reflection of a certain majesty which radiated from the personality of Christ, an influence as divine as any manifestation of the Divine which ever has appeared on earth. If I am asked whether I feel I can — whether it is in accordance with my nature — to offer him reverent worship and homage, I reply: Certainly! I bow before him as the divine revelation of the highest principle of morality." In other words, what the Buddha is to Buddhists, Jesus was to Goethe! And it is not going too far to say that is a very often a true representation of modern thought on the subject.

Notice Goethe's expression, "according to my nature". That gives the clue to modern thought since Hegel. It has been the basic principle that in the depths of his self, in the so-called ideal self of every man, he is divine, is in continuity with the divine. The real is the rational, the ideal, and so far as man partakes of that he is one with the divine. Thus the Divine has been unfolding himself in the human race, the absolute extended in time in a great evolving process as we have it in Hegel. It is in the consciousness of men of the ideal that the Divine comes to consciousness. At the bottom there is a secret identity of man with God. What place does Jesus occupy in this process? "Jesus only brought to completion what the best of men before him had desired." (Weinel: *Neutestamentliche Theologie*, p. 226) "As the author of the perfectly spiritual and ethical religion Jesus is above all other men." (Ritschl, *Rechtfertigung und Versöhnung*). That is the place accorded to Christ. If Jesus is the most perfect incarnation of the moral and religious ideal, then his influence can consist only in the intensification of the movement which is already present in humanity towards the ideal. He is only taken into account as a dynamic, and therefore, relative factor. (See Brunner: *The Mediator*, p. 88) In the end Jesus is but the Teacher, the example. What really matters is right relation with God when he and I stand face to face alone. The decisive step must be taken by me alone. I give birth to the ideal in men or the actualisation of it; Christ is only the midwife. No one else can take my place. What are we to do then with Jesus? Well the best we can do is to say he is the Archetype of the religious man, that is, through the special endowment he had of the consciousness of God. What Christ does is to aid man in the work of assimilating his consciousness of God the Father. Thus the nearer the man is to Christ, the more aid Christ gives a man, and the nearer the man consequently gets to God the Father, the less does Christ count in importance, the more unnecessary does he become!

We cannot go further in an elucidation of this modern docetic Christology. It must be clear now, at all events, that the essential place of Christ as *God in Person*, as the Mediator who is both very God and very Man in his incarnate Person, is repudiated or lost. Modern man wants to help himself; he thinks he is free and already at one with the divine at the bottom of his soul — poor wretch, when all the time he is bound in the bondage of precisely this autonomy! He wishes to save himself, and brings in Christ by the way as a co-partner - Christ may indeed be called the revealer of God but as such he was merely the possessor of a specially great but impersonal divine power and divine spirit called the Truth! And here the docetic Christology passes over into Ebionite Christology, for Jesus is nothing but a Man who was highly endowed by God, raised even to divinity. But the union of Christ with God is ethico-religious, not essential. If it does not pass into Ebionite Christology, then in the struggle between personality and Idea which Christ's person exhibited, personality as the weaker party, is defeated. (See again Brunner, *op.cit.* p. 267) For the idea, the truth, the teaching of Jesus, which he illustrates in his life, possesses the quality of absoluteness which his personality does not.

In an interesting article in the Encyclopedia, *Religion in Geschichte u. Gegenwart,* Prof. Karl Ludwig Schmidt (my old New Testament Professor in Basel) has shown that the New Testament tradition presents the activity of Christ always as an intermixture, impossible to dissolve, of word and deed. (See also Barth, *op. cit.* p. 458.) What Christ does and is, is what he reveals. He is himself the revelation he gives of the Father, and that not in a merely symbolical way. Jesus is not a symbol which speaks about God, but a symbol who actually conveys God — that is, a symbol which is one with the reality it conveys. Thus, as the Word, Jesus is not just a word about God, or merely one speaking from God. As the Word he is spoken in the place where God is, the correlative of God. In other words, he is the Word of God in such a way that *one cannot apprehend the Word without apprehending God, and one cannot apprehend God without apprehending Christ the Word.* These two are held together in the act of faith in an indissoluble unity. If a break is made between them, and the approach is made in either of the two directions indicated above, in the historical-naturalistic way of Ebionitism, or in the rationalist-idealist way of docetism, then there is no place for a real revelation of God. For it is only when the Word of God *is* God, when the Revealer of God *is* at the same time the Revelation itself, that there can be real revelation. Both Docetism and Ebionitism mean the denial of revelation, and hence the denial of either the humanity or the deity of Christ: and as we have seen a denial of either one always merges into the denial of the other too. If Christianity is to mean anything it must mean that in Christ we do have a real revelation of God to men. Therefore Christ is himself *alethos* and *teleos, God-Man.* Both sides of this must be maintained in Christianity. The Church in its major Councils and in the best of her theologians has always repudiated one or both of the alternatives we have considered: of Christ regarded either as the apotheosis of man, or as the personification of God, the divine idea. The New Testament itself bars these alternatives. Indeed the New Testament can be understood only if it is seen that it has nothing to do with these approaches. If it is not seen that the New Testament teaching is within faith then all one can do is to take up an adoptionist attitude or a mythological view of Christ. But while the New Testament does indeed think of the humanity of Christ as very real and while it does think of Christ as the express image of the Father, the Son of God, it does so in a different way altogether from either of these false views. For it views both the humanity of Christ and his divinity in his wholeness from the point of view of the revelation that came with Christ, from the point of view of the *new Dimension* which while gathering up the elements of truth in both of these two alternatives transcends them and sees both together in a single unity.

The starting point in the New Testament is neither Jesus the hero nor Christ the Idea, but *GOD IN CHRIST* is the first and basic fact. It is within this "Whole" which comes first to faith, in this new dimension, that faith takes its rise and theology develops in self-orientation. God in the midst of men - *Immanuel*! This is grasped immediately, not as a synthetic but as an analytic statement. (see Karl Barth, *op. cit.* p. 463) There is thus no primary knowledge of Christ from which a start is made later to develop into faith - what changes into faith is not knowledge but want of faith! And that change does not involve the dialectic that we have been discussing. "In distinction from the assertion of the deification of a man, or of the humanisation of a divine idea, the statement of the divinity of Christ is to be understood in the sense that Christ reveals the Father. But this Father of his is God. Therefore to reveal him is to reveal God. But who can reveal God but God himself? Certainly no exalted man and certainly no descended idea can do that. Both are creatures. Certainly the Christ who reveals the Father is also a creature and his work a creaturely work. But if he were only a creature, then neither could he reveal God, just as surely as the creature cannot take the place of God, or act in his place. If he reveals God, he must himself be God, whatever be the relation with his creatureliness. And in that case he must be — for this is a case of either/or - complete true God, without deduction or limitation, without more or less. He is not "all but" and he is not "somehow" God. By every such limitation his divine Being would be not only weakened but denied. To confess him as the revelation of his Father, is to confess him as being essentially equal to this Father of his." (Karl Barth, *op. cit.* p. 465)

If we recall our discussion on the knowledge of the Trinity as grounded in and based on revelation we see that there is no real revelation in the complete sense of the word as we have it in Christ unless God reveals himself personally in Christ. That involves the identity of the One who reveals and of that which is revealed. In Christ we do not have a mere message; God himself speaks — that is the immediate asseveration of faith. In the existence of this Person, Jesus, God is Present in a final way, such that Christ is not simply the bearer of a Word but *is* the Word itself or rather himself. If this is not the meaning of revelation in Christ, then Christ is mere symbol, merely the bearer of an idea that can be detached from his Person. "But this would not then be revelation; for he would then be less than a prophet, not more. It is only this identity of the divinely authoritative Word and the Person which constitutes the fact that he is 'more than a prophet'. Thus his Person is not the transparent veil through which gleams the divine, but he is himself the divine; hence he is not that which is divine, but God." (Brunner, *op. cit.* p. 273 f.) This means that faith in the Person of Christ yields the doctrine of the Trinity: and it has been this doctrine that has kept the doctrines of the Christ and the Spirit pure from the inroads of corrosion in the Church and outside of it. It has been the bulwark against mythology on the one hand, and against the deification of man on the other — while it destroyed Arianism finally.

The Christian doctrine of The Trinity in relation to revelation means that the only genuinely personal Word of God is that which exists concretely in a person — that which has become a person. It is precisely on this fact that the Old Testament revelation hangs as well. It is only with this hope that the prophet dared to lift up his voice and say "Thus saith the Lord" - all those words were loaded with the future Word that was to come, and they are to be thought of rather as proleptic revelations of the Christ. They are fulfilled, and finally substantiated when the Word actually comes to pass and does become Person. Apart from this the Old Testament must remain a problem, just as the fact of sin and Law remained a problem for Paul until seen in the Cross, as he says in Rom 3:23 f. They are only planets which do not shine in their own light. Of course they conveyed light, those words of the Old Testament; but were not that Light which lights every man that comes into the world already on the way without which there would have been no light but darkness, gross darkness. It is thus that Abraham and with him all the faithful saw the day of Christ and rejoiced. That light came; at last the Word who was eternally with God came into the world, a Light to lighten the Gentiles and a horn of salvation to Jacob. Here alone in a final and ultimate way does God pronounce his own Name, in Christ the Lord. Here alone do we have the Word, or Son, upon whom all other words like planets draw their light, for here alone do we have a word who is *identical* with the Speaker. Here alone does God actually give himself wholly to the finite. The questions which we ask here confronted with this Word, with the Christ, are questions that must arise in the face of such other ways of regarding the Christ, and they are questions which carefully considered and answered with courage, yield the proper dialectic of faith for a formulation of a true Christology. They are these and the like (cf. Brunner. *op. cit.* p. 280).

Is this Word which we have in Christ really God? Is God like this? Or is this Person only a divine instrument of revelation — and do we wait for another? Do we have God here in his inherent reality? Is it really God's own proper Name which is here manifest? Or is it merely the form which contains something entirely different? Is the self-communication of God something different from God himself, or is it precisely this God who communicates himself, who is the real and true God, the essential Deity, the Divine Name? Is the form in which God comes to us something which differs from his real Being? Or, on the other hand, is this will to descend, to seek fellowship, to give himself, the actual will of God, so that both his "Coming" and his "Being", his Self-revelation and his independent inherent Deity, his Self-communication and his Essence, are one and the same?

It is this question — this question, for they are all the same — that we answer in the affirmation of the Deity of Christ as of absolute significance for faith. For it is this affirmation which alone guarantees us the revelation which Christ brings. In the Bible revelation is never mere form, but always at the same time, real content. The fact that God's Word has come to us is indistinguishable from its actual Truth; but the word of revelation is true in so far as it comes from God, and it is acknowledged by us as true as far as we acknowledge it as an actual word, the Word, which has come from God. It is the fact that the word has come from God which makes it legitimate as such. For that which only claims the right to exist on account of its content is a general and timeless idea. To recognise the word of revelation as true means to admit also that it has actually come; and this means that we listen to it with the knowledge that this word has actually come from God. Thus it is only when we perceive who the Revealer is that we are assured of revelation at all. It is the fact that God reveals himself that *is* his love; in the very fact that he comes down to our level, that he comes to us, that he seeks us, that he reveals his heart, his will, that he suffers for us — that betokens God's very Grace. Thus it is only when we see that the Revealer really is God himself that we perceive that God is One whose inmost Essence or Being is Love, whose inherent Reality is Personal, and that he exists for us. God manifests himself to us in revelation as the One who communicates himself, as Love. Because the communication, the Word, is himself, therefore in himself he is One who gives himself. But that he is the One who communicates himself we cannot conceive otherwise than through the thought that in himself — and not only in relation to the world — he is Loving, Self-giving One. (For this see Brunner, *op. cit.*, p. 279)

Again: "A Human being may be as moral and religious as he likes, he is still merely a man, and as such he has nothing to tell me about God. For either he merely tells me something which I can examine for myself afterwards, then he is a `teacher', and stands on the same level as I do; the only difference between us is that he is a few paces further on. Or he may really communicate to me something of the mystery of God: it is not he who speaks as himself; indeed, it does not really matter to me *who* he may be at all. His word is a prophetic word. But there is a further possibility: he himself may be in his own Person this Divine Word, coming from the realm which lies beyond all human possibilities. Then he cannot be man, a man like the rest of us, including the man of genius and the prophet, but he must be the Son of God, he in whom the word of revelation, the secret word in which God speaks his own name, a human being, has actually become flesh: he is the Christ. Then he speaks and acts as God himself with Divine personal authority, no longer in virtue of a divine commission, but in virtue of his Divine Being, as the Son, to whom the Father `has given to have life in himself'. This is the perfected Word, the One which has actually come to us, the Word in whom the Divine Truth and righteousness, which was separated from us by the great gulf made by the Fall, comes to us himself and imparts himself to us as truth, righteousness life: the Word in which God gives himself personally to us, because in the Word he is personally present, as the bridge over the gulf between us and him, as the Mediator." (*Ibid.* p. 228)

What, then, shall we say the significance of Christ for faith is? The significance is this: that not only do we here hear the Word but we see it; that not only do we here have the Word of God coming to us but we have it active as well; here we have not only a Word from the beyond of the *Word*, but we have the Word itself, or rather himself. In the Prophets the Word came too, but it was a Word from beyond and about the beyond. Here in Christ faith finds the Beyond itself about whom the other Words, the prophetic words had spoken. God is not only speaking here, but *speaking in Person*; and God not only is speaking here in Person, but is *acting in Person*. In Christ we have One in whom the Word and the Work of God are one and identical. Thus the great significance of Christ for faith is that it is *The Person*, yes, the personal existence of the Lord Jesus Christ, which *is* the Word. The disciples do not listen here to the Baptist; he pointed to another. The disciples listen to One who is himself *The One*, to whom all else pointed. They listen to One who directs them to his own Person. "Come unto Me", he says! Christ stands on the other side of the frontier where God only stands, within the realm of the Divine Majesty. This is the fact from which faith starts out — Christ as the "Visibile" Reality of God, and not only the "Audible" Reality. *His Person is the Word*, not a word about the Word, but one and the same as the Word, identical with the Word. It is his Person who is the Gospel! It is his Person which arouses faith and maintains it as the divine Object of faith. He is as such the correlative of God — there is no Word about the Father which is not Christ, there is nothing about the Christ which is not a Word about the Father. As Barth puts it: "There is no Jesus per se, who might perhaps later acquire the additional predicate of a bearer of the revelation of God. Just as there is also no revelation of the Father per se, which later might also be apprehended in Jesus, by way of an instance and in a pre-eminent form. But Jesus is the revelation of the Father, and the revelation of the Father is Jesus. And actually it is in virtue of this *is* that he is the Son or the Word of the Father." (*op. cit.* p. 472) "Christ confronts us all as the One who is himself God, as One who does not seek God as we do, but who brings God to us, as One who does not tremble before the judgement of God, but who knows that he is himself on the other side of the Judge of the whole world, not as One who must endeavour to enter into the Kingdom of God, but as One who in his own Person brings in the Kingdom, even though in a hidden way. He is One who descends to earth, instead of ascending to heaven like the rest of us. He is not One who has to make up his mind, but is One who is the focal point of all decision, the `only begotten', the `only' Son of God." (Brunner, *The Mediator*, p. 247 f.)

CHAPTER 6

The Incarnation

The Christian doctrine of the Incarnation is perhaps the most distinctive feature about Christianity regarded as a system of Truth. Its teaching here is quite alone in all thought. Other religions and philosophies have held or postulated theophanies, but none has really asserted an actual incarnation of God, such that *One Man is very God and very Man, vere Deus et vere Homo*. For all thought outside Christian thought it is this which is the greatest *scandalon* or stumbling-block! That the Christian faith associates in this way the Eternal God with a contingent fact of history seems to be an insuperable stumbling-block for human thought, and the greater that stumbling-block becomes, the more difficult systematic thinking becomes!

It is at the bottom a refusal to face the *Incarnation* squarely that is the root error in false Christologies. Thus both the Ebionite and Docetic Christological formulations ultimately entail a denial of the fact that God as God really became Man. On the one hand, Ebionitism instead of starting with the Incarnation, started at the other end and reached a deification of the Man Jesus which entails a double denial of the Incarnation because in the end, the very humanity of Christ is impaired. On the other hand, Docetism started with denying the real humanity of Christ which is either unreal and only apparent, or it is finally regarded as unimportant, since the essential significance of Jesus is held to be not in his Person but in the divine Idea that he represents or mediates. As such Docetism passes over thus into Ebionitism and constitutes again a double denial of the Incarnation, for the Divine Person is transmuted into a abstract idea, and the Person of Jesus is regarded as a mere symbol. Against both of these mistaken Christologies the Christian faith maintains in the strongest terms the full fact of the Incarnation, namely, that the Very Word of God who was in the beginning with God and actually was God, and through whom there was not anything made that was made, really became flesh, took upon himself the humble form of a servant and dwelt among men. The significant words in the doctrine is the word "became" with the predicate "flesh" immediately following.

It is this "became" (*egeneto*) that is difficult, that causes all the trouble, and that brings forth the vehement denials in this-worldly thought. The truth is that it is humanly actually unthinkable; it is an incomprehensible idea or term applied to God! We cannot interpret it, that is, relate it to the rest of our knowledge. It cannot be explained, that is, so related to the rest of our knowledge that it is given a central place within a systematic coherent body of truth. In fact, this word "became" actually shatters all human thought about God, and like a hammer smashes it all into relativity. The keenest minds have always seen this; alas, it is often only professing Christians who have failed to see the incredible drastic reality which it denotes. Even pagans like Celsus in ancient times and Nietzsche in modern times knew well what the Incarnation meant, as it was promulgated by the Christian faith, and that is why it was abhorred by them or whittled down into something that meant its very opposite! That is why too most philosophers have looked askance at this doctrine of Christianity or laboured in vain to reconcile it with their own thought or their own thought with it.

Here, then, in the doctrine of the Incarnation, we have the great dividing line between Christian thought and all other religious or philosophical thought; and it is here that the Christian Church must stand or fall — the doctrine of the Incarnation properly conceived is an *articulus cadentis aut stantis ecclesiae* - by it the Church stands or falls! Hence it behoves us to approach it with the utmost care, and, in the light of the truth we have already discussed, to face the facts squarely without any yielding to the temptation to look at it obliquely, thus missing its main force: the force of the Fact that *God himself became Man, and became man without ceasing to be God, very God, and yet without impairing the very humanity he assumed.* We cannot approach the question logically. We must think of it frankly and clearly without demur. We may not approach it *a priori.* We can approach it only *a posteriori,* only through faith looking at the actual event after it has come to pass, and see it in the light of the revelation of God given in it and the act of redemption there wrought for us men and women.

We will do well, before actually entering into the discussion of the positive content of the doctrine, to bracket it off, and to discuss some of the implications which it involves, implications which bear so sorely on human thought and life. The very fact of the Incarnation creates for itself out of the world of life and thought a background, and it is in the light of this that we might do well to turn our thoughts to the Incarnation first. It is here too that the issues involved will be raised to their most precise intensity, and then, with a clear idea of the issues and difficulties involved, we shall be able to tackle the central question of faith.

1. The Implications of the Incarnation

A. If God became man, then there was a movement of Eternity into time. That is one of the central facts, indeed *the* central fact, of the Incarnation. When we think of it that after all has been the whole message of the Bible, the *movement* of living acting God toward men. This is the Christian doctrine of *Grace*, that God in his sovereign freedom has taken the initiative of Love toward men. The whole implication of revelation is just this, that in it we have a movement of God in the direction of men, and not a movement of men in the direction of God. This revelation is fulfilled completely in the Incarnation. Before this God had drawn near, but now he has come. Eternity has moved into time and taken up an abode in time. By this is not meant, of course, that a piece of eternity has entered time, or has been inserted into time and as such has an existence in a section of time, therefore a certain circumscribed existence. It means that in the Incarnation Eternity without diminishment has entered time without its diminishment and dwells in time in temporal form, without of course ceasing to be what it is.

The essential point, however, for our consideration at this stage is just this movement of Eternity toward and into time. We must note a number of the implications contained here in this word "became", *egeneto*, or in this word *movement*. We must remember that fundamentally Eternity is what God is; Eternity is God-in-action. The point with which we are first confronted, then, is that in the heart of Eternity there is motion. Eternity is not static. God is not what Aristotle called "the unmoved Mover", nor is God impassible, in the philosophical sense of the word which we repudiate. This means that Eternity is an eternity of action, therefore of relation, yet of the One who is always himself, the *I am who I am*, the ever unchanging and abiding One, whose freedom is not conditioned, but who is ever free to be himself, and who is Love. Now this cannot possibly be grasped and understood by thought. Our rational thought operates with the principle of continuity, and therefore systematically developed operates with a conception of an or the Absolute in which or in whom all particular relations, motions, and distinctions disappear. Thus the very idea that Eternity actually moves into time, without of course ceasing to be Eternity — that too is an impossible thought for philosophy. In philosophical thought time always tends to disappear, to be swallowed up in a timeless eternity or just timelessness, and therefore any question about time is simply a question about appearance not reality. Time is thus regarded as essentially appearance or phenomenon and not really or ultimately real. The Universal or Absolute by definition cannot be thought of as having anything to do with time relations far less as involved in them. Thus there is no love or motion in the God of Aristotle; there is no purpose in the God of Spinoza; there is no Personality with reciprocal relationships in the Absolute of Hegel! There time and Eternity are thought of as logical correlatives and the stronger finally negates the weaker — Eternity, time. The Absolute is the All in all.

Here in Christian thought, however, we have quite the opposite approach — the concept of the "Incarnation": *the actual coming of the Eternal God into time.* What does that mean, then, but that Eternity establishes relations, real relations, with time?! In Time, yes, it is actually *in Time*, that we are confronted with Eternity. Eternity meets us in Time. Eternity itself has advanced to meet time, and time stands still, as it were, before this advent. This means further that time must be real for Eternity, that time relations are posited as real events for Eternity, and it is here, at least, that time has its justification as something real — that is, in the Incarnation. Therefore time may not be resolved away as ultimately unreal. Hence we may not pass by the human Jesus, the historical Christ, and think only of his teaching in terms of eternal timeless ideas. The significance of the Incarnation is just this that "the Eternal Word who is God, the personal and historical existence of the Christ". The Word has *become* flesh — *egeneto sarx* (ἐγένετο σάρξ). Eternity comes into grips with Time — why of course, Eternity, Holy Eternity, does not annihilate time, we cannot understand, but have to refer it simply to the Wonderful reality of the Love and Grace of God. That is what the Incarnation betokens, a gracious attitude of Eternity toward time, evident in the acts of God in forgiveness and reconciliation.

This, of course, does not mean that Eternity condones time or whatever takes place in time, no more than forgiveness of sin means the condoning of sin. The coming of Eternity, the entry of the Eternal into time, of the eternal God into time, betokens Grace that is to say, the "eternal" forgives time or deeds that take place in time, even when it negates or condemns them. For it is precisely the condemned deeds in time that are forgiven. Hence we cannot run away with the idea that because Eternity enters time, that all is well with time, that thereby time is simply ratified and substantiated, or that the Incarnation of God guarantees to people that their existence in time is essentially in union with Eternity. The very contrary is betokened as we shall see!

B. And so the second implication of the Incarnation is that the world as it actually is, is *not* right with God or rightly related to God — the Incarnation presupposes what is known as the "the fall" of man, and the reality of sin. The created World has lapsed from its proper relation to the Creator, has fallen away from God, and so in order to recover the world, in order to redeem it, the eternal God himself enters the world in and through the Incarnation of his eternal Word in that fallen world, in order, certainly to condemn sin in the world, but also to destroy sin and save the world. The fact that the whole of Eternity had to be set in motion in order to save and redeem mankind, the fact that God's Only Begotten Beloved Son had to become incarnate in the world in order to restore men and women to fellowship with God, shows the depth of their need, and the dire reality of sin and its judgment. If it took the coming of the Eternal God into time, as happened in the birth of the Lord Jesus Christ in the world, in order to redeem time, there must be a fearful chasm, utter separation, between God and man — and that is precisely the meaning of original sin. As Anselm said, sin means sin against the infinite Majesty of God, and therefore sin is infinite in its results; it means infinite guilt, absolute separation, and impassable Abyss, *Abgrund*, as Barth calls it — which man cannot pass over or bridge.

The Incarnation, however, is not to be understood as a metaphysical necessity. This means that we cannot dare to say, therefore, as some people in the history of Christian thought have claimed, that even had man not sinned, even if the world had not fallen, God would have become incarnate. The Incarnation is not and was not due to any necessity within God's Being or to any kind of immanent principle or law in God. The Incarnation was an act of utterly free love, sheer divine love, "uncaused love", as it were, and was as such a revealing and saving act of pure grace. Further, because the act of God in the incarnation was a real manifestation of divine grace, it thereby reveals that there was a desperate need for salvation in the world; it means that the incarnate coming of God was essentially redemptive in its nature, a movement of pure unmerited divine grace toward a world that had somehow "fallen" from him.

It is that breach between the world and God that provides the meaningful perspective in which the incarnation is to be understood as essentially a *redemptive* event. It thus reveals the meaning of the Incarnation, while it is the actual happening of the Incarnation of the very Son of God himself, that reveals the depth of the breach, or of what is called the "fall" of the world, and of man, from God. We cannot say that the Incarnation would have taken placed had the world or man not fallen away from God as if it was due to an imperfection in the world which was inherent in the world from the creation — which was the view of F.R. Tennant of Cambridge. Such a conception is Gnostic or Manichaean, and entirely alien to the message of God's self-revelation in Christ. The purpose of the Incarnation relates rather to sinful fallen humanity; not therefore to humanity as such, but to *fallen* humanity. The Incarnation is not to be understood as the perfection but the restoration of the creation. We shall see later what an uproar this has created in the history of thought — but the coming of Christ always creates an uproar! How could it help but create an uproar in such a world as this? The Incarnation had to do with the reconciliation between sinful man and a wrathful God. It means that God himself has come in grace — and it is precisely because *he* has come in grace and forgiveness, that it might be said that in contrast we have the greatest revelation of his divine wrath. "No one", writes Bultmann, "has spoken more forcibly of the wrath of God (although without using the word) than Jesus, precisely because he proclaims God's grace. Because he conceives radically the idea of the grace of God, he makes it plain that God's forgiveness must be for man an event in time, that the relation of `I' and `thou' exists between God and man, that

God stands opposite to man as another Person over whom the man can have no sort of control, who meets man with his claim and with his grace, whose forgiveness is a pure gift." (*Jesus and The Word*, p. 203, Eng. tr.) That implies that the Incarnation in itself was and is a revelation to man of the fearful need which brought the coming of Christ to earth. Apart from this coming we would not know either of the mercy of God or of our own dire need. And it is because the Incarnation has taken place in such infinite and unconditional love, because the Incarnation meant the plucking from the Bosom of the Father of his only begotten Son in his purpose to save the world, that we may by contrast get a glimpse into the black darkness of sin that yawns between us and God. But thank God, the Incarnation does not only reveal to us something of that fearful gulf of darkness but reveals the divine provision for our salvation from judgment and damnation and opens the way for us in new life and resurrection. That darkness, however, is something to which we must give serious attention, for it means that those who turn away from God the Holy One, who precisely in his Holiness must himself turn away from the sin of humanity sinner, disclosed to us in the terrible cry of Jesus on the Cross: "My God, my God, why hast thou forsaken me?"

It is there in the sacrifice of the Lamb of God bearing and bearing away the sins of the world, that our desperate condition as sinners becomes revealed, but also the incredible love of God in Christ in his incarnate Son who for our sakes became one of us and one with us bearing our sins in his vicarious humanity to redeem and save us guilty sinners from judgment and damnation. It is there in the passion of the Lord Jesus, and really there alone, that we can take the idea of guilt seriously, knowing that we ourselves cannot lift a finger to remove it. It is in the past and out of our control altogether. It is only when we dare to look at the crucified Saviour, crucified for us, that we can and may be saved. It is only the man who has lost all hope, who is reduced to abject despair, and finds there is no way to God, who is ready to see the real saving significance of the Incarnation. He alone can believe in God, and he alone can trust in a real coming of God to the world. Emil Brunner writes: "A man can only be brought to a full sense of his own complete helplessness when he admits that `God himself must come to me, hence I must indeed be so far away from him that I cannot possibly find the way back myself.'"

C. We have now to consider a further implication of the coming of Eternity into time in the *act* or *event* of the *Incarnation* itself. We have already glanced at it: the truth that the gracious coming of Eternity into time disqualifies time, but redeems it. *Gratia non tollit naturam, sed perficit.* (thus Thomas Aquinas!) This is an implication or corollary of the last point — but it is here that we see where the chagrin of modern Renaissance man comes from — for it means nothing less than the smashing of all his cherished hopes, the surrender of his self-will and vaunted human autonomy by a condemnation of it as sin, and indeed the disqualification of the rights of man, for man is now forfeit before God; so in fact it means ultimately the disqualification of civilisation and the great and magnificent tower of Babel which man has built and goes on building, a judgment of it all as a form of "Titanism", however refined and aesthetic it may be! It is thus that men like Nietzsche cry out against Christianity, for it means nothing short of the reversal of all human values, the subversion of all that is the product of man, of man in time. It is not often that Christians have seen this truth — and it has been left to a pagan minds like Celsus, as I remarked before, to show the Christian wherein the genius of Christianity lies. What is the message of the Incarnation in this respect, but that when we have laboured in the vineyard, as Jesus said, we all receive the same reward, whether we have laboured all day and borne the heat and burden of the day or whether we have but laboured for one short hour before sunset? That is not fair cries the modern man, cries Nietzsche, as well as the classical man, Celsus! Of course it is not fair when judged from the values of time that we human beings have set up, the values of a fallen world: but in the Kingdom of God all these values as such are utterly undone and disqualified, and the sentence of death is uttered over all: "There is no difference." "All have sinned and come short of the glory of God". There is no difference! That is a hard saying of St. Paul, but precisely the truth that we see in the parable of Jesus. It is here, then, that we arrive at the great difficulty natural man has of the Incarnation. We must look at it in the face.

The coming of Eternity into time means that time, the time of this world of ours, is disqualified. It implies the condemnation of time although, as we have seen, time is nevertheless real, and that there is a place in the heart of Eternity for time, time redeemed, real time. It is, however, the fallen world — this present evil *aeon*, or this present evil age that Eternity disqualifies. It does not, of course, disqualify time as such, but rather indicates that time as such (if there be any such thing as time as such!) has a place in Eternity which is not static monotone but God-in-action. That is the meaning of the Kingdom of God as Jesus preached it at the beginning of his earthly Ministry, the preaching of the Kingdom of God which would overthrow this present order ruled by human pride and moralised evil. But while Jesus came to overthrow the old order, he came to set up a new one, a new Kingdom, a new time. He entered this evil time in order to bring it to judgement and death, but with the promise of renewal. He died on the Cross in and for the world; but in his resurrection from the grave he gave it new hope, and with this resurrection there was the promise, and also the beginning of a new Order and a new Time.

Thus in a real sense the Resurrection might well be said to be the completion of the Incarnation. Consequently if in one way the Incarnation means the end of all history, yet in another way it means the proper fulfilment of it - in and through the mighty Word of God incarnate in Christ. History had lost its proper destiny in the Fall of mankind, and was pressing toward a wrong goal, but its proper goal is promised and fulfilled in Jesus Christ risen from the dead. We must not think of the Incarnation as the peak of history, the flowering of the race, the height of civilisation and all that! The Incarnation means something utterly different. Nor does the incarnation mean that once when the world was old and weary with age, and humanity was struggling and dying in agony and thirst, in a nostalgia for the beyond, that God renewed the world again, brought about a new Spring in the Incarnation in which he infused new life, so to speak, into its veins, brought new vitality and a new lease of life. Such thought when found in Christianity — and I have often heard it preached in our country — is little short of a humanistic paganism. It is the old Greek myth of Ceres baptised into Christianity or the Egyptian myth of Isis and Osiris redivivus!

The Christian understanding or doctrine of the Incarnation is exactly at the opposite pole from all such thinking and nostalgia. It means the end of all that. It means in fact the end of all *human* thought, the end of *human* hopes, but the coming of a really *new* Order, to which no continuity in history may be drawn. But just because this new order is really new, a wholly other, it does not mean, and cannot mean, an historical extension in the time of our world, but rather its final and complete transformation, when the time of our world will reach its end and a new time will arrive, which is not to be thought of as an eschatological gathering up and a transformation our worldly historical worldly time into a crisis of decision. History as such, is disqualified, history of our world, our history as such is disqualified, disqualified even while it was used even in the Incarnation, for it is renounced on the Cross. Thus we may not think of the Kingdom of God as an historical extension of time, but as bringing in what is radically new and which cannot be construed in terms of the world that waits for its final transformation and renewal at the return of the incarnate and resurrected Lord Jesus Christ.

It is just here that we face one of the issues where the Incarnation challenges modern and ancient man most. Christianity sees history as a whole to be under divine judgment and needing radical transformation. Man, however, likes to regard history as normal, or if not normal as it actually is at any given moment, as something that is really adjustable through human efforts, so that it is within the power of man to improve history. This implies that there is not much radically wrong with history and is actually characterised by progress. This assumes optimistically that our world and its time are not really fallen, that man is not essentially wrong, but that what is wrong is a set of individual and incidental features within humanity or history — but these features may be removed. Hence there is no belief in the dire corruption of mankind or of the race in spite of its appalling history. Original sin is not realised, not realised precisely because it is disliked. People don't like to think that they are out of gear, that they have fallen from God, that they are on the wrong side of a break with reality. They do not like that because it means that the coherence of the world, the balance of things is upset, but believe or want to believe and that a really world and new time will come about through human progress.

Yes, in spite of the appalling events of our time, people like to think of history in terms of as a vast human progress which will end up in a fulfilment of creation. The Incarnation, however, comes with another message, with the message of Daniel: *Mene, Mene, Tekel, Upharsin*! "Thou art weighed in the balance and found wanting"! There the divergence of the Incarnation from the world is most wide, or deepest, and is very apparent in the doctrine of natural evolution or continuity. That is the basic thought of our modern life and practice. There is no principle so thoroughgoing, so far-reaching in its implications as this belief in progress. Continuity has become the warp and woof of our humanistic outlook and the temper of our mood. It has indeed become a basic category of our understanding! Indeed Kant included it in his Principle of Causality. In the first part of his book on the *Philosophy of Religion*, he actually denied it in the doctrine of radical evil; but he had hardly denied it when he saw how disastrous it would be for his whole system and he made a compromise in the last half of the work which meant its denial. Yes, he appeared to realise as no philosopher did really realise properly, not excepting Schelling, until Kierkegaard, that to deny the principle of continuity would mean that he would have to accept divine revelation and become a Christian. It might be said in fact that no philosopher can *as such* be a Christian! A proper study of David Hume ought to have taught the modern world that long ago.

To be a Christian means precisely that this principle of continuity is denied, for he Christian message is one of repentance, rebirth and renewal, and calls for the confession of sin, of failure, and the recognition of original sin. It means that the world has broken away from God and is so hopelessly astray and wrong that it takes the whole of Heaven to come down to its rescue! That Eternity must come to time means that time cannot save itself. It means that if Eternity *does really come to and into* time, then time is not in touch with Eternity; it means that time is discontinuous with Eternity. Were that not so, then the Incarnation would not be a real coming of God to the world, but a flowering of humanity toward God. Were that not so, the movement would not be from God to man, but one from man to God! It is thus that Ebionite Christology like all philosophy, starting from man, ends by denying man, and making history and time merely docetic! The Incarnation means that the Divine is not present in the world in any natural fashion, is not immanent within the world *as* the world would like to have it.

In contrast to the world's optimistic belief in progress the Incarnation means that Divine truth must be *revealed*, not discovered but be *given.* The Incarnation is an irruption of a mighty Divine Word or love and grace from above which pierces through the continuity of this world and breaks it open. The monologue of the philosopher is broken, the soliloquy of the mystic is broken, and there is a great interruption — the entrance of a Word from the beyond! Hence the disturbance creates an uproar. Men don't like to feel that the continuity of things has been broken, that the comfortable theology that they have built up is to be questioned; they do not like to believe that their tower of Babel is Titanism and must be cast down; they do not like to feel that the "balance" (see Brunner, *The Mediator,* p. 107) is disturbed.

That Word of God always confronts us with a definite challenge. That is why the eyes of Jesus are as a flame of fire and his teaching is like a two-edged sword! The Incarnation denies the harmony of the world, and it denies the possibility of finding truth and salvation in any other way than through a real coming from the other side. It must be Christ or Goethe, a German friend said to me, when faced for the first time with the challenge of Christ in its stark nakedness. The issue today is either the Renaissance or the Resurrection. The Renaissance with its assertion of the rights of man, with its fundamental principle of continuity with the divine, with its glory in man, is diametrically opposed to the Message of Christianity. "Choose you this day whom you will serve!" Driven from pillar to post, modern or Renaissance man has been taking refuge in the realm of moral and social values, for there, he thinks, he is at least safe. There, whatever be the criticism that pursues him and dogs his steps from Christian and pagan alike (!), he thinks he will be able to find a safe haven, for it is through moral and social values and actions that man must approach God. That, of course, has been the dominant note in the latest phase of modern thought. This, however, only means a return to the moral compromise rife in Protestantism today, to the idea of self-justification not least in its socialised form. Faced with a new Paganism modern man refuses to fight, but effects a compromise identical in principle with that which gave rise to modernism in the Church. I must not go further into this here, but suffice it to say, that the ethical and ethico-social approach to religion of our day is little short of a refined form of group egoism, for the kind of love or altruism which it advocates as bringing man into continuity with God, is one determined by and dependent on the quality, beauty and value of the whatever objective he prefers to commit himself. It is not real love or even some form of altruism that motivates him personally or socially; but what one might call "caused" love and is ultimately a form of desire and self-expression, personal or social. It is evidently very different from or even a denial of the kind of *agape* love revealed in the Incarnation.

The revelation of the Lord Jesus Christ, precisely because it is *revelation*, imports a very different approach, for it means the reversal of all human values, ethical and socialist as well as others. The Word of the Gospel not only attacks our vaunted human values but the human ego, the human personality of which we are so inordinately proud today. Christianity attacks the very centre of the moral will, the self-esteem of moralism and every self-justifying ethical approach, the self-sufficiency of moral energy. "I ought, therefore I can", says modern man. And that is finally the essence of anti-Christianity. For the Incarnation says the very opposite. It is because you cannot, that God comes.

Hence, to sum up this point, the message and meaning of a real Coming of Eternity to Time, the Gospel of Grace, is regarded as an absurdity and an offence. Indeed an Insult! "The will of the self-sufficient modern man reacts violently against this assistance which is only offered to those who have learned to despair of themselves. This is degrading to humanity; it is treating humanity as a minor and stripping it of all its rights; it is intolerable! In its most earnest form, in the form of personal dignity — or, as Christianity calls it, in the form of self-righteousness or a righteousness which is of works — reason here revolts against the claims of the Christian revelation." (Brunner, *op. cit.* p. 115) The point of view here in antithesis to Christianity may be summed up in the words of the Pagan Aristotle : "He who lives according to reason is the special object of God's love. For if the gods, as s commonly believed, take thought for our human affairs, we must rationally conclude that they take most pleasure in that which is best and most nearly related to themselves, that is, in our reason, and that they reward those who live according to reason. It is clear that this is most of all the case of the wise man. Therefore it is he who is most loved by God." (Aristotle, *Nic. Ethics*. X., 9)   A still more obvious return to the humanist principle of salvation through merit arises when optimism is related to the growing secular emphasis upon a social or socialised community more than to the individual, or to humanity as a whole. It is the hope that in a moral hierarchy which will be gradually built up, the Kingdom of God will come on earth when the individual will be able to overcome the moral tensions between good and evil which he could not do otherwise! Here humanity as a whole, since the Incarnation and the teaching of Jesus, it is urged, is continuous with the divine. Jesus leads the way as the Elder Brother. As individuals we must not regard ourselves too important, however. Here the emphasis is on social relations, cooperatives (good as they are), which, of course, is a sign that man has lost his real connection with God and is seeking to find support somewhere else! This idea of human development or continuity even in a social way is, however, assailed by the Incarnation as well. For history and time are still under the judgement of God, and we cannot regard God, or the Eternal as somehow extended and developing in time in this way. This is, however, an idea firmly rooted in the modern mind, and that is why it resents revelation and the supernatural so violently. "The thesis of the Christian religion, however, is the very opposite: that no moment in historical existence is in its right place, nor can it be justified. It is against this desecration of history that the modern mind revolts when it turns against Christianity. It feels itself menaced and injured. Thus the idea of continuity in the philosophy of history is rooted in the same fundamental thought as the modern idea of continuity in general, that is, in the assertion that our given existence is continuous with the divine." (Brunner, *op. cit.* p. 118)

It is thus up to us as Christians to think this matter through, the question of continuity or discontinuity: for here Christianity and all other ways, ethical and religious, part direction and company. Here is the either/or fork in the road — the one is the broad way that looks fair but leads to destruction, the other is the narrow way that looks forbidding for it faces an abyss and a deep canyon, the pit of sin which must be but cannot be bridged by us, but the other way leads up to Mount Zion! The Incarnation challenges all thought and all men and women to a decision, because it is the coming of the Eternal into time. It is round this that the battles must be fought out, whether the assertion of continuity, the self-assurance of Renaissance and modern man is true, or rather, why it is not true. Here lies the key to the understanding of the Christian faith and its opposition to the modern mind. (See again Brunner, *op. cit.* p. 121)

D. A fourth implication of the Incarnation is a setting aside and indeed an uprooting of all our own knowledge. This is a corollary of the fact that the coming of God in Christ means a disqualification of our values, of our self-asserted or vaunted rights. Among these rights are included the right to be able to know God of ourselves. When revelation comes it means that we have a revelation of something that was hidden, a revelation of God in Person who was not therefore knowable impersonally - therefore not known otherwise or knowable elsehow. This means at once that all our previous categories of thought are punctured; they cannot contain this new knowledge vouchsafed to us in Christ, and therefore we may not pigeon-hole this knowledge in previously acquired thought-forms. Out of its judgement upon these thought-forms the revelation that is given in and through the Incarnation will create new thought-forms, nay, a new language, the language of the Spirit, which will be used by the Spirit to convey the spiritual realities. This must be taken seriously before the depth of the Incarnation can be probed at all — the fact that the Revelation of God in a personal and acutely personalised way through the Incarnation, means *eo ipso* a refutation of other knowledge, it means a relativising of it all. When we see Jesus Christ face to face all else fades into the background, into insignificance, and Eternity itself shines forth. This is a light brighter than the noonday sun which flashed upon St Paul on the road to Damascus, and it turns our light into darkness as it blinded St Paul. Here we are really confronted with the absolute and it destroys all relative approaches to it from the other end.

Karl Barth asked on one occasion: "Would God be God if he met us in any other way? Would he be the Source of all being and Creator of all things, unless, in comparison to him, all being had to be disqualified as not being, and all things recognised as estranged and fallen away from the good and perfect life which belongs to him alone? And can man conceivably enter in to him except through that door of death and hell which is the perception of his remoteness from him, his condemnation by him, and his powerlessness before him? We meet our doom upon the rocks of imperishable truth, but that is the only way we may be saved from the sea of mere appearance and delusion. The devastating negation under which we live has its positive, obverse side." (*The Word of God and the Word of Man*, p. 168 f.)

We are not to think, however, that the relativisation of all extraneous knowledge is just a relative matter itself; it is not a relative relativisation but an absolute relativisation — it is that because it is concerned with *sin*. The relativisation here has not to do with any relation of the metaphysical absolute to the metaphysical relative both of which are merely imaginary symbols and logically negate one another, but here in the Incarnation of God's eternal Light and Truth, we have to do with a coming that is unique in Holiness and Truth because it is the ground of all goodness, the ground of all truth, and the ground of all being. And precisely because this upon which we all depend has to come and draw near to us in personal presence, we know that the gap which separates us from God is, not a metaphysical or natural gap, but an unnatural one, a sinful one, but a real one.

We must think of and think through the whole matter religiously. In the face of

Jesus Christ I know that I do not see God anywhere else but here; in the self-assertion of God, and in this divine revelation my self-assertion in the matter of knowledge is judged and broken; in the absolute surrender that I make to him, my other allegiances are given up and forsworn. You cannot be a Christian and a philosopher (that is trust in philosophy) at the same time! Pascal was the first to point that out to the modern mind. It is true. We may pursue other thought as a kind of propaedeutic, as a mental discipline, but we cannot give our allegiance to it and at the same time give our allegiance to the Lord Jesus Christ. Christ comes with quite exclusive claims, as the *only* Way, Truth and Life. To acknowledge his Lordship or the reality of the Incarnation is to forswear these other claims. "No one", writes Prof. Daniel Lamont, "who claims his rights as a rational being, can be a Christian." (*Christ and the World of Thought*). Revelation undermines all other "revelations" as false.

2. The Incarnation in its positive meaning

The Incarnation means a real coming of God to man, in which God gives himself *for* and *to* man. These two facts must be held together in a single thought, though they may be rightly distinguished. This coming of God to the world of men is his redeeming action in Grace, and Love. His self-giving is his Love, his will to seek people, men and women and children, and to bind them together again in a fellowship of love with himself. But in this fellowship what constitutes "Love" is God's loving self-giving to men, and what constitutes "Grace" is his self-giving which flows out of the superabundance of his Love toward us who are not in the least worthy of it. Thus, his love or self-giving, as Grace, is not to be regarded as prompted far less as "caused" by any obligation to men on the ground of value or merit. However, we must note that this self-giving of God to people in Jesus Christ, is the giving of God, that is to say, the Transcendent God in the fullness of his Majesty and Glory. He does not give something, or something like himself. He does not send a saviour or mediator who is not himself, but his self-giving is actually a *self*-bestowal of the Great and Holy God, the Lord and Creator.

Thus the Love of God which is found in this self-giving of God involves the bestowal of God in all his fullness (what St Paul called his *pleroma*) to men and women; it includes therefore the self-asserting claims of God as God and Lord. The self-giving of God includes his self-assertion. Who is it, he who comes to men at Bethlehem? It is the Lord of Glory! Who is it that gives himself to men in Love at the Incarnation? The "I am that I am", the Lord God Transcendent in Majesty and exclusive in Holiness. The self-bestowal of God means, then, the bestowal of his holiness as well as his love. The Incarnation of *God* in Jesus Christ means as well, therefore, the coming of God as Judge and Saviour. These two thoughts must not be separated in any conception of the Incarnation. The Incarnation is not just the Incarnation of love on earth. It is not the personalisation of love or the hypostatising of kindness on the part of God toward sinful men. The Incarnation is the Incarnation of the *Lord God* with whom there is no changing, nor shadow in turning. It is the Incarnation of the God who created the world; it is the Incarnation of the God who chose out Israel for a divine mission as a people to whom would be committed the oracles of God, and from whom God would bring forth his Christ, among whom God would himself take flesh and tabernacle among men; the Incarnation is the Incarnation of the God of Sinai, the God of the Law giving; it is the Incarnation of the God who proclaims his name as "The Lord, the Lord God, merciful and gracious, long-suffering and abundant in mercy and truth, keeping mercy for thousands of generations, forgiving iniquity and transgression and sin, and that will by no means clear the guilty, visiting the iniquities of the fathers upon the children, and upon the children's children, unto the third and to the fourth generation." (Exodus, 34:6 ff.)

Let us not think lightly of the Incarnation — for through it we are called into the very presence of the Holy God whose name is Love. He who comes is meek and lowly but comes as he who has a fan in his hand who will thoroughly purge the garner. Hence he has come to send fire on the earth, to bring a sword, and to judge the world for all judgement has been committed unto him. That is what his holy *Self-giving* means, for it is the Self-giving of God, *of God*, the only God who will have no other gods before him and whose eyes are too pure to look on evil; it means the self-giving of God to men without any diminishment in his nature or character or purpose. When therefore the Holy God gives himself to men, when the Holy God loves men, sinful and fallen men, he can love them only by slaying them! *"Si Deus vivificat, facit illud occidendo,"* said Luther, "If God makes alive he does it by slaying"! The coming of God in Jesus Christ means that death, and indeed the death of our death, is the way of life. Death the great enemy of mankind is defeated and turned into the very gateway of Heaven. To meet the God, then, who comes, is to meet One coming apocalyptically with garments dyed in blood, as the Redeemer in glorious apparel, travelling in the greatness of his strength, speaking in righteousness mighty to save. In him we meet One who treads the wine-press alone, treading the people in his holy anger and trampling upon them in his divine wrath until his garments are stained and sprinkled with blood; for the day of vengeance has arrived with his coming, and the day of Redemption has drawn near, but that is the Lord Jesus Christ of Calvary. But it is withal, however, a day of *loving-kindness and infinite mercy*, for in all their affliction *He* is afflicted and in his love and pity *He* redeems them, bears them, and carries them as in the days of old. (Is. 63.1 ff.) We must take the Coming of God to judge and redeem mankind seriously.

We must take this *Self*-giving of God in earnest, remembering that it is the Self-giving of the Holy God. Who dares to take such a gift? Who dares to say thank you for the fire of God's transcendent majesty and holy love? It is only when, like David, we prefer to fall into the hands of the living God - fearful though it be! — that we can understand, with the gravity that is appropriate to such a coming, the profound meaning of the Incarnation. It is only when, so to speak, we pluck the sword of God out of his hands and thrust it through our own bosoms, when smitten before the Holy Presence of our Advent God, we bow ourselves in sack-cloth and ashes, in broken hearts and contrite spirits, that we can look up and see the forgiving love of an ineffable Redeemer who comes at infinite cost to himself, who comes in travail over the birth of human souls and in that travail himself to die. If it costs pain to be born it costs pain to give birth where sinful men are concerned. "To mock at this Evangel is the jest of him who never felt the wound?" (Carnegie Simpson, *op. cit.* p 168)

We cannot think for one moment of the Incarnation apart from this two-fold way of looking at it, in holiness and love. We must think of the Incarnation, in terms of both the Cross and the Resurrection, which were the ultimate goals of Christ's coming. We must think of the Incarnation in the light of Christ's self-bestowal in love and his self-assertion contained in that act. Without this self-assertion the Incarnation cannot be thought of as the Incarnation of *God*, for God *as the one*

Lord God asserts that there shall be no other gods before him, and asserts that his Transcendent Majesty shall be the exclusive law of the universe. Not to do so would be for him to abdicate his very Deity. The very fact that God himself comes to earth means that he comes to assert his claims. Jesus Christ, in his parable, is the Son sent from the far country to collect the dues on the vineyard, to maintain the claims of God on earth, and to this end everything has been committed into his hand. But at the same time as he comes to demand the utmost from men he comes also to save them from the world of sin and evil in which they are involved. He comes to give *Himself* in infinite love and grace to them and to restore the lost fellowship of the human race with God, to bridge the chasm in the fall of man from grace.

We must think then of the Incarnation as an act from God who in his boundless Love and infinite Grace comes into a world that has separated itself from him through sin and which precisely as Holy Love he must and does resist in it its contradiction to his Being and Nature. He comes to condemn and destroy that sin, and in his infinite, and infinitely costly, Grace to redeem men and women, bringing them to a knowledge of himself and restoring them to fellowship with the Triune God. The Incarnation thus betokens for us Life and Knowledge; both are bound up together by the bonds of fellowship with God without which they may not be given or received. But that fellowship has been broken, and there is a quarrel between God and man; a serious breach has taken place, and therefore in achieving that end the Incarnation represents at the same time the way in which the God of absolute Holiness and of infinite Love God acts to settle the quarrel, to forgive man and restore the broken fellowship, at cost only to himself.

We must not think of any of these various purposes as accomplished at any time before the other, but rather of them all as accomplished at the same time and in the one supreme comprehensive act of God's Self-humiliation from the Cradle to the Cross. We cannot therefore properly think of the Incarnation apart from the Atonement, or of the Atonement apart from the Incarnation. Nor may we separate the work from the Person of Christ for they are one, and it is the work of the Person and the Person who does this work, that together make the whole life and work of Jesus of Nazareth significant as fraught with saving Power, as pregnant with Eternity. We may think of these various purposes entailed in the Incarnation in the language of the Fourth Gospel. The Incarnation means that the Word which was in the bosom of the Father and was God has become flesh and *tabernacles* among men; and we behold his Grace and Truth. Thus the Incarnation of the Living Word means that he Jesus is the Way, the Truth, and the Life. Or to use other equivalent terms from the same Gospel, Christ is Love, Life, and Light. None of these may be thought of separately, for they all belong together and merge into one another in a central act. Now for purposes of further elucidation we may do well to think of the Incarnation in this three-fold way.

1. The Incarnation means Love

It is the Way of Love. This Way of Love is the Way from Eternity into Time, the way which God takes in becoming flesh. If the Holiness of God involves the unapproachableness of God in his Transcendent Majesty, the Love means the nearness of God in which he draws nigh to bestow himself upon the contrite spirit and broken in heart. Here at the Incarnation we have something that never happened before. Certainly God had ever drawn near to men, had walked with them as he did with Enoch, talked with them face to face as a friend as he did with Abraham, revealed himself as he did to Moses, but never before did he actually descend in *Person* out of his Eternity in this fashion and don the garb of man. The Old Testament saints and prophets had one Word on all their lips: He is Coming! All their fellowship with God hung on that fact, and God drew nigh to them on the basis of that coming; but now the last in the row of prophets lifts up his voice and shouts, he has come! *Behold the Lamb of God*! At last the God who draws near has broken through time and entered the sphere of our self-alienation to be near us, to take on our flesh, to live as a Man among men, to live with them, to talk with them, to bear and take away all their sins, and to restore them to Fellowship with the Father. He is thus the Way of sheer limitless Love.

We must be careful here — especially today — in thinking of God as love. "'God' and 'love' cannot be read simply as an equation. Love, it will be granted, is the bestowal of self; but if so, the self that gives must form the *prius* or ultimate fountain of such self-giving. Love, in other words, is conceivable and real only as an expression of personality and such an expression as does not create, but presupposes the personality which is expressed." (H.R. Mackintosh, *The Christian Apprehension of God,* p. 194 f.) The Love-act of God in the Incarnation is thus an intensely *personal* act on the part of God in real *self*-bestowal. It is not simply love. The Incarnation means that GOD loves, and loves us; but God cannot therefore be resolved into Love. Therefore we may not construe the Incarnation simply in terms of love; rather must we construe our idea of love in terms of the Incarnation! It is in this way that Christianity reverses all our values. For example: it reverses our idea of Fatherhood. When we know God as Father we must confess that we as such do not know what real fatherhood is! Our fatherhood which we know is only fatherhood so far as it is named after the Fatherhood of God (Eph. 3:15), and *not vice versa*! That is what the Incarnation must mean in all of our human and Christian life. But we must consider this matter more deeply.

A. The first thing we must note, and note emphatically, is that God is himself the Subject of the Incarnation. The Incarnation is an act of God, very God, an act of the one Eternal God himself. That means that the origin of the act lies outside time altogether, quite apart from our world. To understand that is to understand half of Christianity, for it means to understand what the Grace of God is. In this sense the Incarnation is not an historical event, for it does not arise out of history, nor is it presupposed by history; but it is rather an invasion of history and an interruption of history and takes place in the midst of history. It upsets history! It breaks into it and makes a radical new beginning — but all that simply because it is an act which starts from outside history altogether in Eternity, and yet enters history. If it were not such, it would be robbed of all significance; it would not be divine revelation; it would not really mean fellowship with God and therefore Light and Life and Love! But just because it is an act of God himself, and because it is *God* in Christ reconciling the world unto himself, is it fraught with all its tremendous power and significance for Christianity and the world that we are aware of. Thus we must take seriously that "both the "sending" and the "being sent" are eternal." (Brunner) That the Incarnation starts from the other side of reality altogether, that it starts from God, that it originates in himself alone, makes the Incarnation what it is, and gives us the faith which may depend on it utterly.

The Incarnation means accordingly that God does not wait for men to seek him but that he has and does come seeking them, his lost children! God does not wait! He does not wait for us to be good; he does not wait even for us to try! God's love is not a calculated love, it is not prompted or "caused" by anything in us. God does not love us because we are of value or because we are worth loving! The initiative lies absolutely with God, and not even a passive stimulation is to be attributed to mankind. God's love does not take on its colour and value from the nature of its object. Our Love to God may and does. We love him for what he is and love him only because he first loved us. Our love is thus quite different from his love; ours is a responsive love, created, creaturely love. His is uncreated, and itself creative! His Love is grounded in itself, in the Holy Trinity, and does not depend on our being fit or good or having value. Thank God for that! Were it not so, there would be no salvation for any of us! And yet man in his pride dares talk about the infinite value of the human soul! As if he could compel God to love him, as if he could deride God if he did not love him! As if he could use it as a lever against God and force him against all justice to love in spite of evil, in spite of God's own intrinsic nature, as if he could force God to banish punishment and abolish hell! "God has to love me; he will not finally condemn me; because he would not be love otherwise!" To talk like that is not to understand the Love of God in the least! To talk like that is in reality to betray pride and secret fear — it is not really the love that casts out fear! It is a love created by fear! That kind of love is the kind that starts out from human love and which is then foisted upon the Almighty. And it is so plausible because it deals with "love", and it is hard to gainsay such an argument because the word "love" must itself be contradicted and a new "Love" must be substituted — the *AGAPE* of God, as the New Testament calls it. No! We cannot think of God's love as forced love, even if the force be the fact that "we are of infinite value". That doctrine is not a Christian one but its opposite; it is the assertion that God's love is not spontaneous, not free, overflowing, abundant, luxurious love such as we know the Love of God to be. You can never say God "must" love; for that is to say that God "ought" to love; and that is to say that God does not Love! does not Love as God Loves, freely, royally and sovereignly. There is nothing so perverted today in our Christianity as a false cheap view of the Love of God and consequently there has rarely been such a perverted view of Christianity as there seems to be today.

If we will take seriously the fact that the Incarnation really rises in Eternity, in the self-grounded Will of God to bestow himself unconditionally upon men and women — we shall get a real insight into a love that will shatter all false views, and transform the world. The other kind of love has at its heart a refined form of egoism, a deep-seated self-centredness, and its loud insistence upon external social relations can well be a sign that it is internally ruptured in its connection with the Creative Love of God. The characteristic thing about the Love of God is that it is always due entirely to his sovereign initiative, and is entirely free from any obligation. It is the spontaneous overflow, the uninhibited outflow of the Divine Nature. To think of there being a Law in the Divine nature which makes God love, is to misunderstand it quite as much as to think of something in man which demands that God love him. It is God who moves freely toward man in the Incarnation of his own accord. This is a work which, as I have remarked before the *Confessio Scotica* referred to in terms of "*ultro*". It is absolutely unprovoked — and we cannot point to anything which gave rise to it. *God's Love is an ultimate fact and knows no "Why?"*

When we take this in earnest we see that the Christian religion is utterly different from anything else. Its emphasis is entirely Theocentric, and thus Christocentric. Its question is not: How can man come to God? It has to do with the

Fact that *God himself comes to man*. If one iota of the Incarnation is surrendered as a spontaneous real coming of God to man, the whole Christian religion is impaired in its uniqueness and distinctiveness. God is central at every point. It is what God himself in his infinite love does and says that saves man; it is what God himself does and says that matters in the Christian life; it is what God himself does and says that is the beginning and the end of everything. Immediately we get out of this absolute God-centredness, this strict theocentricity, Christianity is surrendered in principle — whether we say with the Roman Catholics that the ultimate duty of man is to save his own soul or say exactly the same thing with Neo-Protestants who assert that the business of the Christian Church is to cultivate Christian personalities. It is neither; and in both Christianity is betrayed by a subtle anthropocentricity. In both the real significance of the Incarnation is lost, for in both it is a movement of man toward God, and not a movement of God toward man, that is ultimately dominant. We must remember that in the Bible all our "religion" is rendered valueless by God. The final meaning of the doctrine of justification is that even the concept of religion, our religion, is stripped of all meaning by the Divine act of revelation and reconciliation - that, and that alone is true Religion. Because everything depends upon the coming of God himself, therefore, from the very outset it is a divine movement towards the world. "This is the whole point of the Christian revelation, for in every other form of religion the subject is treated from the opposite end of view: how can man come to God? The change of direction also provides the basis for the other characteristic of the message of the Bible...Not the flight of the individual soul out of the world but a coming of God into the world, to his people. Thus here not only is our religion swept away, but also all the individualism which is connected with religiosity." (Brunner, *The Mediator*, p. 294f.)

The Incarnation, then, means Theocentricity, means *Grace*; God's love is absolutely uncalculated and incalculable. It is overwhelmingly extravagant love, unconditional in its self-bestowal; that is to say, unconditioned by anything outside itself. That is why God's love actually comes to seek sinners and to save them; that is why it reverses all ethical standards and institutions. Before God actually came in Christ these no doubt had great value and their proper place even in relation to God, but now that he has come they do not count in that way any more; they are the propaedeutic that must be set aside before the Reality. That God has come means that the central factor in everything must be God's *own Person*, the Person in whom he confronts the World. That is why Jesus always points men to himself: *I am*. This is Love, this self-grounded Love, God's giving of himself to men. He, as coming from the Father, is Love. We have to do with him alone.

B. Christ's coming therefore established a utterly new relation between people and God, a relation not possible before that time, although evidently in certain ways proleptic to it, as in the Self-revelation of God, as the "I Am", in the Old Testament. The coming of God in Christ means an unmediated relation to God, mediated only by himself. We are not here concerned with goodness or religion or cult; we are concerned with the fact that in Christ Jesus God creates a *new* relation between human people and himself which actually penetrates behind all the other relations and tensions of people and transforms them by God's giving himself to them. This is a self-giving which generates a surrender and love on our part. It is not just to love that we are called in Christianity, but to *this* divine kind of Love. The fact that God has drawn near means that it is this relation that must come first: everything else, second. I cannot love God through loving my neighbour. I can love my neighbour truly and only through loving God. To love God through loving my

-88-

neighbour is to assert that the Incarnation is not a reality, the reality it is, that relation to God is still a mediated one. To love God through my love to my neighbour is to move toward God. It does not know a movement of God toward man. What is religion in its reality but having traffic with God: to glorify God and enjoy him for ever? What is religion but having that traffic with God which is begun and maintained by his creative Love? Until devotion to Christ immediately is absolutely central; the true Christian relation to God is not discerned. True love to my neighbour, goodness, "religion", comes only by the way and are properly only by-products of this devotion to Christ. We cannot really be religious try to be religious; we cannot really love our neighbours by trying to love them; we cannot be really good by trying to be good. We can become properly good only by the way, as it were, spontaneously. To cultivate Christian personalities is nothing short of a secret cult of self! Such people only lose their souls in cultivating their own love to others. After all to cultivate a Christian personality is to start from ego-centricity, to cultivate a refined form of selfishness, therefore! You cannot make your face shine by washing it or purifying it! You can only look at God, keep your eyes fixed on Christ, and your face will shine without your knowing it, reflecting the Glory of Christ himself. "Moses wist not that his face shone." To go and look in a mirror to see yourself spiritually is to prove that you never looked properly at God, but were looking at a projected picture of your *own* self!

The Incarnation imports a fellowship with God that gets behind all such self-centred attempts and cults. It means sheer unrestrained and spontaneous love for God in Christ which itself unconsciously transmutes all one's activity into Christ-like activity. And so all our own self-conscious, self-groomed ethic is done away with in the Gospel of the Incarnation. The Incarnation imports a quite new kind of relation that strikes behind the tensions of good and evil, love and hate, as we know them, in our relations with others, whether in family, society, or state etc. These relations are all relativised by the new kind of relation which flows creatively from the Incarnation, from the incarnate Love of God in Jesus Christ. This new relation of ours to others, supplants our ego-centred relations to them, cutting behind them and transforming them, and creating, in its operation under the power and guidance of the new love flowing from Christ, new norms and new forms and new channels of love. But so soon as I turn my attention to these forms themselves, these norms or channels of love, I lose true love, for true love flows spontaneously from an immediate vision of God in Christ. Unless God in Christ be everything, everything else will be nothing! The love that transforms things, that overthrows my petty goodness and my selfishness, that overthrows my self-centred ethics and all my own cultivated ways of behaving and worshipping. True love of others is generated in the heart of the believer by the Holy Spirit; but the Holy Spirit operates in that way in and through us only as our eyes are fixed unselfishly on the Lord Jesus Christ.

This is then what the Incarnation means for us — that out of his sheer Love God has come to restore man to such a fellowship with himself. Man has fallen from it; he lives in a world detached from God in which all he can do is to try and grasp at God through goodness or earthly love, through the cultivation of his personality in harmonious relations with his fellows. The immediate presence of God and his self-bestowal to us in Love means that he has come to set aside all those self-centered approaches and to bring us into immediate touch with himself, into a personal relation with God which will change the whole world for us and ourselves as well, not least in our relation to and with others. It is an utterly new relation in which one no longer lives unto himself or herself, but unto Christ, in which the point of reference is not one's own self or that of the neighbour or that of society or state but solely and absolutely Christ Jesus himself. And precisely because Christ has come in order in his Love to establish that relation between himself and all men and women, does the immediate and personal relation to Christ involve or carry with it a relation to people and the whole world that will be revolutionary — everything is for Christ's sake. It is not the giving of the cup of cold water to the thirsty that counts, it is not the kindly behaviour of a good Samaritan that is of value, nor even martyrdom, the giving of my body to be burned, but *all that for Christ's sake alone*. Unless this love takes hold of us; unless we see through Christ's eyes, unless we exercise our will through the Will of Christ, unless we feel through his affection, unless we act through him, we do not live Christian lives at all. That God really has come in Christ means that he must have central place all the time and all the way; that salvation is *his* act of love and grace, and the fruits of it as well. The Incarnation means the Christian has one primary duty, to "Look unto Jesus the Author and finisher of our faith" — all else follows.

C.   A further point we must note here is that the Incarnation means the inhomination of God in one specific Man, Jesus of Nazareth. The Love of God in Christ takes a particular Way, and that is *The Way*. There is no other way to God or his Love than in and through Jesus Christ which God has established once for all. God does not assume some kind of ideal humanity in his incarnation in Christ, for such a humanity would not be near us, it would not even be personal. God has assumed a specific personal and historical existence in Jesus Christ, and we may not therefore stray across country away from him. We cannot occupy ourselves with thought constructed by us out of him, or free ourselves in any way from *this* historical Person; for to do otherwise would mean that the humanity which God has graciously assumed in Jesus Christ for our sake was not real.

We must think then of the Incarnation as the specific act of God's love in which he has concentrated all his action and salvation, all his Love in Christ in a final and absolute way. In the Lord Jesus Christ we have the full and supreme Self-giving of God to men, and his supreme Self-assertion to and for men. That the whole of Eternity has come in Christ means that we have here an act which is utterly unique and quite decisive for the world. There is nothing mythical about the Incarnation; it is not something that may run in cycles; nor is it a necessary event. It is particular and historical, once for all; and because it, or rather *he*, the Lord Jesus born of the Virgin Mary, is the one point in time at which and in whom Eternity enters directly into time, and as such it means also the crisis of all history. That Incarnation is absolutely unique. Here is an event which cannot be related to history as such. Because it originates in Eternity alone, because it has no antecedents in time, it has no relations with and in time as other historical events have. An ordinary historical event is one which can be related to the rest of history, one which fits into the temporal pattern and continuity of things; but this event fits into nothing. It cannot be accounted for by history and is not continuous with time but with eternity. It thus has an element of Uniqueness which stamps it out as absolute. We cannot sit in judgement on it; we can only wait to hear (or see) what it has to say to us. Here we have an event that breaks through the even-ness of history from the beyond. It is therefore in its way the abrogation of history. Coming from Eternity it is the one event which is of all-decisive importance; Eternity comes to time and time is called to decision.

That is a supremely important element in the Christian revelation which some modern Continental theologians are insisting on so strongly — its *Einmaligkeit*, its once-for-all-ness. The coming of Eternity into time is a final event and as such cannot be repeated. Therefore we must take a decision toward it that is also correspondingly final and complete. The Incarnation of God in one man, a Man who has no existence apart from the Incarnation, means that to this one Man we must turn and nowhere else. It is another way of asserting the absolute Theocentricity, and the Christocentricity, which uniquely characterises the Christian Gospel and Christian Faith. That has been well expressed by the poet Browning in a couplet from *The Heretic's Tragedy*:

> The Lord we look to once for all
> Is the Lord we should look at all at once.

It is for this reason that the religion or worship of God that Christ founded in his own Person is so exclusive, and even intolerant at least so far as the Truth concerned. It cannot in the nature of the case demand anything else than absolute decision. No one can stand before Jesus Christ and be neutral. To accept him properly is to look "once for all" and "all at once" — and that is so because when we face him we are face to face with the Eternal God; in his Presence we are freed from the bonds and shackles of time and the fallen contingent world. Face to face with Christ we are face to face with an active Eternity, God himself Incarnate, who generates faith and love within us; who blesses and changes, brackets and countersigns our decisions so that they are works of eternity in our hearts, so that faith, our very own faith, is yet a gift of God. That is why to know God is properly to be known by him, and to love God is properly to be loved by him. That is why the Incarnation betokens a radically new relation with God, a new Love that transcends all other relations, gets behind them in its ground in the Eternal, and creates new issues and values not known before.

2. The Incarnation means Life

It is life to the dead. We must not think of the Incarnation as a natural event even in the order of God's thought for the world! The Incarnation like the Love which it manifests is not a "caused" event, but took place freely out of sheer divine love to a sinful and lost world. It is not, therefore, to be confused with an act of Creation. While it is creative, its significance lies in the fact that it is not creative out of nothing so much as creative out of death or our mortal existence. In other words, God has come to restore life; he has come to resurrect man, to remake him. The Incarnation means God's drawing near with a will to fellowship, but the very fact of his coming unveils the fact that it applies to us who are out of fellowship with God, to human beings who are aliens and at enmity in their minds toward their Creator and God. We are therefore shown to be living in separation from God the Author of life; we are "dead in trespasses and sins", as the Bible says. The trouble is that we don't really know it — not till we look up and see the Life which Christ brings. We are really aware of our enmity to God only when the Christ comes to create fellowship between God and us and us and God. It is the Word of God which tells us that we are rebels against his Grace, and that by taking our own way over against his Love we have taken a way in contradiction to God, and have put ourselves under God's wrath; the sentence of death is pronounced over us. The Incarnation means that God has come into the very midst of that, our enmity to and contradiction of him, and therefore the Incarnation imports an act of Reconciliation. Here in the Humiliation of Christ we have a Bringer of peace, a coming of God himself to reopen the intercourse and re-establish the fellowship we have lost, "the mercy of God triumphant in wrath over wrath." (Karl Barth, *Church Dogmatics*, 1.1, p.468) The Incarnation means Life through new fellowship, through Incarnation.

We must not think that the Incarnation *eo ipso* brings new life and reconciliation. The Incarnation is the primal step in the act of God's work of salvation which culminates in the incarnate vicarious life of Jesus Christ, from his birth at Bethlehem to his   and his death on the Cross and is completed in the Resurrection. We include here the fact of Reconciliation because the Incarnation cannot be understood without it. Properly speaking the work of reconciliation is not completely wrought out till the actual crucifixion and resurrection. It was on that ground that Jesus could forgive sin; that is why he so often followed his Word of forgiveness by a miracle; an act of victory over evil as a sign that he could and would forgive sins not only in word but in actual power. That is why the Resurrection follows the Cross. The Forgiveness is validated by new life; and it is itself the gateway to new life. That we have already in the act in which God comes in our humble flesh sharing with us his fellowship and breathing words of forgiveness; seeking out the lost sinners, the dead sons; the publicans and harlots; and restoring them to fellowship with God and so to new life in him, through his Forgiveness — that *is* reconciliation.

What after all is our life but that which we receive from God in fellowship with him? We were made for God and our lives are dependent on him. We have been created in the Image of God, that is, were made such that the Love of God created in us a way of corresponding conformity to God's love. We were "fellows" called to Divine fellowship, to sonship. It is sonship which is the real meaning of "image of God", the relation begotten in us by the Spirit of the Son of God — and that Spirit is Love. "A man looks into the mirror and beholds his image, or someone shouts and the cliff echoes his cry. We have been created by God that we should reply to him in the Word of Love with which he has called us into Life." (Brunner, *Our Faith*, p. 52) The Image of God in his redeemed people is simply the faith which works by Love, the faith in which we are *assimilated into the likeness of the Object of our Faith*, the faith in which we *con-form* to God, in which we are *transformed into the Image of Christ* from glory to glory — that is, become sons and daughters of God in Jesus Christ. That is what it means to have life, to live in and out of God, to be nourished by the Grace and fellowship of God, to be one with him in will and heart and soul, one in communion and communication. Our life is hid with Christ in God, bound up with the Word of God through the Word in the bundle of Life. All our springs are in him. To be in the Image of God is to be in the Spirit '*en Pneumati*" which is the subjective counterpart to being in Christ '*en Christo*"; for it is the Spirit who moulds us into the Image of Christ, who shapes our faith till we conform to our Redeemer, who begets in us new life and love and light. This is what religion properly means — this fellowship with God in which the Love of God is the supreme all-creating power and norm. For us to live is to love God and be loved by him; to live is to have communion with him, to walk and talk with him in response to his call and his word.

But all relationships with God have been broken. Our relations with God have been severed by sin so that we no longer live unto God but to ourselves. Instead of giving ourselves to God, we have seized hold of them for our own end; we have usurped God's love and seized autonomy; autonomy is sin. As St Paul wrote to the

Romans, "Whatsoever is not of faith is sin". In our unbelief we human beings have fallen from God, and therefore fallen from conformity with him. We have lost the Word and are grown deaf in sin; we look no longer on the Face of God, and therefore have lost his image and glory; we are turned to enmity against God. The central point in every human being is his relation to God. That has been shattered by sin, and man is become an impersonal person; for that which makes really him personal, the Love or Word of God, now is turned to criticism against him. As Emil Brunner has written: "So far as his attitude towards God is concerned his nature is perverted, spoiled, lost. It is God's Holiness and righteousness which make us aware of this subjective fact as an objective fact; since our attitude towards God has been perverted, God's attitude towards us has also been changed. It is not merely subjectively from our point of view, that guilt lies between us and God, but objectively, from the point of view of God. This is what constitutes its gravity." (*The Mediator*, p. 443 f.) Thus relations with God are closed from both sides — man is cut off from God in his sin, and his sin is confirmed in its being sin by the divine opposition or resistance to it that is, God's wrath! *And yet God loves us in spite of that.* In his sin, Adamic man is torn from his roots in the eternal and is banished from the garden of fellowship with God. A flaming sword bars the way back: the Holiness of God. Torn from his roots in God, man loses his life; he is dead and all that he is, is forfeit, condemned. He disintegrates. What else could he do, if he were made for God and his whole life is dependent on God and fellowship with him? His character collapses; and his development is *eo ipso* a development in and toward sin. The actual sins he commits are but manifestations of the real sin, the rupture with God, the rupture therefore within his soul; that is why human personalities are always such contradictions and puzzles; why you never find a really integrated personality except in Christ Jesus. Men and women are all "eccentric", that is to say, they are torn out from the true "centre" of Life, God to whom they ought to live and do not and cannot now in their fallen ad estranged condition. They are thus contradictions in themselves, as well as contradictions in relation to God. Real life for us human beings, women and men, true life is simply living with and in God; but we have fallen out with God and from that Life. Like a fish taken out of the water, he dies and putrefies (C. H. Spurgeon remarked somewhere that when a fish dies, it begins to stink first in its head — so with us men and women!). The sin or death in which we are engulfed is the opposite of faith and life — it is autonomy and separation from God; and therefore our minds are at enmity toward God.

The event of the Incarnation betokens the fact that God in his utterly astonishing love has come into our fallen world in Jesus Christ to reconcile us again to himself and to restore us to our lost place in his divine Love, to restore human beings to the centre of his or her life which is in God, to remake eccentric human beings and to them to their to true centre in God. He comes to offer peace at cost to himself. He comes to reconcile but that means that this business of sin, this business of our wayward human autonomy, must be dealt with; that means that there must be forgiveness. "Can two walk together except they be agreed?", as the prophet asked. Can God and man have fellowship if there is sin thrusting itself between God and man? Therefore sin must be radically dealt with and put away; the cause of the enmity between God and man must be destroyed, before such fellowship can be restored and really new life begin again in which a human being may have his or her soul renewed through divine nourishment and love; in which the image of God destroyed and lost in them may be renewed by the indwelling of the Holy Spirit who brings them into conformity with Christ who as the Son is the "express image" of God the Father.

The rift to be overcome through the Coming of Christ, God incarnate in our midst, is two-fold. On our side, there is enmity toward God, our very minds have been warped and our souls characterised by a radical self-sufficiency and selfishness. On the other side, God's self-affirmation as God, in his claims upon his creatures, is critical of their self-willed being and sinful activity as human beings. Consequently as One and Holy, God's very Nature resists and judges us sinners. Both of these sides are expressed in *guilt*. It is our guilt that bars a renewal of fellowship with God and it is guilt that must be judged and put away or be destroyed. The feeling of a guilty conscience is not all that there is in guilt — that is the subjective side of it. Guilt before God echoes the objective reality of God's judgment upon sin. The sinner's feeling of guilt is the echo of that judgment, the subjective counterpart to it. Our conscience condemns us; but corresponding to that registry of sin in ourselves there is an eternal register which judges us and before which we cannot stand. St. Paul expressed that in referring to the "handwriting of the ordinances that are against us." (Col. 2:14) The gravity of the situation is that to this handwriting God has appended his signature. God is not mocked and he does not wink at evil. He takes our guilt seriously; and he does so as God whose holiness and love have been violated. He cannot merely erase the register against us, for he cannot and does not cease to be who he eternally is in his Holiness and Love.

We must not think at all that God hates the sinner, the sinful human being whom he has created and whom he loves. He loves the sinner but hates sin, and cannot merely erase the register against us, for he cannot and does not cease to be Holy Lord God. God does not cease to love the sinner. What God does do, however, in reconciliation is an act of his holy love, humiliation and vicarious suffering. He annuls the handwriting of the ordinances that are against us by paying our debts himself. And so Christ Jesus himself, God incarnate, comes among us sinners as one of us, comes to love us but also to judge our sin and forgive us - "Blotting out the handwriting of the ordinances that was against us", as St Paul expressed it. God incarnate in Christ Jesus bears our sin, takes our sin away, and nails the judgment against us on the Cross. It is in that very act of God in the crucified Lord Jesus that we see our both guilt and God's Mercy — that is the Amazing Grace of God.

It was for this reason and on this basis that God could and did become Incarnate, and came among us and became in Jesus one with us, sinners though we are, that he might take away our guilt. That is what took place in the birth and life of Jesus as "Immanuel", *God with us*. He came into the world to bear the sin of the world. All through his incarnate life God the Son identified himself with us in our fallen humanity, took our sin and our guilt vicariously upon himself, and was crucified for us on the Cross, bearing our sin and the divine judgment upon it. In his vicarious life and vicarious death under the judgment of God, our sin and guilt are done away. But he carried our humanity in himself right through death to the other side, to life, and so is able to bring us guilty sinners life through atonement, forgiveness, and reconciliation. In his death all died, and in his act there was made once for all real objective reconciliation for all people without exception. In Christ all men were damned and in him all men were elected unto salvation. That is the objective side of reconciliation. In his incarnation and vicarious life and death the beloved Son God came to be one with us and bear the sin and guilt of the world upon himself. The curse of sin that we should bear he has taken upon himself.

Jesus Christ the Son of God went to the Cross because we sinful and guilty human beings could not endure the presence of the Holy God. But in the humiliation of Christ for our sake God has been brought near and we are reconciled to him, for the obstacle was taken out of the way, and we are saved from our sin and guilt. The good news of the Gospel is that *God loves us in spite of sin and reconciles us to himself*, for in the words of Brunner: "God's Son had to go through this shambles really to come near us." (*Our Faith*, p. 84) How and why anyone can still rebel against God, the God of such infinite Love, it is difficult to understand, but such a rejection of the Love of God in the Lord Jesus, is part of the very irrationality of evil and sin in taking the way of unbelief and bringing upon the sinner the damnation which the Apocalypse speaks of as "the wrath of the Lamb".

There is another subjective side of our reconciliation in Christ Jesus, the enmity in our mind must be destroyed, the mind of sinners being forgiven. Our alienation must be put away; we must be brought to accept forgiveness, to admit our guilt just as God in Christ Jesus took it upon himself for us. We must acknowledge that what he in Christ Jesus took upon himself was ours. We must thus appropriate the very judgement of God on our sin that was pronounced on the Cross and executed on the Person of Christ. And now the Cross is the instrument of God's Love directed upon our hearts, to bring us to the same humiliating spot. We, too, must go to Golgotha and be judged and forgiven, and be forgiven in being judged. Forgiven we must be made over again, made to partake of God in Christ, related anew to the Fountain of Life, replanted in the Eternal, re-engrafted in the Word of the Creator; we must be renewed by God's Love. And thus once again we may partake of fellowship with God through the Spirit, a fellowship grounded in Christ. We become like Christ in Love, because of his Love or self-giving. To be forgiven, to be reconciled to God is to be in Christ, to be united with Christ, to partake of eternal life in Christ. The incredible fact, however, as I have noted, is that some people for whom Christ died and rose again strangely and un-understandably reject Christ and bring upon themselves the final judgment of God.

3. The Incarnation means Light, Truth.

We cannot think of the Incarnation as bridging divine revelation and forgiveness without at the same time bringing to us light or knowledge; nor can we think of the Incarnation as effective in our lives and souls apart from a real understanding of it, or apart from an actual initiation into the Mind of Christ. We must not think, however, that this Light can come to us apart from the reconciliation which the Incarnation and Cross in God's atoning love, bring to us. We cannot know God properly until we partake of his forgiveness and until we know that we are sinners really forgiven. That appears to be a paradox, but it is fundamental to the act of faith. In conscience we know only God's law and through it, but in our bad conscience, we have a very distorted view of God, which is not of God. Until the barrier of sin and guilt has been removed, and removed subjectively as well as objectively, we cannot get away from the Wrath of God or our own enmity and depravity of mind, or really and personally know God in his Self-giving and Holy Love, and enjoy him. We can know God personally only in love. Faith works by love, and it is only as in love answering to God's love for us in Christ we surrender ourselves to that redeeming Love that we can really know God, know him in truth, in his Truth. Knowledge of God is only distilled out of the fellowship with God, under the power of the Word which conforms us to God in faith. We can know God only as we become like God, as through the Holy Spirit we take on again the Image of God, as we reflect his Glory, as we become sons and daughters of God in Christ, as the Word of God echoes in our hearts creatively calling forth from us response in love to God's love. There is no true knowledge of God or of Christ apart from reconciliation and forgiveness. While there is objective revelation, and objective forgiveness and objective reconciliation, while there is an objective Christ, we may pass all these by and pass Christ by and not know it, or blind ourselves to it.

It is important for us to learn that our knowledge of God depends on our hearing, God's Word, not on ourselves apart from our hearing. (See Karl Barth, *Church Dogmatics*, I.I, p. 467 f.) Both the hearing, a real hearing, and forgiveness take place together. There is also a hearing in which we disobey and a hearing which gives way to deafness. "To him that hath shall be given, but from him that hath not shall be taken away even that which he hath", said Jesus. Thus the Word of God tells a man that when someone cannot hear the Word, it is because he or she does not want to and is actually living in disobedience. The way he/she lives his/her life is a refusal to listen to what God says to him. Man cannot hear the Word because he is always robbing himself of this possibility of hearing it.

The point that calls for our attention just now is not how man does come to have faith, but the fact that the Incarnation means that God himself has come to establish relations, fellowship and communion between himself and us in which knowledge of God will be imparted. "God opens up his will and operation to us. He does not treat us as he does dust or clay, although as his creatures that is what we are. He does not leave us simply subjected to his creative power, controlled and moved by his creative power, in order to fulfil his purpose in us. He seeks us as those who can let themselves be found. God converses with us as those who are capable of hearing, understanding and obeying. He deals as the Creator with us, but as a Person with persons, not as a force with things." (Karl Barth, *op.cit.*,p.466.) "Though hadst not sought me, hadst Thou not already found me." (Augustine and Pascal). The possibility of hearing the Word lies thus in the Creative impact upon us by the Word itself, not in us apart from our hearing, but in the Word's letting itself or rater himself be heard, and in the Word's own action upon us.

And so we come to the very important point that the Incarnation betokens a coming of God himself to the World and therewith a revelation and a knowing of God which we would not have known apart from this coming: the fact that *the Word was made flesh*. The fact that the Word is made flesh is the possibility of its being known or seen or heard by us human beings. The possibility lies within this "became flesh". We recall that the Incarnation as the actual self-revelation of God means the setting aside of all other knowledge about God as invalid. The Incarnation means that the philosopher *qua* philosopher cannot be a Christian, cannot accept revelation. To be a consistent philosopher like Kant is *eo ipso* to repudiate grace and revelation. To become a Christian Kant would have had to become converted and become a little child, as Jesus said. Thus as my old Professor Daniel Lamont (the mathematical physicist in New College, Edinburgh), used to say to us: no man who claims his right as a rational being before Jesus Christ can be a Christian — he has to give up that claim in the face of the Incarnation, for the Incarnation means that this is the way God has provided for us really to know him. It is in a child-like attitude to Christ Jesus that we really begin to learn and know of the Kingdom of God, and can become Christian! We must take that in earnest and very seriously. Certainly it is a blow to our pride; it cuts us to the quick. It is what the Greeks call *moria*, folly. And every non-Christian Greek

> Yget out, really?
> "Mines of Morg" from
> Lord of the Rings.
> - Mirs of Folly

thinker since that time has said much the same thing about the Incarnation and Resurrection of Christ in their exclusive claims; that it is folly. No! We must be humble before the Incarnation; and as we look up into the face of the Lord Jesus Christ in honesty we shall humbly know that there is no other face which reflects God's Face and his Grace: that here in Christ Jesus, the Word of God become flesh, we have a revelation of God which was not possible otherwise; that here we have a revelation of God, a knowledge, which no philosopher, however clever as a philosopher, could possibly attain.

That is not to say by any means that this is anti-intellectualist. Those who assert that of men who take revelation seriously, as Pascal once said, put themselves into the suspicious category of those who have not enough intellect to understand what it is all about! That is nevertheless an argument that is hurled at men like Karl Barth: that he is an anti-intellectualist because he is in earnest about God's incarnate self-revelation to us in and though his Word. That accusation is a clear indication of the fact such an accuser has been mentally unfit to follow Barth, while the very fact that he has been unable to apprehend Barth shows the intellectual depth of Barth's works. For Christians to repudiate philosophy is not to repudiate reason but to repudiate reason acting on its own, or rather, to repudiate a particular field of thought for another.

The difference between Kant and Pascal was not a difference in the claim to use reason but a difference in subject-matter and in the field in which reason is at work. Reason cannot work on empty nothing; it must have some subject matter. The question is what subject matter? Is the subject matter to be found in man and the natural world? If so how can that lead us to God? Or is the subject matter to be found in a revelation of God in Person? In both cases it is reason that acts when man reflects upon the subject matter. But it must be added also, it is in the case of reason's reflecting on revelation that we have the truest activity of reason (and not therefore in philosophy or metaphysics) because only in its treating of revelation does reason get away from the circle of its own self-enclosed autonomy, and escape from its own shadow-world. Let me quote a few lines from Nicholas Berdjaev in which he begins his important book, *Freedom and the Spirit*: "Abstract metaphysics are based upon the hypostatising of the phenomena of man's psychic life and of the natural world, or still more of the categories of thought, that is to say, of the world of ideas. It is in this way that metaphysical spiritualism, materialism and idealism come into existence. But concrete living realities have always eluded these metaphysical doctrines. Abstractions of reality or the abstract ideas of the knowing subject were taken as constituting the essence and fullness of reality. Abstraction and the hypostatizing of abstractions created both spiritual and materialistic metaphysical systems. Life was identified as material or spiritual nature, and the substance, a thing, nature. Ideas are also substances. Metaphysics in all its (divergent) tendencies was naturalistic and hypostatizing. It understood reality on the analogy of that of material objects. God and Spirit are a reality of the same order as the material world." (p. 1) "The process of hypostatisation beloved of metaphysics and theologies and the objectification and erection into absolute of certain moments of spiritual life, cannot acquire that perfect significance to which the dogmas of faith lay claim." (p. 5)

Against all this self-constructed subject-matter which reason by itself works with, the Incarnation is a protest, so far as that subject matter is imported into religion. Philosophy has its own rightful place, but it must not usurp the place of God's self-revelation or it destroys itself in its conceit. The Incarnation is the great attestation by God of the way the human mind is to think when it thinks of God. In Jesus Christ and his revelation we have the full and final revelation; that is, in him we have *the* Subject-matter of faith, the Object of faith which is Truly Subject. He becomes the Way, the Truth and the Life. He is in his Reality and Truth the summation of all the forms of thought which men may use of God. Thus the revelation of God in this definite way, personally, relativises all other ways of trying to reach him, and puts them out of court once and for all. Now that we have the reality there is no sense in speculating about what we could or would naturally conceive God to be. Our business is to look at Jesus Christ and trust him. And the place of reason lies working on the subject-matter which he has is given in and through this revelation. The theologian must be wary of surreptitiously introducing his own self into the subject-matter, for that is always what philosophy does when it intrudes upon the Christian's thought. Philosophy is said to be man speaking in a loud voice about himself, and that must be silenced in the courts of the Christian sanctuary!

What, then, does the Incarnation say of God in the way of theological knowledge?

1) The Incarnation of God in Jesus Christ means that we may really have knowledge of *God*, and may speak about him in our human language. It means that God comes personally to us in his self-revelation. This point we have discussed often before, and its negative side already in this chapter. What we must think of here is the fact that in knowing God we have a knowledge of the Unknowable. This is an underlying principle here. In order to put what I have already said in this respect in a fresh way let me quote a few sentences from the French theologian and thinker, Malebranch: "Of all things that come to our knowledge we know none but God by himself... For though there be other spiritual beings besides him; and such as seem intelligible by their own nature; yet in our present state there is none but he that penetrates the mind and discovers himself to it. Tis God alone that we see with an immediate and direct view; and possibly he alone is able to enlighten the mind by his own substance...It cannot be conceived that anything created can represent the infinite, that Being without restriction, the immense Being, the universal Being, can be perceived by an Idea, that is, by a particular being, and a being different from the universal and infinite Being." (*The Search after Truth*, 111: 7:2) Notice in the above quotation that Malebranch points out that God can be known only through himself, and that therefore he must be known in person and immediately; that therefore there can be no analogy to him through the creature. The whole point of the Incarnation in the face of this is that God has taken Human Form in order that *we* who can think only in terms of human forms may really get to know God. → Don't have to leave the sphere of human speculative

In the honoured words of Athanasius: "Seeing that men, rejecting the contemplation of God, as though sunk, as it were, in an abyss, kept their eyes downward, and sought for God in nature and the world of sense, fashioning as gods for themselves of mortal men and demons, therefore the loving and common Saviour of all, the Word of God, assumes a body and as a man dwells among men, and meets the senses of all men, in order that they who think that God is corporeal, may from what the Lord effects by the deeds of the body know the truth, and through him may recognise the Father." (*De Incarnatione*, VIII.15) Again: "It seemed to be especially fitting to the Saviour to do all these things, in order that, since men were ignorant of his providence in the universe, and did not understand his divinity through created beings, they might at least from his deeds done in the

body look up, and receive through him an idea of the knowledge of the Father."
(IX.19) "It was not in the power of any one else to change the corruptible into
incorruption except the Saviour himself, who at the beginning had made all things
out of nothing. And it was not the part of any other to create anew than the express
image of the Father to restore again to men the image of that likeness. And it was
not the part of any other to make render the mortal into the immortal, than of our
Lord Jesus Christ, who is Self-existence. It was not the part of any other to teach
men about the Father, and to overthrow the worship of Idols, save of the Word who
orders all things, and who alone is the true Only-begotten Son of the Father." (X.20)

Reflecting on what has actually taken place in the incarnation of his Word in
Jesus Christ, we can say that for revelation to be real revelation to us it must be
mediated to us in our forms of thought, and therefore that God's self-revelation
must take human form. By taking human form through the revelation of himself in
that incarnate way in Jesus Christ and communicating himself to us in and through
him, he will make us conform to his image, the Image of the Word, and so transform
us into the Image of Jesus Christ. It is this transforming by conforming to the Word
of God in Christ that is of such great significance in the doctrine of the Incarnation
as Athanasius wrote of it in his *De Incarnatione*. The Image of God in man is the
Word of God incarnate in Jesus Christ, and only as a man comes to know that
incarnate Word or *Logos* of God, and is conformed to the *Logos*, does he become
truly rational, of *logikos*, imbued with the Word; but, as Athanasius added with a
sparkle of humour, he who rejects the *Logos* or Word of God and does not therefore
become conform to his Word or *Logos*, is thus irrational, or *alogos*, or a "donkey"!
(In modern Greek the word for a donkey is also "alogo"!)

This is, of course, in direct contradiction to all other ways of thinking. Thus,
for example, Socrates is made to say in the *Republic of Plato*: that education is
fundamentally getting a man to think for himself and ask himself questions and
answer them himself. The function of the teacher is simply maieutic. "If I am right,
certain professors of education must be wrong when they say they can put a
knowledge into the soul which was not there before, like sight into blind eyes."
(518) Opposed to this Christianity does claim to put a knowledge into a man's soul
which was *not* there before. This comes by the divine Word (such as even Plato
sighed for in the *Phaedo* 84 c-d). We do not set out "on the raft of our own
understanding" and negotiate the sea of life on "human opinion" as best as we
may. On the contrary, we set out from a "word that will more and surely and safely
carry" us through. That is the fundamental and inalienable doctrine of Christianity
that "The Word became flesh and tabernacled among men." Thus what
characterises Christian knowledge is not a Socratic dialogue which is really a
monologue, but a dialogue with the Word who addresses us in Person, in the Lord
Jesus Christ. Truth is here what is actually communicated by the Other addressing
us from the Beyond, which we could not have otherwise. It is granted that
revelation, to use some words of Schleiermacher, is not so much a communication
of doctrine as the impartation of life, but while it is the latter, it is also the former —
and that is the side we are concerned about at the moment. "Revelation did not
come in a statement, but in a person; yet stated it must be. Faith goes on to specify.
It must be capable of statement, else it would not be such; for it is not an ineffable,
incommunicable mysticism. It has its truth, yet it is not a mere truth but a power; its
truth, its statement, its theology is part of it." (P.T. Forsyth)

The import of this is that the renewal of man in the Image of God, in the Image
of Christ, the Word of God made flesh, will be possible only by personally

communicable truth — and truth that will not be obtainable from human nature as such. It is the *Incarnation*, while meaning that God may be apprehended only in a human "form" (and therefore in human language and categories of thought), which means also that we cannot apprehend Christian truth in a general way, but only in this precise "form", Jesus Christ, the Incarnate and a historical form at that. Hence we must repudiate the idea of Fichte, voiced for the modern world that "It is the metaphysical element alone, and not the historical, which saves us." We must listen to Paul when he says "Faith comes by hearing and hearing by the Word of God." The holy Bible is, as it were, the intellectual Incarnation of the Word of God in Christ Jesus, and which we must now use to confront our eyes and minds with the Form which God assumed in the Incarnation. It is folly to focus our attention on man as such, because God assumed man's form — for that would be to think that the humanity of Christ as such was the Word of God and to think of God only in human terms or in terms of humanity! But while we now must turn our eyes and our hearts to the Bible, we must not, of course, make the mistake of thinking "as if the Book were God, and to read it were the whole function of a soul; as if God had concentrated himself in a Book, and left the field of operation wholly in its hand." (Edward Irving, *Collected Writings*, Vol. 2, p. 392) Nevertheless, unless there is an actual ministration or handling of the bare facts or truth, there is no way in which the Spirit of God can get a purchase on men's lives. It is high time that the anti-intellectualism which has reigned so long in the Church should cease. The Holy Spirit does not work in sub-rational ways or non-intelligible ways in the hearts of men. "God's Spirit is no magical stream of power, but always speaking Spirit" (Brunner), speaking the Word which is Christ and which we find in the Bible.

2) While the Incarnation means that God is revealed to us in a human form, it does not mean that God is human; or to put it the other way around, that human creatures as such can reveal God. Christ Jesus as visible to the human eye, and as audible to the human ear as human "form", is nevertheless object, and creaturely object. It is through Jesus Christ that the revelation comes, but really through the very Form which he took in his Incarnation. In the same way must we think of his intellectual Incarnation, as I have called his relation to the Bible. The words of the Bible themselves are not the Words of God, but they are the vehicles of the Word, but *really* the vehicles of the Word. We are to worship the humanity of Christ no more than the humanity of the Bible. But of course we cannot separate the humanity of Christ from his Divinity for his humanity as such has no separate existence or self-existence. It is the Spirit of God who reveals the Lord Jesus Christ to us. We must know him as well as the Bible *kata Pneuma* — according to the Spirit. It is the Work of the Holy Spirit to transmute the objective revelation of God in Christ, of Christ himself — that is knowledge of Christ as Object — into a subjectively real revelation — that is knowledge of Christ as Subject whom we know personally only as we are known personally by him. But this we can say, that in the objective self-revelation of God in Jesus Christ, while we do not have a duplication of what God is as he is in himself, (for we shall never know God as he is in himself but only in his act of self-manifestation in Christ), we do have through the Spirit a revelation of who God is and what he is like. What God is in Jesus Christ, in Holiness and Love, in Grace and forgiveness, in power and word, God is, and is eternally and unchangeably, antecedently in himself. Thus there is given to us in the Incarnation a real unveiling of God to us through the Holy Spirit. The fact that the Word dwells among men is not automatically a revelation of God to them, but this revelation is a mystery of the Kingdom of heaven, as Jesus called it,

communicated only to the response in faith — through the Spirit. To the believer there is thus a real and complete revelation of God in and through Jesus Christ. We must take these two points seriously. In Christ we do have a real revelation of God, and no where else do we have this. The Incarnation of God in Christ being thus final and complete means that there are no dark spots in God's Being and character which are hid from us and unrevealed in Christ. Christ's own Person, albeit in human form, is a guarantee that God is like him, that in Christ we have a real knowledge of the very heart of God, for God and Christ are *One*. The Revealer and the Revealed are one, and what God communicates or reveals in Christ Jesus is not something but his Very Self. All our knowledge of God comes certainly in human language and human thought forms but distilled only through the Person of Christ. It is by keeping our thought of God rigidly along this line that we can keep it pure and true. We must learn *to think of God exclusively in terms of Christ,* and to think nothing of God which will not pass the censorship of his Person and Revelation. This is nevertheless a difficulty for us all. Christ did not assume a general humanity or an ideal humanity but he took upon himself one definite specific form in Jesus, and it is through looking at him, listening to him, and believing in him, that we may really learn of God — not elsewhere or elsehow. Just because God has invaded humanity and his Word has invaded the human language, that does not warrant us in searching the human language for God, in examining the human categories for knowledge of God. We are provided with only one *Form* where we may find God; and there are only certain words, the inspired words connected with that Form, the Incarnate Word of God, that we may use to gain knowledge of God. The temptation is to stray across country, to run here and there and to find other ways of knowing God. But God became incarnate solely and in Jesus of Nazareth, and only there *in and through him* may we hear the Voice of God or feel the touch of his Spirit on our souls. The Incarnation means that at this one point, which God had carefully prepared throughout long ages by proleptic revelations and education in a particular race of people, God has appeared among men in a way that men may at last have personal dealings with him, may overcome the enmity of sin, the bane of broken fellowship, and may receive Life and Love, and withal a new knowledge of God in the conformity of trustful and submissive faith. The riches entailed here are so great and so wonderful that St Augustine felt he could sing: *O beata Culpa*! when thinking of the Reconciliation and humiliation of Christ. We cannot think of our *culpa*, our fault or sin, like that, but we can in humility and humiliation rejoice at the transformation, wrought by God, at the Victory in which Christ has turned death to Life, by dying, darkness to light by veiling himself in our flesh, life and power by bringing the Omnipotence and Life of God to dwell within the compass of human weakness.

Let me close this Chapter with a quotation from Luther:

"For I have often said and continue to say that men should remember when I am dead, and guard against all teachers, as men ridden and led by the Devil, who aloft in highest position begin to teach and preach God nakedly and separately from Christ, as hitherto in high schools they have speculated and played with his works above in heaven, and what he is, thinks, and does by himself, etc. But if thou wilt fare securely and rightly touch on or grasp God, that thou mayest find grace or help with him, so let thyself not be persuaded to seek him elsewhere than in the Lord Jesus Christ, nor go round about with other thoughts and trouble thyself or ask anent another work, than as he hath sent Christ. Upon Christ set thy knowledge and study, there let them also bide and take hold; and where thine own thought and reason or anyone else leadeth and directeth otherwise, but close thine eyes and say: I should and will be aware of no other God save my Lord Jesus Christ." (*Sermon on John 17:3,* 1528, Weimar edn: 2.28, p. 100).

CHAPTER 7
The Pre-Existence of Christ

Strange as it may seem to fully fledged faith in Christ this doctrine of the pre-existence of Christ has been one that has been much controverted throughout the history of the Church. The motive for it seems difficult to fathom, but it is usually the result of a very bald faith in Christ and a very meagre conception of the Deity of Christ at the best. This tenet of Christian dogmatics cannot be treated as a side-issue; nor is it a derivative that is not of fundamental importance. The doctrine of the pre-existence of Christ has, after all, to do with the *eternity of Christ*, and without the eternity of Christ there can be no real Incarnation of God. The doctrine before us is contained in the immediate asseveration of faith in Christ as divine, as Lord and God, as St Thomas confessed to the risen Jesus, "My Lord, and my God" (John 20.28). We have been too apt to use the word "divine" loosely without stopping to think about its meaning. There cannot be two senses of the word "divine" any more than there can be two realities meant by the word, any more than there can be two Gods! To assert that in Jesus we encounter God, we must be prepared to admit that in Jesus Christ we encounter the One and Eternal God, very God, the God from and unto all Eternity.

Of course we do not start out with any idea of the pre-existence of Christ, which is then applied to interpret the Incarnation. On the contrary, we start always with the actual confrontation of Christ as the Incarnate Word. Starting with Jesus Christ we acknowledge *God* in Christ; we acknowledge Christ as *Lord*, therefore as *God* in human form, as one eternal God among men. Now the point here is that in this revelation of Christ in which we encounter God himself, we do actually and really have to do with God. In the Lord Jesus Christ the eternal God does not impart something but his very self; here in him we have to do with an act of God identical with himself, with very. That must be in essence the way we are to think of the Pre-existence of Christ. From this we may and must branch out into a full apprehension of Christ in his cosmic significance and power.

The Biblical Basis.

1. It has sometimes been remarked that Jesus nowhere expressly speaks of his pre-existence in the Synoptic Gospels in an open way. I feel that this has often been taken too glibly at its face value. There are times in the Synoptic Gospels where we must admit that while Jesus did not teach it as a specific doctrine any more than he taught his own Deity as a specific doctrine, he nevertheless implied it in a way that is fundamental to his Person. "Every attempt to conceive of him as becoming the Son of God makes shipwreck on the unconditioned character of his self-consciousness." (H.R. Mackintosh, *The Person of Jesus Christ*, p. 29) In the light of the Synoptic Gospel accounts of Christ's own words we can say with Mackintosh "that no convincing reasons can be given for denying that Jesus

himself spoke expressly of his pre-temporal life." (*ibid.* p. 446)

This is borne out by the Fourth Gospel, whatever the view of its composition is, unless it be taken to be simply and wholly spurious, for the many times that Jesus spoke of his unique relations with the Eternal Father cannot but go back to the historic words of the Jesus Christ himself. It is sufficient to say without going into the matter more deeply that the whole of the New Testament presupposes that he was pre-existent, that in him *God* came to men. It is however in the light of the resurrection and the descent of the Holy Spirit that the words of Christ are themselves fully to be understood, that his saving work and his divine Person are to be understood in a way that carry along with that understanding, belief in his pre-existence. And it must be that our faith in Christ as eternal arises in the same way as the faith of the New Testament writers did, and not in some other way or on some other ground. The whole of the New Testament is unanimous in asserting that Christ was related to the Father in personal and intimate ways that transcend all temporal terms, in ways characterised by an absoluteness and unconditionedness that involved Eternity. Such assertions are found all over, in the epistles of St. Paul, of St. John, and particularly in the Book of Hebrews. It is significant too, that it is in the latter where the humanity of Christ, his human suffering and priestly nature as representative of men, are emphasised so very strongly, that we are given the strongest statements about the pre-existence and eternity of Christ's Person, as increate and unbeginning. The New Testaments writers had such a faith in the Lord Jesus Christ, the beloved Son of God who is himself God, that human words fail to express that truth in its length or breadth, height or depth. They were continually reaching out after ever new ways and ever loftier superlatives to express their faith in Christ the Lord as equal with God and supreme in the whole of Eternal reality. It is particularly when they come to think of the Love of God that they discern and affirm that in Jesus they had a divine Saviour who transcended all time and all finite relations in the magnificent and transcendent scope of his divine glory and being. The pre-existence of Christ is not with them a postulate of faith, nor an addendum to it, but an *integral part* of faith in Christ itself, as necessarily involved in our trust in him who for our sakes *became* poor. As we shall see the whole significance of the Incarnation, and of revelation, is dependent on taking this "became" on the part of Christ seriously as his own act. He became poor, a servant. In him it is God from all Eternity who had come to seek and save the lost. Were that not so we would still be under tutors and not yet having to do with God himself in Person.

2.   We learn that this faith of the Apostles is the immediate result of the confession of faith in Christ as *Lord*. Christ Jesus comes to men precisely as their Lord. Now of course the word "Lord" carries with it to the Jewish mind the identification of Jesus Christ with *Yahweh* or Jehovah: and Jesus himself claimed as much when he said that before Abraham was "I am". But the confession of him as Lord is itself the result of the recognition of the fact that the disciples knew that in Christ they were confronted with one who actually is *Lord*, that is to say, Lord over the World, the Creator. That is why they called him by the name of the One in the Old Testament who had revealed himself as the One who existed in his own right eternally without tense, *I am*. To Jesus that Name which carried with it the idea that it is without tense is applied, on the ground that he authenticates himself as Lord in that very sense. He is Lord over all created being, free of his own right, free to be himself and to be what he would be, the Lord over life and death, over sin and evil. The Lord is thus the One who in his own Being and Person transcends time and its limitations.

Like the first disciples when they followed and accompanied Jesus day after day, and week after week for three years, and found themselves exclaiming "it is the Lord", "It is *Jahweh*", so we today bow before Jesus, and say with them, "it is the Lord", and worship him as the very Son of God, God of God. "Jesus is Lord", he *is* Lord, therefore the Lord. There is but one Lord, the Lord of heaven and Earth who was and is and ever shall be. Thus the Lordship of Christ carries with it the attestation of his pre-existence. Indeed we can safely say that his Lordship would have no real content were it not for the fact that it did do so. His Lordship is not a borrowed authority; it is not one that he holds in another's right. *He* forgives sins, *he* heals, *he* raises the dead, and now today he saves you and me, and we worship him. He is divine, yes, but the divinity is his own, not the lustre of another: his own, therefore existing in him and existing eternally in him by his own right; and therefore in an absolute and unconditioned way that transcends all the relations of time and involves Eternity.

3.   Pre-existence of Christ is even more evident in the fact that faith acknowledges Christ as the Son of God. As the Son Christ is the Only-begotten Son of God involved with God in such a way that he is the Son of the Father and the Father is the Father of the Son - the Son and the Father are correlative to each other. If the Father is Eternal and pre-existent, and eternally existent, so is the Son pre-existent, and eternally existent; for we know neither the one nor the other without the one or the other. That Christ is in this unique relation to the Father means that he is co-eternal with the Father. "The union with Father as increate and unbeginning." (H.R. Mackintosh, *ibid.* p. 446) That is why the creeds spoke of Christ as *eternally begotten of the Father, and consubstantial with the Father.* This is implied in the Son's exclusive and adequate knowledge of the Father. It is upon this basis that the whole of the Fourth Gospel was written, with the very significant Prologue: *And the Word was God.* The Work and Person of Christ take on their significance only when they are seen to be personally anchored within Eternity, to be on the divine and eternal side of Reality. The Word who became flesh was the Word who was with God in the beginning and was God, and through whom time itself had and has its beginning.

Thus strictly speaking the word "pre-existence" cannot be applied to Christ because he is the origin of existence itself. In him all things consist, and have their creation. The fact, then, that the Son reveals, really and adequately reveals, the Father, carries along with it, as we have had occasion to note already a number of times and shall do again, that the Revelation of God in Christ is one with the Revealer.

What God is in Christ, Christ is in himself. More, what Christ is in revelation, he is antecedently in himself, eternally antecedent. Such revelation only can have eternal content and eternal validity — that eternal Content is the eternal Reality of God himself. That is to say, in communicating himself to people, Christ communicates the Eternal God to them. If Christ is the Son of God for us, he must be the Son of God for God, that is to say again, the Son of God antecedently in himself and in Eternity, one in divine Being with the eternal Father. Were this not so, that Christ is very Son of God antecedently in himself, therefore pre-existent, it would mean that God is resolved into humanity, the humanity of Christ. It would be to deny that Christ the Son of God became man, while asserting that he is yet the Son of God.

The temptations to diverge from this central, pivotal, point in Christian dogma were countered by the explication of the correlative Sonship of Christ as his consubstantiality with the Father. That is to say, Christ is the express Image of God, the brightness of his Glory, the Image of God's Being or Essence or Substance. On this essential likeness of Christ to God Luther remarks: "Here Christ is the image of the Father, so that he is the likeness of his divine essence and not made of another nature, but is (if one may so speak) a likeness of gods, which is of God and has divinity in itself or of itself, as a Crucifix is called a wooden likeness of Christ, being made of wood. And all men and angels are made in the likeness of God, but they are not likeness of his Essence or Nature, nor made or arising out of his Divine Nature, but Christ has arisen out of his Divine Nature from eternity, his essential Likeness, *substantialia imago, non artificialis aut facta vel creata*, which has his divine nature completely in itself and is also itself, not made nor fashioned of somewhat else. For if he had not the entire Godhead of the Father in himself and was not complete God, he could not be nor be called the likeness of his essence because the Father would have something over, wherein the Son was not equal or like unto him, so he would in the last resort be quite unlike and in no wise his Image according to the essence. For the Divine Essence is the most individual of all, indivisible, so that it must be *entirely* where it is, or must not be at all." (*Die drei Symbola oder Bekenntnis des Glaubens Christi*, 1538 Weimar. edn. 50, p. 276 and p. 277)

4. If Christ is divine, then what Christ is in his acts, he is antecedently in himself. That we must think too in relation to his act of Redemption. The Redemption, the word of Forgiveness which comes from Christ, cannot be only a temporal word or event, but must be eternal in nature. The Redeemer must be eternal. "Only the eternal God can save; Christ is Saviour; therefore in eternity both before and after, Christ is one with God. He who fills the soul's horizon can be no mere incident of human history, but must have his roots within eternal unbeginning Deity. Otherwise, in the last resort it is a Man who is given, or assumes, the central place in faith's universe, with the inevitable result that theology, while remaining Christocentric, ceases to be theocentric." (H.R. Mackintosh, *op. cit.* p. 459) "It is only kept theocentric by the unflinching faith that the Christ in whom we believe is not merely One who lived a life of uninterrupted fellowship with God, so constituting the perfect exemplar of religion, but One whom we are justified in referring unequivocally to the Divine side of Reality, not as having attained that place progressively, nor seen as having received it by privileged election, but as having emerged in love (from the bosom of the Father)." (*ibid.*)

Here we touch again with point 2 above, because it is as Redeemer that Jesus is Lord and Creator; his redemption touches our very existence, and we know him to be the Creator. Only the Creator can recreate as he does. Only the Word without beginning, only self-existence, as Athanasius said, can take the part of restoring and recreating our existence in God.

5. The pre-existence of Christ must be seen also in the fact of its bearing on the humanity of Christ as one with his Deity. Unless this Man has a relation with God transcending that of a prophet we still wait for another, for an Incarnation of God. The Incarnation itself presupposes the pre-existence, and without the Incarnation the whole structure of the Christian faith would collapse. It is absolutely essential to the religious experience that the relations with Jesus Christ be relations that are not on a merely human level, that the Humanity of Christ have its ground in an action of the eternal Word of God. Unless there is this essential relation in being between Christ's humanity and eternity we are not assured of either real relations with God or eternal relations with him. If the Love of God in Christ is not one that came from all eternity, then the significance of Christ is *vastly* altered. Haering

writes in his *Dogmatik* (p.449): "The love of God which acts on us in Christ the Son, is so utterly God's love and the active self-disclosure of His Being, that it is eternally directed upon Him as Bearer of this Eternal Love. And this not only in the sense of pre-existence — for then He were but the temporal and historical correlate of God's eternal love — but even irrespectively of His earthly existence; God's love directed upon Him is the Love of the Father to the Son in the secret of the eternal Divine Life, or, to put it so (since no other terms are possible), in a real pre-existence. Also, to take the other side of the same conceptions — this Son, loved eternally of God, is not only sent by the Father into the world: He has come by His own loving act."

6. The whole discussion of the pre-existence of Christ hinges on the fact that Christ manifestly, antecedently and therefore is eternally in himself what he is in his revelation and saving activity. This of course does not mean that his humanity is eternal, but that his Person is eternal, and that his divine *Person* is not human but Divine. Such a relation as we believe Christ bears to the Father could not have arisen within time. The life of Christ was itself the obverse of a heavenly and eternal deed, and the result of a timeless decision before that life began here. "His emergence on earth was as it were the swelling in of heaven." (P.T. Forsyth, *The Person and Place of Jesus Christ*, p. 271, cf. also p.269) The dialectic of this discussion yields the doctrine of the *Trinity*. We see that clearly in the act of the Incarnation as a real act of revelation in which God reveals himself; that is to say in which the Subject is the eternal God himself, and yet in which the Object of that revelation is one with the Subject, the Revealer. Therefore we do not say that God is Father, Son, and Holy Spirit, because he becomes Father, Son, and Holy Spirit to us, but while we only know him because he becomes so to us, he only becomes Father, Son, and Holy Spirit to us precisely because he *is* first and eternally Father, Son, and Holy Spirit in himself alone. The doctrine of the Trinity which involves the very root and ground of Christian truth all in itself is the guard of truth here. If there is no such dogma as the Pre-existence of Christ, there can be no Trinity: and the central basis of Christianity would then be cut out. The Trinity and Pre-existence of Christ are tenets of faith that stand and fall together.

CHAPTER 8

The Humiliation of Christ

In this chapter we are to think of the road the Lord Jesus Christ travelled from heaven to earth, the road of Humiliation and of Grace. We are not concerned with the "how" of the Incarnation. That is really quite beyond our knowing, and it is useless trying by the use of psychology, human psychology at that, to understand even in the least way "how" it was possible for God to become Man, or "how" Jesus could be the divine. When it is realised that the Person of Christ is divine and not just human, but nevertheless divine Person incarnate in human form, it will be obvious that we can find no analogy whatsoever to enable us to understand what took place in the event of the Incarnation. What we may do, however, is to trace as far as revelation allows us something of the way that the Son of God took from the bosom of the Father to our valley of humiliation, from being in the form of God to being in the form of a servant, without of course ceasing to be the Son of God himself. "For ye know the grace of our Lord Jesus Christ", wrote St. Paul to the Corinthian Church, "that though he was rich yet for your sakes, he became poor, that you through his poverty might become rich." (2 Cor. 8:9)

1) Jesus The Incarnate Servant

The first part of that way or becoming that we must consider is that described in the verse above and those in Phil. 2:5 ff, to which we have already directed our thought, but which we do well to consider more fully: "Let this mind be you, which was also in Christ Jesus: Who, being in the form of God (ἐν μορφῇ θεοῦ) thought it not robbery to be equal with God (τὸ εἶναι ἴσα θεῷ), but made himself of no reputation (ἑαυτὸν ἐκένωσεν) and took upon himself the form of a servant (μορφὴν δούλου), and was made in the likeness of men (ἐν ὁμοιώματι ἀνθρώπων γενόμενος. And being found in fashion as a man (ὡς ἄνθρωπος), he *humbled* himself (ἐταπείνωσεν), and became obedient unto death, even the death of the cross."

Here we must consider first the question that is raised by the verb ἐταπείνωσεν (*etapeinosen*) or the noun κένωσις *(kenosis)*, which literally means "emptying". Let me say at the outset that this passage has been vitiated in interpretation by making it out as an attempt to explain *how* the Incarnation took place. It does nothing of the sort. Here a correct exegesis is as important for Christology as is any other passage in the New Testament, for it appears to me that it has been a wrong understanding and interpretation of this passage that has led to the so-called, but damaging, "kenotic theories" of the Person of our Lord. Here we need only call attention to some salient features in the teaching of St Paul about the incarnate Person and humiliation of Christ as the Son of God.

The first point to be emphasised is the statement that Christ was equal with God and was in this equality in the form of God. The equal with God refers to their consubstantiality, to use credal terminology, the fact that they were one in substance or being; the form of God refers to the style of God which Christ set aside for the "style" of man. (cf. P.T.Forsyth, *op. cit.* p. 307) The point is that this is the act or movement of divine *Grace*, as Paul expressed it in the Corinthian passage: "You know the grace of our Lord Jesus Christ, that, though he was rich, yet for your sakes he became poor, that you through his poverty might be rich" (2 Cor.8.9). That was what Professor Mackintosh, my old teacher in Edinburgh, said was "the infinite mobility of his absolute grace bent on the redemption of the Lost." (H.R. Mackintosh, *The Person of Jesus Christ*, p. 473.) Christ came out of his eternity, put off the garment of his divine Majesty and put on the garment of humility. In so doing he did not change in essence or in consubstantiality with the Father. He did *not* empty anything out of himself — that is an absurdity - but emptied or poured his Personal Being out of the form of the Divine into the form of the human; far from emptying anything out of himself, he emptied *himself,* his *whole self,* out of one *morphe* or form into another, out of the divine into the human, and so assumed the characteristic fashion (σχῆμα) of a man. *Morphe* (μορφή) does not, however, refer to the physical, but rather to the volitional side of the external form. The "form of a servant" corresponds to his "form" as a man, the *morphe* to the *schema,* the fashion or habit of a man. Thus putting off the "habit", so to speak, of divinity, he donned the "habit" of manhood, and of *real* manhood. The expression "in the likeness of men (ἐν ὁμοιώματι ἀνθρώπων)" does not mean "in the appearance or superficial likeness", but in the *concrete likeness* of men (the Greek word is ὁμοίωμα, *not* ὁμοίωσις). There is no reference in the text to an act on the part of Christ emptying something or anything out of himself, but of his emptying "himself" his whole self out of one form into another. We cannot think of that, therefore, as involving the setting aside of certain attributes and the diminishing of others. What are the divine attributes, the attributes of God but very *God himself* acting in certain relations? The divine attributes all go back to the divine Aseity and are grounded in it. They are here the Divine Aseity in the freedom of God's action turned outwards towards us. Therefore we cannot think here of God as putting off or laying aside any of his divine attributes to become incarnate. As a matter of fact we must think of him as employing them in the Incarnation. For the Incarnation means surely that the full Divine Being or Aseity goes into action, that God, very God, moves towards time and into time; that the immanent personal relations within the Godhead are projected, as it were, between eternity and time, and particularly between Christ and God, in the God-Man himself. There in Christ it is God himself in action, acting no doubt in a different way from other ways as in the creation, for in the Incarnation there was a really *a new movement* of God. Thus the Incarnation and the Humiliation of Christ are not to be understood in terms of any change in divine attributes or of a *kenosis* or a emptying of any of them out of himself at all. Rather do we understand here in this action of God among men what the attributes of God really are and what they involve for us as well as for God. The whole Deity of God must remain in Christ if Christ is a real Incarnation of God. The fact that he reveals himself to us as *Lord* contains that in itself. God cannot as God abdicate any of his functions or attributes, any of his proprieties without abdicating Deity, without ceasing to be God — and that is unthinkable.

The mischief in this discussion was started, I have no doubt, in the view that the "emptying" meant an emptying by God the eternal Son of "something" out of himself; whereas the text in reality says that he emptied *himself* out of heaven on to earth, out of Eternity into time, and yet did not cease to be eternal, or cease to be what he ever was. The fact that Christ is Lord, is Jehovah, means that he was the "I am that I am". We cannot adopt the so-called kenotic theory without doing violence to that truth.

The so-called "kenotic theory" is ultimately a theory of *how* God and Man can be conceived together in Jesus of Nazareth. We must stick close to the doctrine of the Trinity to avoid such exotic ideas as are often promulgated in the theory. What the Lord is in Jesus he is antecedently in himself. We do not know of another Christ than that Christ Jesus, though we do know him in his fullness after the resurrection as we do not know him before. Still it is the Jesus Christ before the resurrection who constitute and provides the reality and objective basis for the exalted Christ, and it is the objective Jesus Christ who is the basis of the revelation of the Holy Spirit. It is in him that we know God the Father, and without him we know nothing of God. It is only because in Christ we meet God the Lord that we are able to know what Lordship means. Therefore we cannot bring any preconceived ideas of Lordship to interpret the Lordship of Christ. Our interpretation of this passage from Philippians, and what it actually says about Christ, must be gained from Christ himself and his self-revelation to us throughout his incarnate life. Thus it is in starting with Christ that we reach a doctrine of the Holy Trinity which became and is the safeguard of all our Christological and Theological thought. What God is in Christ he is antecedently and eternally in himself. We learn that he does not first become this and that in Christ, but though there we know it for the first time only, he was this and that before and in himself in order to be this and that in Jesus of Nazareth.

It is clear that we must think of Christ as deliberately taking on himself *the form of a servant* in order that we human beings in the form of our human being which he came to share may behold him and know him. The Lord Jesus Christ, our Saviour, in and in accordance with his infinite condescension and grace, "had to" lay aside his magisterial insignia, his effulgent glory, for our sinful eyes to see him; else the brightness of his glory had blinded us altogether. In other words, we are to think of the form which Christ took in his incarnate self-humiliation, as a veiling of his divine Nature. We cannot look upon the naked Glory of God, or upon the naked Word of God, but may and can look upon the Glory and Word of God only in a veiled way or a refracted way, as it were. To look directly upon on the pure holiness of God would mean death, for no man has seen God and lived. This is partly the reason for asserting that we may never know God as he is in his ultimate Being or Divine Essence. Hence the very fact that Christ stripped himself of his heavenly habit, his divine glory and magisterial form, was an act of pure uninhibited Grace toward us. "Though he was rich yet for our sakes he became poor"! It is an act of sheer mercy that God veils his glory and only allows us to see it as we are pure, for it is only the pure in heart who see God. This thought is nowhere better expressed than in the lines of Binney's hymn:

> Eternal Light! Eternal Light!
> How pure the soul just be,
> When, placed within Thy searching light,
> It shrinks not, but, with calm delight,
> Can live and look on Thee!

The spirits that surround thy throne,
May bear the burning bliss;
But that is surely theirs alone,
Since they have never known,
A fallen world like this.

Oh, how shall I, whose native sphere
Is dark, whose mind is dim,
Before the Ineffable appear,
And on my naked spirit bear,
The uncreated beam?

There is a way for man to rise
To that sublime abode:-
An offering and a sacrifice,
A Holy Spirit's energies,
An advocate with God -

These, these prepare us for the sight
Of holiness above:
The sons of ignorance and night
May dwell in the Eternal Light,
Through the eternal Love.

Instead then of thinking of an emptying out of himself we are rather to think of the *humiliation* of Christ the only begotten Son of God an emptying *himself, his* very Self, out of a form in which we could not behold God into an incarnate form. And at the same time we are to think here of a redeeming act in which Christ takes upon himself our flesh in order to destroy in it the sin that is there enthroned; and think too that it is only as he renounces this flesh burdened with our sin in his vicarious life and death on the Cross that we really may and do behold God, a beholding of him in Christ Jesus that culminates in the Resurrection Glory. But unless very God himself is there in Christ, unless the whole of heaven is in Jesus of Nazareth, we cannot be saved by him. For Salvation has to do with *God, very God*, and the work of Salvation is primarily a work by *God himself* and his incarnate work among us men and women and children. Thus were Christ not very God our ground of Salvation would not really be *by God and in God*. If the Incarnation is to be of the significance that it is in our Christian faith, in Christianity, it must be a *complete Incarnation* of the One God. Only God in his fullness can save us from the wrath of God, and his holy judgment upon our sin; it must not be anything less than God in all his might and power and holiness who is our Saviour — our Redeemer cannot be a second-class God.

What does the New Testament Revelation mean, then, when it speaks of Christ as having become "poor" for our sakes? Once again all we can do is to describe the road which he actually trod, and not to say *how* he became poor or to explain his becoming poor. His poverty must mean that he laid aside the form of the Divine. He did not confront men as the Lord of Glory. It was one of the temptations of Christ, as we read in the Gospels, to come among men with all the glory that was his, and so to compel men to believe in him. But he deliberately set that aside temptation and took another way, the way of humility and poverty. He donned the beggar's garment, as it were, in order to persuade the beggar that God was in earnest about loving and forgiving him, and at the same time to work out in and through his lowly incarnate life on earth the way of reconciliation. Thus Jesus' "poverty" must include all that he was and did in this lowly incarnate life on earth, in the actual way of his *humiliation*. In that he exercised all the powers of full Divinity. He was the Lord free to act as he would among men, free to be a Man among men, without ceasing to be the Lord. He would not have been Lord were he not free also to be what he actually became and was savingly among men. That is omnipotence, to be so wise and omniscient as to bring himself so close and savingly present to men and women - that *is* his omnipresence.

We must realise that these attributes are not of the same kind as our activities and abilities which go under the names of potence, science and presence, raised as it were to the nth degree (omnipotence, omniscience, and omnipresence), but different in kind altogether while including within their scope also the freedom to be at will personally manifest in our way with our potence, science, and presence. His very freedom was one in which he was able to be this, and to act thus, without at the same time ceasing to be what he in virtue of which he was able to be this, and to act thus among men. A right knowledge of the attributes, accordingly, will not trouble us here, while the idea of a "kenosis" or "emptying" of attributes, or even a condensation or concentration into essence-form of the Divine capacities or properties, is irrelevant to the situation. Christ's "poverty" will thus mean two things, corresponding to his work of Salvation and Revelation which interpenetrate each other. It means the act of Jesus in which he comes to us and to be among us in such a lowly way in the company of publicans and sinners, in the humble form of a servant in which he may reveal himself to us in a way in which we human beings may really know him. It means that he, the Lord of heaven, stoops down to our low estate setting aside all the effulgence of his glory that our weak eyes may behold the meek and lowly Jesus and through him have them lifted up to know him in his Deity and Glory. It means that with the lowly Christ we are carried up to his Glory, from seeing him only in the form of a servant we accompany him till he is raised up above all and given the name that is above every name. Then too, the poverty of Christ means that he has actually come down to be one with us in our poverty, and stooped to enter our frail mortal flesh, the flesh of sin under the judgment of God's holy law and its curse, all in order that he may exercise within that compass his saving power to destroy sin and death themselves and deliver us from them. He is the Strong man of his own parable who invades the other's house and by his power subdues him.

That is what Christ did; he defeated evil by the Word of his power, cast out Satan, and finally even broke through the bands of death. But he had to enter the strong man's house in order to bind him, and subdue him. By taking our flesh on himself the Lord Jesus exposed himself to the fierce assault of evil and sin; then he advanced to meet sin at the summit of its achievement in rejecting him, and slew it on the cross there destroying it when it was working its worse, when it was slaying him. And so he condemned sin in the flesh and carried his saving activity right to the Cross and, as the Creed says, "he descended into hell" which he burst open by his holiness and the power of his Resurrection. It is there that we see what the Omnipotence of God is: in the life of the lowly Jesus, in his triumph as Christ on the Cross over sin and death, and in the glory of his resurrection from the dead and his final defeat there over all the powers of evil and darkness.

In this discussion we must be careful not to switch off the initial path of faith in which we confess Christ in our encounter with him. The confession of faith is that Christ is *Vere Deus et vere Homo*, "truly God and truly Man". From this double assertion we cannot budge an inch. And to the question *Who* is Jesus Christ? we must always answer in these words, "truly God and truly Man". The *how* of it all is utterly beyond our knowing, but the *fact* of it we must assert in certain faith. That the Lord Jesus Christ was "Truly God" must mean here not simply Divinity or Deity as such, but the one, the only, proper, eternal God. Thus we must think of "God" here *"in der ganzen Fülle der Gottheit"* (Barth, *Kirchliche Dogmatik*, 1/2, p. 146), that is in the complete fullness of the Godhead. It cannot be held that there was a change in God when he became flesh. He who became flesh in Jesus Christ did not cease in any respect to be what he ever was and is. The miracle is that he became flesh without at the same time ceasing to be what he was, True God. And yet he became True Man!

However, that Jesus Christ is truly God and truly Man does not mean that in Jesus Christ God and a Man were alongside each other, but it means that Jesus Christ the Son of God, and therefore *himself* God, was and is also a true Man. We must take earnestly the sentence that "God became man", remembering that the *Subject* was and is always God. That is to say, the Subject is God himself and as he is in himself. The predicate "became man" is not a necessary predicate of God, but one which God freely assumed for our sake. Thus even in the assumption of flesh it is God, True God, who assumed Flesh, and not a diminished God in any sense. This means further that the Man Jesus who the Word became has no existence apart from the "became flesh". The Man Jesus is the Creature of the very Word who became flesh; the Creature who is in the Incarnation astonishingly also God. Since this so, we must say that the reality of Jesus Christ consists in this: that he, *God himself is Personally present in the flesh*. God himself in Person is Subject of an actual human being and existence. Indeed, it is only because God himself in his own Person is the Subject of the act that this being and existence have reality at all. (See Karl Barth, *Kirchliche Dogmatik*, 1.2, p. 165).

If we remember that it is God, the same God before the incarnation as after, who is always the Subject in Christ, then kenotic theories will be found to be quite irrelevant. "This Man would not be God's revelation to us, God's reconciliation with us, if he were not, as true Man, the true, unchangeable, perfect God himself."(Karl Barth, *ibid.* p.166) This becomes clearer when we say that the Son of God was not made flesh, but he *became* flesh himself: that is to say, it was an act of his freedom, of his Grace and transcendent Majesty, in assuming human flesh. His becoming flesh was not an event that in any sense contradicted his Godness, or in which he imprisoned himself as the kenoticists would sometimes have it. It is his own free act in virtue of his own Deity as Lord, in his own right and power. If his Humiliation which is his own *Self*-humiliation includes suffering and pain even unto death, then they are his own chosen experiences; he takes them upon himself. He is not to be thought of as conditioned by anything outside himself and so limited or imprisoned in space and time. He freely took the form of a servant (Phil. 2.7); he took the seed of Abraham (Heb. 2.16). Thus to say that the Word became flesh means that the Word in actually becoming man took up our flesh and clothed himself with it. He "assumed our human flesh". That seems to get us over the difficulty which the English, "he became flesh" might seem to indicate; namely, that in becoming flesh, he became something other than he was! But that is not the sense of the sentence. He became flesh means that he became flesh without ceasing to be what he ever was - that is, *he* freely assumed flesh, *he* freely became flesh, as he who was in the full sense, God's Word, or God's Son, or simply, God. And God cannot cease to be God. "The incarnation is inconceivable, but it is not absurd, and it must not be explained as an absurdity. The inconceivable fact in it is that without ceasing to be God the Word of God is among men in such a way that he takes over our human being, which is his creature, into his own Being, and to that extent makes it his own Being." (Karl Barth, (*Kirchliche Dogmatik*, 1.2. p.175.)

This union of God and Man in Jesus Christ is called in theological terminology the "hypostatic union" — *unio personalis sive hypostatica.* Here we have true God and true Man in such a way that the Manhood is not diminished or impaired, and real Manhood in such a way that the Godhead is not diminished or impaired. There are thus in Christ Jesus two natures but the two natures are not to be thought of as mixed or identified in Eutychian fashion, nor separated in Nestorian fashion. The Union between Word and Flesh, God and Man in Jesus Christ, is a Union of a Personal kind, due to the Fact that God in Person is acting here. It is only on that ground that we may legitimately speak also of a union of natures in Christ; but therefore not such a union as might imply that either flesh or Word passed into the other to be the other. The union is to be thought of as the Chalcedonian formula expressed it, *asughutos,* without confusion, *achoristos* without separation. We must think of God as Personally present to every believer, but in each case of this kind the believer has an individual personal existence, though dependent on God, nevertheless one created in a distinct and separate existence from God; therefore in an independent existence that is yet relative. Here, however, because the act of the Word with which he assumes flesh is also the act with which the human existence of the Word comes into being, the human existence of the Word has no separate existence from the Word — that is from the Personal reality, action and presence of Christ Jesus as himself God. Hence the Man Jesus is not be thought of as having an existence or reality alongside that of God the Son but as indivisibly one with him, and thus as one with God, and as such, is God the Son. This Man Jesus is identical with the Presence of God himself among men. Thus we must think of the Humanity of Christ as the predicate of his Divinity, assumed by God in his inconceivable condescension (Karl Barth, *ibid.* p. 163). Wolleb: *Pesonalis unio est qua persona Filii Dei upostasin suam humanae naturae communicavit.* (*Compendium*, 16, 4.)

We must take it simply that this "hypostatic Union" of divine and human natures in the one Person of the Lord Jesus Chris is a downright act of God. It is manifestly incomprehensible to us — more comprehensible than any miracle: that God and man should really and actually be so united in Jesus Christ; but that is nevertheless the central truth and dogma of Christian Faith. The Eternal Word and Son of God has "come down" from his Glory and Majesty and without becoming different has become like us and one of us. He has so taken our human likeness upon himself that he is now here for us and really and altogether here: he is to be sought and found only in his human reality or existence in Jesus; there is no other Form or appearance in heaven or earth other than the baby Jesus in the manger, than Jesus of Nazareth, than the Man on the Cross, in which we may find the very Word and Son of God. Jesus Christ alone is in hypostatic union with the Son or Word of God, and therefore to pass Christ by is to pass the Word of God by, and to pass God himself by, because the Word and so God himself is to be found nowhere apart from the human being or existence of Jesus Christ which the Word has taken to be his own for ever and ever. Certainly now that the Incarnation has taken place God may not be known by us apart from or outside of Jesus of Nazareth and of Calvary. Before his coming while he was yet on the way men learned of him through the shadows he cast before him, but now in the Meridian of his full glory there are no shadows, and we have the full Reality of the Word himself united to Jesus Christ. Here and only here is God's Word, here and only here is God's only begotten Son. If we are to take the Chalcedonian *asughutos*, without confusion seriously, we must also take the other Chalcedonian terms seriously too: the *adiairetos* (without division) and *atreptos* (without change). God and Man are not separable or to be confused in Jesus Christ. There are not two separate Persons in Jesus Christ but one single Person. Where Christ is, there is the unique undivided Person. Luther says "Where thou canst say: Here is God! There must thou also say: So is Christ, the Man also there." (*On the Sacrament*, 1528) Where the Word is there is also the human existence of the Word. Where God is there is also the Humanity he assumed in Christ. That is, then, the meaning of *"the Word became Flesh"*. Now that the Word is become Incarnate, we cannot have the Word except in incarnate form; we cannot have God without having Jesus. We cannot really have Jesus without having God. God is not Man, and man is not God in Christ, but they are so hypostatically united that we cannot have God without having Christ Jesus.

The Council of Chalcedon was very wise in discerning that these Christological questions could be stated only in negative terms. Barth asks on one occasion whether we can do anything more than simply write a prolegomena to Christology. We cannot certainly fathom what the hypostatic Union of two Natures in One Divine Person means, though we may understand something of what is involved in it. There are things that we know cannot be asserted of Christ, of either his divinity or of his humanity, and these we can make clear as far as they interfere with true Worship and trust in God for salvation. The fact of the hypostatic union between the two natures of Christ is a miracle and as such beyond our grasp. It is evident that this is the way in which God acts with men, for in the other works of God with which we are concerned in other Christian doctrines we see much the same kind of thing being asserted as having taken place. Thus in the act of election and faith we have a similar movement or miracle in which the act of decision is wholly man's act, and without diminishment of human capacities but rather with a heightening of them, yet it is still wholly a divine act through the Holy Spirit. Augustine called the Incarnation of the Word a sort of prototype of justifying Grace, for the Word of God relates itself (or rather himself) to human nature as Grace to sinful men. The Act of God in relating himself to men in Grace reflects on its level the kind of Divine action in the altogether unique hypostatic union of the two natures in the one Person of Christ. This principle can be traced throughout the whole of Christian theology!

2) The Virgin Birth of Jesus

This is part of the road which our Lord travelled from heaven to earth that must now come up for consideration. It is one that has provided a great deal of controversy and a great deal of superstition or misinterpretation in the Middle Ages, which has sometimes reduced the birth of Christ into the world into a serious travesty of the truth. However, we may not balk at a consideration of this matter because of superstition or wrong interpretations of the event of Christmas. Nor on the other hand may we shy clear of facing the question from a fear induced by the intimidation of natural science. Science has nothing whatsoever to say on the matter and all its pronouncements in this regard are quite beside the mark. We must not start out with a minimised conception of God such that a miracle like the Virgin Birth of Jesus is automatically excluded from sane consideration. We are to think of it as we must think of all the other miracles and particularly as we do the miracle of the resurrection of our Lord at the end of his earthly life: the Virgin Birth of Jesus and the Resurrection of Jesus complement one another. We are here thinking of the beginning, of the entry of the Son of God into temporal and earthly conditions; thinking therefore of a downright *act of God* — which in the nature of the case will be incomprehensible. We must be prepared for that with any act of God in time and in relation to earthly conditions. Once again the Virgin Birth has nothing to do with the "how" of the entry of Jesus into the world, but is part of the Road along which the Son of God travelled. Of course it cannot be understood if it is treated as a theory of *how* Christ became man! It is not that at all; it is rather an account of something that happened as the Son of God became man, a sign of his entry into time as the Resurrection was a sign of his exit out of time conditions.

The signification entailed in the *Virgin Birth* of our Lord is the important event to which we must now give our attention. We must not think of it in any biological way at all. The *Virgin* Birth means that the birth of Jesus is not to be biologically understood. It points to the secret of Christ's Person, the incomprehensibility of the hypostatic union, the character of Christ's Birth and Person as a fact in which God alone works and in which God may be known only through God. To the questions why? and whence? and how? we can only answer with the Virgin Birth that God begins with himself alone. Of that the Virgin Birth is the Sign, and so this miracle confesses the utter hiddenness of the *Vere Deus et vere homo*. The Virgin Birth means that neither Ebionite nor Docetic Christologies are in place, but asserts that the Person of Jesus Christ is to be understood only spiritually, that is after the Holy Spirit, *kata Pneuma*, as well as ontologically, *ex Virgine*. Just as Jesus was conceived of the Holy Spirit, so no man can say that Jesus is Lord but by the Holy Spirit. That is to say, we cannot conceive of him as Lord but by the Holy Spirit. It is this secret of the Christ, the secret of Revelation that the Virgin Birth indicates or signifies.

The Virgin Birth indicates this secret — the secret is the Divine origin of Christ, conceived of the Holy Spirit, the inner mystery of the hypostatic union of True God and True Man. Of that inner meaning the "born of the Virgin Mary" is the outward sign. They may be thought of as form and content of the Incarnation-act of God. But while the Form is not the content, and while here the outward sign is not the actual hypostatic union of Very God and Very Man, nevertheless it is the Form in which this content, Jesus, first appeared on earth. In the same way the empty grave at Easter is the sign, the outward signification of the inner act or content of the Resurrection. But can we conceive of the Resurrection of Christ apart from this form, from the empty tomb? Can we likewise hold the "Very God and Very Man" truth of the Incarnation without lapsing into either Ebionitism or Docetism, apart from the Womb of the Virgin? Certainly the history of Christian thought seems to show that where the outward form or sign of these miraculous acts of God has been repudiated the inner content has inevitably gone along with it. We might almost say there is something like a "hypostatic union" between the inner content and the outward form in the Resurrection or the Virgin birth!

Does this mean then that the Reality of the Incarnation of the Word of God in Jesus Christ such that he is very God and very Man is not known apart from the Virgin Birth, that it is impossible to acknowledge Jesus Christ as Lord apart from acknowledging his miraculous birth? I think not. It seems possible for people to realise the meaning of the Incarnation in spite of their "weakness" here! But that does not mean that the Church has a right to repudiate it or leave it out of its creed. The Church knew well what it was doing when it raised the witness to the Virgin Birth to be an article of belief, for there it has been set as a Watch upon the secret of Christ's Person, which means it would not be well for any one to hurry past without consenting to it. It is thus a warning that those who prefer to take their private ways are very liable to go astray. But fundamentally the Virgin Birth belongs to the Confession of true faith, and those who prefer to pass it by should at least have courtesy enough for such a redoubtable article of Church belief to respect it through silence on the matter. (see Karl Barth, *op. cit.* 1.2. p. 198)

One of the very first things we must say about the Virgin Birth is that it is a Miraculous — that is to say a sheer act of God in time. This means that the act which takes place there is not an event in continuity with time, with the rest of the world of events. It is to be understood as proceeding from God himself alone, thus an act done in God's own right and freedom. As such it is a sign of the fact that the hand of God is at work there. Barth writes: "The sign must indeed signify. In order to signify, it must itself have something of that which it signifies; it must be noetically and ontically analogous to it. Herein is the Miracle of Christmas analogous to that which it signifies, to the secret of Christ; it also is based on the fact that God begins with himself in the midst of the continuity of the creaturely world, but independent of it as far as our understanding of his act is concerned as well as far as his own act itself is concerned." (*ibid.* p. 199)

In this respect, Barth goes on to point out, the Virgin Birth is parallel to the Resurrection, to the miracle of the empty grave. Both miracles belong together, and form a single sign with the obvious function of pointing to and pointing out the existence of Jesus Christ as such, among and beside the many other existences of human history, as the single human-historical existence in which God himself, God alone and God directly, is Subject, whose temporal reality is not only ordained and created through the eternal reality of God, but is identical with it. The Virgin Birth at the entry of the life of Jesus and the empty Grave at the exit of his earthly Life mean that this life is bracketed off over against all other human life, and that not first through our understanding and our explanation of it, but as a fact that is bracketed off through itself. It is bracketed in respect of its Whence: it is free over against the arbitrariness upon which we subsist. And it is bracketed off in respect of its Whither: It is triumphant over death under the sway of which we are all fallen. Only within these boundaries or brackets is the Virgin Birth of Jesus what it is, and therefore it is to be understood, as the Secret of God's revelation. To that the boundaries themselves point.

Compared with each other these two wondrous acts or miracles may be thought of thus: The Virgin birth signifies especially the *secret* of Revelation. It signifies the fact that God stands at the beginning where there is real revelation of God, and not the arbitrary cleverness, excellence or piety of a man. That in Jesus Christ God himself comes forward out of the deep hiddenness of his eternal Divinity, in order to be God among us and with us, as becomes apparent in the cognate sign of the Resurrection from the dead, that is grounded in what is signified through the Virgin Birth: here in this Jesus has God really come to us in space and time down and veiled *himself* in our humanity. Thus because he was here (in the Virgin Birth) veiled he must be unveiled, as he was at Easter. The empty tomb symbolises the revelation of the secret. The Birth means the secret of God's Revelation; the

Resurrection means the revelation of the secret.

The two usual credal statements used for this dogma are, *natus ex virgine Maria* and *conceptus de Spiritu Sancto*: Born of the Virgin Mary, and conceived by the Holy Spirit. To the understanding of these we must address ourselves. The "born of the Virgin Mary" means that Jesus, while really and genuinely having a human birth of a human mother, was not born as other men are. The "conceived of the Holy Ghost" means that the secret and origin of Jesus lie *wholly* with God and in his sovereign gracious will alone. Nevertheless the Virgin Birth really conveys the idea that Jesus was a genuine man. It does not teach the idea that Jesus came through the Virgin as water through a viaduct, to use the heretical words of Valentinus. That would be to say that the birth of Jesus was ultimately a docetic one. The teaching of Holy Scripture on the other hand is that Jesus was *really born* of Mary, and she was his *real* mother. On the other hand, while we are to think of Christ's humanity as utterly genuine we are not to think that he was born as other men are, of the will of the flesh, or of the will of man (see John 1.13-14, which in the original Greek text was in the singular: "*Who was born, not of blood, nor of the will of man, but of God. And the Word was made flesh and dwelt among us, full of grace and truth.*" That is to say under the sovereign act of God, not under the sovereignty or act of an earthly father. In other words, in this act, man and God are not co-equal partners. The doctrine of the Virgin Birth is the great bulwark, or ought to be when rightly understood, against all synergistic ideas and all monistic conceptions of faith in God. What took place, took place under the free will of God, in which God alone was Lord and Master, in which the birth of Jesus was grounded in the sovereign creative act of God alone. But that does not mean that the work is an act on the part of God without man, but on the contrary that "man" plays a great part in it all, for in *Jesus* the eternal Son of God becomes *man*, but he *becomes* man, and the man-side of the act is the predicate side alone. This act of God's sheer Grace, this advent of God, as we have seen already in the Incarnation and in the idea of revelation, means a disqualification of human capabilities and powers as rendering possible an approach of man to God. It is *to man* that God comes. But in that God comes, in that God acts in an act which is grounded in himself alone, though among men, there is carried in the words "born of the virgin Mary" the disqualification of human powers. Jesus Christ is not in any sense, even in a co-operative sense a product of human conjugal or any other activity. The fact that he is born of a Virgin betokens the downright reality of God's Grace which begins from and continues in his sovereign initiative. Thus here we have the sentence on human nature to the effect that human nature as such has no capacity, no power, no worth, to beget a Christ, to be the place and ground of divine revelation. Man and God are not equal partners here in the work of Salvation; it is entirely of Grace — "*conceived of the Holy Spirit*". How are we to understand that?

First, we are to see that the coming of the Lord Jesus Christ means that he is in no sense the product of the causal-historical process of nature or of the world. God the eternal Son entered into humanity and assumed flesh and took it to be one with himself in the Person of Jesus Christ. It is a real entry of eternity into time. And incidentally, it is worth asking whether we think Eternity can enter into time in any ordinary way? Does not the fact that Eternity acts here, mean that the birth is a supernatural event, and pure act of God, and thus an act, grounded in itself alone, unconditioned by the activity of anything else, such as a human father?

Second, we are to think of the birth of Jesus as a creation on the part of God, a creative act of the Spirit, in Mary. But here we must not think that there was any sort of marriage between Mary and the Spirit — that idea would simply be heathen mythology. Nor are we to think that this creation was creation out of nothing, but rather creation out of our fallen Adamic humanity, *ex virgine*, out of the Jewess Mary. That is to say the creation of Jesus in the womb of the Virgin presupposes the first creation, and betokens a recreation in the midst of and out of the old. That is a large part of the significance of the Incarnation, that Christ really comes to us, to our flesh and assumes it; that out of our fallen humanity which God has come in Christ to redeem and reconcile fallen sinful human beings to himself, he created and assumed flesh for himself for ever, to be one with it. The humanity of Jesus Christ was real and not a docetic affair. This indicates, nevertheless, the fact that the origin of Christ was an act of God alone, and therefore an act of sheer Grace.

Third, we are to understand the birth of Jesus as a break in the sinful autonomy of man. However, the Virgin birth is not to be taken as casting a slur on marriage or on the marital relationship in the least — though we must remember that all our human acts are tainted with sin, and sin permeates all, even the best of our acts and intentions. We must think here, however, of sinful acts as excluded in the birth of Jesus Christ — that is to say, remembering the nature of sin, as the act of human assertion over against God is entirely excluded — that is to say again, man's sovereignty is excluded. In his own sovereignty or autonomy man is not free for God's Word. And thus the birth of Jesus takes place apart from any act of human will or assertion, apart from human sovereignty, such as epitomised in the act of the man or the father. God himself, God the Holy Spirit, is the actor here, and he alone, in which the act of human assertion is excluded. Thus Christ is not born as a result of human nature, but of an act of the Spirit; in other words, the Incarnation is an act of pure Grace and not of nature. Here in the Virgin birth man has no say in the matter; he exercises no act of self-will in order even in helping to bring about the act of God.

Fourth, it is here that we may discern very clearly the significance or meaning of the Grace of God in its most pure form; and in a form we may do well to take as a norm for our understanding of all God's gracious acts, and of all other theological statements. God takes the initiative and approaches Mary, telling her of the choice of God. She has not to do anything in the matter except under the operation of the Spirit. What she does is humbly to believe, and is blessed because of that, not because of her virginity. The attitude that the believer must take up towards Christ in Salvation is that very attitude of trust which Mary took up: "Behold the handmaid of the Lord!" It is an act of humble willing obedience and surrender to God. And in her there took place the incomprehensible act of God, the birth of Jesus Christ, Immanuel, God with us! We must think of our own salvation in Christ in a similar way. In the address or annunciation to us of the Word of Christ himself, we are called to surrender to him in like manner, and there takes place in us the miracle of *Christ is us*! That is the Christian message. And it is not at all of our active willing. To as many as believe in God, to them gives he the *exousia* or power to become the sons of God! We are born again, to transpose the metaphor, not of the will of man or of the will of the flesh, but of the will of God (cf. again John 1.13f in relation to John 3.1 f). What happened at the birth of Jesus Christ altogether uniquely, happens on another level in every instance of rebirth of men, women and children in Christ Jesus, or when he enters into our hearts and thereby recreates us. Just as in the birth of Jesus Christ there was no foregoing action on the part of human co-operation between an earthly father and mother, so in our salvation there is no Pelagian or synergistic activity either. It is from first to the last salvation by

Grace alone, salvation of men and women and children and among men and women and children that is grounded on an immediate act of God himself, and not on both man or woman or child and God. Christ was conceived immediately by the Spirit — therefore in a Virgin. We are saved by faith, but in faith which is itself ultimately the gift of God, a human act, yes but grounded in God alone (cf. again John 3.1ff). Faith is here not a creation out of nothing, but is creatively begotten through the Holy Spirit in a human child of God, in the sphere of his/her human choices and decisions, not of his/her human personality, but a creation out of it, and therefore independent of it. Thus in no sense is faith a product of our human capacities, thought or ability or insight. The relation between the conception of the Holy Spirit and faith comes out better in the German than the English. In German the word to conceive is *Empfangen* which is the same word as the receive or welcome, *Empfangen*. As Mary welcomes the annunciation of the Word, of the Christ, and receives it, and so conceives: so we receive the Word of God which is engrafted into our souls, and, as it were, `conceive Christ' within our hearts. We simply receive, giving up human capacities and powers. We do not bring the Christ into us, we do not appropriate him or make him real to us and in us. That is the work of the Holy Spirit; our part is humbly and thankfully to yield up all our autonomy and sovereignty, in surrender to the Work of God on and in and for us through the Spirit.

We cannot offer any defence of the doctrine of the Virgin Birth any more than we can offer a defence of any other doctrine in Christian Dogmatics. We cannot prove it; for a doctrine is a way of expressing the insight vouchsafed by the Word of God through the Holy Spirit, and we cannot prove the Word: but we can hear it, and obey it. It seems true, however, that when one really understands the significance of the Virgin Birth, its significance as an act of God's coming grounded in himself and in an act of Grace alone which is as such the archetype of all other acts of Grace, and thus the very essence of our salvation, that one will not be able to treat the Virgin of Jesus lightly and set it aside, but rather embrace it as having a real and integral place in the Christian faith and dogmatics. After all the only proof of any Christian doctrine is its intrinsic significance. To understand this doctrine, the most holy of all miracles, and at the basis of all, is tantamount to accepting it with firm faith. We must not think that Christ is the Son of God because he was born of a Virgin. It was because he was ever the Son of God in Eternity and was God, that he was so born into this world. He was not born as the product of a sinful will, but born of the Holy Spirit; and his miraculous birth is the accompanying sign of his Person; that is to say: we are not even here to separate the Act from the Word. We have seen earlier that in the New Testament the Act and Word of Christ are always one and are only to be understood in relation to each other and as involving each other. Thus too the Virgin birth is to be understood not as the vindication of the Divinity of Christ, but as the Word-Act proclaiming it. It is a piece of revelation; it is itself an act of revelation. In other words, it is a sign or symbol taking place in our human existence of the secret beyond the sign, the mystery of Christ's own Person as Son of God and very God himself. Understood as an act of revelation or as a *sign*, or *semeion* in the Johannine sense, the Virgin Birth will be given its proper place in faith. But while we may not be able to adduce any external evidence for it, we may show how the doctrine is of the same tissue as all the other doctrines of the Christian dogmatics, and show further how it links in with them all in such a close way as to precludes its exclusion. We may show again how the doctrine is a bulwark against forms of christological heresy, and even show

how in the long run denial of the Virgin birth results in Docetism or Ebionitism on the one hand, or in Eutychianism or Nestorianism on the other hand. Without the Virgin birth we could adopt only a heretical adoptionism, an ascent of man to God, thus countering the Grace of God in the Incarnation, or heavenly descent of God to men, a view which would lead us further to a Nestorian two-nature theory of Christ as being two persons in one body. The doctrine of the Virgin Birth has done noble service in playing the role of watchman in the sphere of Christian theology — let him be warned who will depart rom it on his private path! Let him learn that here we are taught not to trust the will of man, or human assertion or sovereignty, but rather in the act of Divine Grace and sovereign freedom.

The Virgin Birth is thus the form and fashion of the true manhood and Godhead of Christ. It preserves *in nuce*, as it were, the truth of the fact that God and man became ONE in Jesus Christ in hypostatic union. It is on the basis of this that we are truly assured of our being reconciled to God; for here there is created in man the possibility of Salvation which does not arise out of or from man; a possibility which is yet of and grounded in the Divine Reality. In Christ Jesus who is true Man and True God is the Mediator and Reconciler in whom God and man are not simply brought near to each other, but in whom God and Man become one for eternity. And in this God-Man we partake in grace, as members of his body, reconciled to God through him and in him, and even it is said, are incomprehensibly partakers of Divine nature!

3) The Vicarious Humanity of Christ

It is St Paul who tells us, that in his incarnation and incarnate union with us, Christ was made in the likeness of sinful flesh; that, in fact, he who knew no sin was made sin for us, that we might be made the righteousness of God in him. Here we are surely faced with a mystery as great as the other we have been thinking of — the relation in Person of the Holy Son of God to our fallen and sinful humanity. We have already seen in the foregoing discussion that the Virgin Birth betokens a break with the sinful autonomy of man. But is not the birth of Jesus one within our fallen race; and does he not as such take upon himself the form of a servant and live under the curse of the law? That is to say, does not the Lord Jesus in his vicarious humiliation take upon himself *our* humanity, *fallen* humanity, and yet without sin?

The word "flesh" in the New Testament generally denotes fallen humanity under the sentence and wrath of God. Flesh is thus the actual form of our humanity under the fall, the form of the man who needs to be redeemed and be reconciled to God. It is to this humanity that God in his great mercy condescends and actually descends: and it is bone of this bone and flesh of this flesh, through his being born of the Virgin Mary that the Lord Jesus assumes. That must mean that the flesh he assumes is not to be thought of in some neutral sense, but as really *our* flesh. He has come to redeem *us*, to destroy our sin in human flesh; and therefore he becomes what we are that he might raise us up to where he is. "He who knew no sin became sin for us that we might be made the righteousness of God in him", as St Paul wrote. We must be careful here. Jesus was no sinful man, but he entered a fallen race and identified himself solidly with every human being man in his/her sin; and came under the curse of the law.

There are two extreme views here corresponding again almost to Ebionite and Docetic views. On the one hand, the humanity of Jesus Christ is represented as man's corrupt humanity, and only maintained in a sinless life with the utmost struggle against sin in the flesh. This was the view of Edward Irving, for example, who held that the sinlessness of Jesus Christ was not due to his own nature but to the indwelling of the Spirit. On the other hand, Jesus Christ has been thought of in a way that holds him rather aloof from human struggles and temptations and weaknesses; an emphasis is placed on his human nature as such that it becomes "vergottert" or deified in its own perfection. Both sides here embody in part real truths, but both equally depart seriously from the position which the New Testament takes up.

We cannot think of Christ's becoming flesh in a sense which would separate his flesh from ours, and yet we cannot think of his flesh as corrupt in the sense of Irving. Nevertheless, we must think of Christ as having entered sinlessly into our fallen humanity in order to judge sin in the flesh and redeem us. We must remember that there are not two separate natures in Christ - there are two natures, divine and human, hypostatically united in one incarnate Person; that the Word of God has really become one with Jesus the Man; that God has really assumed flesh to be one with the Word of God. Now we cannot think of the humanity of this Jesus in whom divine nature and human nature are indissolubly united in any sense corrupt, but in the most supreme sense as Holy. The Word certainly enters human flesh, was truly born of fallen humanity, the son of Mary who was not blessed for any other reason than that she believed the word of the angel, and trusted God. She was part of the Adamic race, of fallen humanity, and our Lord partook of her flesh vicariously. Thus while we must say that Christ entered into fallen and corrupt humanity, we cannot say that his flesh was created out of nothing and absolutely *de novo*, it was created out of fallen humanity, but without the will of fallen humanity. We must therefore think of the humanity of the Lord Jesus Christ in a *vicarious way*, as his *vicarious humanity*. In this Union the flesh of Christ becomes Holy though it is a member of humanity under the curse of the law, under the ban of God's wrath. Thus we are to think of Christ's flesh as perfectly and completely sinless in his own nature, and not simply in virtue of the Spirit as Irving puts it. We must think of him nevertheless as really one with us, as really a member of our fallen race who is tempted in all points as we are, though without sin. Were he not really of us, he would not be *our* Reconciler or Redeemer or Mediator. Were he not really of us, his humanity would be really docetic. If he did not come to bear our sin and to be one with us sinners, he would not be our Saviour.

We cannot think of Jesus as having original sin, for his Person was Divine, and the secret of his Person was not on the human but the divine side of reality. Nevertheless, he entered the sphere of our corrupted humanity and we must think of him as vicariously taking on himself our humanity, and as freely coming under the same judgment and condemnation as we are, not because he sinned, but because in his union with us he loved us even unto death. We must think of the humanity he assumed as thus coming under the conditions of fallen and corruptible humanity — for he was able to suffer, was weak with weariness, hungered and thirsted; his humanity as such was not immortal; but he suffered death and through this suffering was made perfect — that is, he condemned sin in the flesh, and presented himself faultlessly before the Father bearing the sin and guilt of a fallen humanity; he met the curse of the law and as in Gethsemane he vicariously drank to the dregs the cup of his divine judgment on our sin, of the results of humanity's sin. He entered into our condemned state under divine judgment and made it his own, suffered the "Eli, Eli, Lama sabachthani", and yielded up the Ghost under the burden of sin and judgment and wrath, all in our name and in our place, *vicariously* for our sakes. Thus we are to say, like St Paul, that Jesus was made in the "likeness of sinful flesh" *yet without sin,* his Person sanctified the very flesh he assumed from the Virgin Mary, and though tempted in all points as we are he was wholly perfect and wholly sinless. We cannot hope to enter into this profound fact much further; only Christ himself knows what he endured and what he suffered for us, in becoming one with us and uniting himself vicariously to a fallen and accursed race under the ban and wrath of God. But he did actually do that, vicariously, and yet while remaining Holy and sinless, and he was yet "made sin for us", as St Paul expressed. Thank God that though his sinless vicarious life and his humiliation under God's judgment upon our fallen race, he has thereby created a new humanity even out of our sinful flesh and has placed it eternally in the heaven. And in our faith we in Christ are hid with him in God, are assimilated to him, sinners though we are, reconciled, redeemed and recreated in *Jesus,* the One who is *Mediator* between God and man, the Captain of our Salvation. Let no man think crudely or contemptibly of the humanity of Christ vicariously made sin for us, but let no man think Jesus' vicarious humanity as such to be any more than human, for it remained human in his incarnate oneness with God the Father. He was God-man, perfectly One with God and perfectly one with us.

4) The Sinlessness of the Lord Jesus

We have now, fourthly, to think of the absolute sinlessness of Jesus Christ, and of his temptation in respect of his Manhood and Deity. Here we are to think of the Christ who with full knowledge and in great love entered our sphere of sin and temptation and met sin squarely and defeated it. He came as the eternal Word of God who was made flesh, the eternal Son of God become man who could not sin, and through his very entry into the world of sin and temptation betokened by the very fact that he *entered* it, and was not the product of it, he would not and did not sin. Therein Jesus fought and won, one who had to win, who had already won in fact in his holy determination to become Incarnate. God was in Christ reconciling the world to himself. How could God sin? How could God deny himself and rebel against himself? But this God incarnate, who as and in Jesus entered human flesh laden with all the consequence of sin and of the fall of man, bearing their dread weight under the judgment of God on him, with all the temptations assailing him that characterise fallen humanity, *did not sin, for they could not prevail over him*. And yet we are not therefore to conclude that the humanity was not real, that he did not really suffer under temptation, that he did not really have to meet sin at close quarters. He entered *our* humanity precisely that he might so struggle with sin at close quarters and defeat it in human flesh where it had enthroned itself. He came into our dwelling, the meek and lowly Jesus, but stronger than the strong, in order to cast out Satan and bind him. In that he was tempted thus in all points as we are, in that he faced, really faced Satan and evil in the flesh, he is able through his victory over them to help us and bring us the succour that we need so much. How can we have freedom unless the strong man is bound, as in Jesus' parable, unless evil itself is faced and defeated? That is what Christ Jesus came to do and does do and did do once for all; and now we in him, through his sinless vicarious, redeeming, reconciling humanity, may now share in his Victory.

Jesus Christ as our Redeemer had to be perfectly one with the Father in will and purpose. That he was, we have no doubt. His was the one sinless and perfectly unspotted life the world has ever known. "Only a sinless person can guarantee the

Divine pardon of sin. If redemption is to be achieved, the Redeemer must stand free of moral evil. As the source of victorious spiritual energy He must himself be in utter oneness with the will of God. The perfect moral health, the unstained conscience, to which he is slowly raising others, must be present absolutely in His own life. If He shed His blood for the remission of sins, it is because He is without spot or blemish. Like to His brethren in all else, He is unlike them here. Yet it is no paradox to say that such unlikeness makes His kinship perfect; for sin had made Him not more a man, but less. Sin dehumanises, and by its entrance the perfection of his perfect sympathy would have been irrecoverably lost." (H. R. Mackintosh, *The Person of Jesus Christ*, p. 401).

And just here is our problem. We know that Jesus, thus perfect, vicariously underwent repeated and dire temptation acute and trenchant in its attack, more powerful than any temptation has ever assailed us. For against him the perfect Son of God all the powers of evil marshalled themselves in full force. We must see here a real temptation, and yet we must say that the victory was bound to be won. Faith will not allow it that Jesus Christ might have fallen victim to temptation, that the divine plan might have been frustrated, that God might have been defeated. Thus the victory of Christ over temptation must be ascribed to the presence of God in Christ, to the fact that Jesus the Man had become *one* with the Divine Word. Christ's personality was divine; ours is human and grows up in the struggle with evil, and indeed it is evil that often makes our problematic personalities what they are. Our fallen human personality lies in the tension of the fact that we have fallen out and away from God, from his Word. It is thus that our human personalities are so contradictory; they are essentially eccentric.

Let me quote here from Emil Brunner (*The Mediator*, p. 318): "Everyone possesses a mystery of personality, which is in no wise identical with his historical personality, with the individual human character which is visible to the historian or to the biographer, and can be grasped by him. This mystery of personality lies behind all historical and psychological perception. It lies even behind all self-perception. As human beings we all wear masks, and we see each other and ourselves through masks. We are mysteries to each other and to ourselves. And indeed this mystery does not consist merely in the sense of individuality; that is our natural mystery, not the mystery of personality. There is the mystery of our created being which separates us and always should separate us from each other. But it is not this with which we are now dealing, but with the personal mystery of responsible being. For to be a person is to be a responsible being. Our mystery is the inmost point of our actual existence, of our self-determination, of the self which is not 'given' but self-determined. For our mental endowments constitute nature, personal possibility. We, however, are not personal only through this 'given' element, but this endowment only develops from a possibility into reality by means of our own personal act, our own decision. Thus it is action as a whole, not individual acts in the historical sense (for these are only the expression of personal being), the fundamental, original act, which constitutes the mystery of our personality. Here alone is the seat of sin; again, this means sin in the total sense, that sin which is the source of all sins, which we cannot perceive psychologically, that which lies 'behind' all that is sinful from the historical point of view — the Fall. The fact that we all wear masks which we cannot lay aside is the result of this original Fall, this original personal act. This is our secret, of which we are afraid, because although it is true that we do not see through it, yet we have some suspicion of the nature of that which lies behind it. We cannot unmask ourselves because we are no longer sufficiently true. But there is a place or point at which we are unmasked: before Christ, in faith. There we see the secret of our personality, there alone where we know the mystery of his Person, where we see him as the Son of God. Our personality, however, remains an object of faith, not an historical form. For as persons we cannot be known, only believed. Our being, as persons, is determined by our attitude towards God.

"The secret of our personality is that having been created by God in his image, in his Word, we have fallen away from God, away from his Word. This is our `eccentricity'; it is this that constitutes our present historical reality, and at the same time our task.

"It is the mystery of the Person of Jesus Christ that at the point at which we have this sinful `person' he has, or rather is, the divine Person of the Logos. For `person' means precisely that which we cannot *have*, but must *be*. Christ has indeed assumed human nature, but not a human person. Thus he may have assumed the possibility of being tempted — the possibility of sin which is connected with the historical personality — but he did not assume the corrupted personality spoilt by Original Sin, that is, the necessity of falling in temptation. To fall in temptation — in spite of Original Sin — is never a natural act, but always and only a personal act. Hence it is said of Christ: he was tempted in all points like as we are — yet without sin. He stepped into the abyss. He entered wholly into human life, even descending to the deepest depths of the `sinful flesh'. He allowed the powers of the abyss to work their will upon him — but he did not make the abyss wider, for that would have destroyed the meaning of his coming. He came in order to enter into the abyss and thus to build the bridge, but not in order to make the gulf wider by his action, to break down the dykes by committing sin himself. Hence, although he assumed human nature with its possibilities of being tempted, even an historical personality after the manner of men, he did not assume human personality in the sense of the ultimate mystery. Instead of the human mystery of personality, sin, he possess the divine mystery of personality: divine authority". (See also P. T. Forsyth: *The Person and Place of Jesus Christ*, p. 285)

An important point that arises now is that the victory of Jesus over sin was not just a moral victory of Jesus the Man. That is to say, it was not a great act of moral conquest, a triumph of the human will; for that would mean that we have in Jesus simply a man who won a great moral victory, a man who reattached himself to the true ground of his being by means of moral conquest, but not a real Incarnation of God. But if we say that he triumphed by virtue of his Divinity does not that seem to say his temptation was mere play-acting? This question has been discussed in theological circles for long under the four phrases : *posse peccare, posse non peccare, non posse peccare, non posse non peccare* (Augustine). These are phrases with which John Baillie used to tease us in Edinburgh! The question is which of these possibilities characterises Christ's action and life in face of temptation. This question we must answer in the light of the whole movement of God to man; for it is the fact that the Person of Jesus constitutes a divine act of God among men that sheds light upon the whole New Testament story and therefore which must be our norm of interpretation here. Thus because Christ is really the act of God, the events in his life will be real. The temptations of Jesus only can be said to be unreal if the act of God in coming into time is itself said to be unreal; the reality of the temptations depends on the reality of the Incarnation, the stark reality of his humanity, therefore. Thus we must look at these for captions in this light and ask which of them represents most truly the life of Jesus as the Divine Word who really became Incarnate. Looked at in this light, the earthly life of Jesus must be thought of as the counterpart to the eternal act of Divine Love, and the earthly repudiation of temptation is the counterpart in human conditions of the Divine repudiation of evil. Thus in the earthly Life of Jesus who is one hypostatically united to the Eternal Word of God, it is the Eternal act of love and renunciation of evil which lies behind that of Jesus Christ. The whole act of God lies behind the words of Jesus: "Get thee behind Me, Satan". And so when we think of the ability of Christ we think of the ability of God even when we think of him incarnate in Jesus as meeting and overcoming temptation in his humanity. Thus when we think of the freedom of Christ we are to think of that freedom as grounded in the perfection of the Word, and therefore the ability of Christ must be thought as an ability which is a manifestation of that perfect freedom toward God. This will become clear as we examine the expressions before us. But before we begin, remember that we think of them all in the light of another: *non peccavit*: he did not sin. And when we remember that the ability of God is not something that we can determine *a priori* but only *a posteriori*, then we shall see from the very beginning that what Christ did actually do in resisting temptation was the very ability of God; what God does do is what he can do, and there is no other "can" apart from what he does do. Thus what Christ did do was what he was able to do, and apart from that "did do", there is no other "able to do"! In other words we define Christ's "can by what he did do, his omnipotence by his very acts". That leads us immediately to the conclusion that he was not able to sin because we see that he did not sin — and that is the correct conclusion as an examination of these four possibilities brings out.

1) *Non potuit non peccare* - he was not able (unable) not to sin. The negatives here make it rather difficult to grasp, but it will be seen after a moment's reflection that this is not the same thing as if the two negatives cancelled each other and gave us "he was able to sin", though that is part of the meaning too. The statement that he was unable not to sin means that he could not but sin, he could sin and could not do anything else. This alternative consequently must be rejected *in toto*, for it involves a necessity to sin. This we cannot predicate of Christ, though it is predictable of fallen man.

2) The next two that come up for consideration must be taken together as contraries of one particular kind of freedom or possibility — *potuit peccare*, and *potuit non peccare* — he was able to sin, and he was able not to sin. The natural thing to do seems to predicate this freedom of Christ, the ability to sin or not to do so. That is to say, he was free in a moral tension to go one way or the other. But this we cannot do for two reasons. i) It presupposes that Christ was neutral in the first place, and that he meets the alternative without any inclination to the one side or the other — which is tantamount to denying that he had a divine Personality, that he was one with the Eternal and perfect Word of God. Thus Christ cannot be thought of as facing the temptations in a neutral sense at all. ii) This kind of freedom implies that Christ is within the moral tension, which is also tantamount to denying his divine Person, his nature as one with the Word of the Eternal who is above all moral tensions. To predicate this of Jesus, says Camfield, is a "piece of sheer humanism and moralism, not to say presumption." *(Revelation and the Holy Spirit,* p. 275) This will be seen when we remember that we cannot attain real goodness through the law or through ethics. Ethical goodness is only attained through struggle in opposition to evil, within a moral tension. Against this we must affirm that real goodness is done easily, spontaneously! The goodness that is done through the moral tension is after all only relative to the evil which is its opposite;

it is not real goodness. Thus the goodness which I do because I ought to do it, is not goodness which gets me round the ought; for the more I pursue goodness through the "ought" the more clearly do I see what the "ought" means. Thus the "ought" is ever receding and ever in front of me; and if that is so, if no matter how much I do what I ought to do, I am never what I ought to be! Here true goodness is unattainable. Thus Barth says that man condemns himself to death by asking the questions about `the good', because the only answer is that he the man is not good, and from the point of view of the good powerless. To start with this ethical freedom within the moral tension means that man starts within the ring of his own self, in a never ending circle in which he is found chasing his own tail! This is what Paul calls the `curse of the law'; we are all caught in a circle in which we have become trapped by our own autonomous striving! Now this is nevertheless the kind of freedom that man has. Indeed man has hardly got even that. We must think, I feel, that unfallen man had this neutral freedom to do one thing or the other; he was able to sin, or able not to sin. Fallen man, however, is not so able not to sin, precisely because he does not come neutral upon the scene like Adam; he comes with an inclination already toward one direction; that is he comes with the overwhelming impulse toward evil. But even should he be able to do what is ethically good in the face of evil, which we must admit, though we cannot say that he can do any act that is actually perfect even ethically, he has not yet attained freedom, precisely because he is bound up in his own autonomy; that is in bondage within the moral tensions of good and evil. He is never free to do the good spontaneously but only a relative good which is still questioned or condemned by a further "ought" in front of him. It is seldom realised that the moral "ought" implies in it a judgement that I am not what I ought to be; that is to say, when the moral "ought" or the Law or even the ethical ideal is taken seriously, it contains an annihilating condemnation upon him who is striving towards the "ought" or the Law or the ideal! Thus we are to think of the moral tension in itself as the result of the Fall of man; in fact ethical goodness, as the relative goodness gained within moral tension is itself a result of sin! You cannot thus really have goodness in the ethical sense without sin; consequently if goodness is to be had the moral goodness must be transcended and the conformity to the Law or the demand contained in the moral "ought" or the summons of the ideal must be attained another way altogether. Moral goodness rightly pursued must be ever destroying itself (cf. here F.H. Bradley and A.E. Taylor!) This is the eternal problem of the suicide of goodness when it is properly pursued and which is not sufficiently discussed in ethical theory.

The point about this freedom which is characterised by the expressions "able to sin" and "able not to sin" is that it is a freedom controlled by the nature of the person with this so-called freedom. If the person is entirely neutral he may be free, but if he has a nature such as we have he is not really free precisely because he is free from God — that is where the paradox and contradiction of human personality come in — man is free to do sin, but not free to trust God. He is not free of himself to trust God precisely because he is — even while he thinks he is so free — asserting his autonomy before God which is itself the very sin that he thinks he is free from! Thus we arrive at the paradox that for a man to be free in this sense not to sin is itself a bondage! And that bondage is all the more bitter and tragic because by persisting in his freedom and autonomy man is not aware that this self-assertion is parr of his very undoing! And consequently, it is only when man realises in revelation that he is not free or that his freedom is itself a form of sin and bondage that he surrenders his freedom or bondage, for they are thus the same, and do gain freedom for the first time in a heteronomy to God. In bondage to Christ a man becomes free for the first time. As the Scottish hymn writer George Matheson wrote: "Make me a captive Lord, and then I shall be free!"

Another point we must notice is that there is no such thing as a freedom of indifference, that is a freedom which is really neutral; that is caprice. Freedom means freedom to do something; and freedom to do the good means servitude to the good; and freedom to do evil means servitude to evil as Paul teaches so plainly in Rom. 6-7 etc. It is the nature behind the freedom, behind the ability that controls the ability itself. That is why we fallen men are really not free even in an ethical sense, because our natures are not free from evil desire. We are able to do only what we like; and the psychological freedom which we all have as living beings is turned not to freedom towards the good but freedom towards the evil, itself a bondage, because of what we are ourselves. A man is not really free unless he can not only control his ability toward freedom but can control his likes and dislikes too; but in order to control his likes and dislikes he must like to do so; and so we are caught in moral *cul-de-sac*! The point is, if we are really to be free our very natures must be changed. That becomes quite clear when we remember the statement of Brunner I quoted above to the affect that our personalities themselves are founded on sin; which is the same as the point I made when I asserted that our goodness is a matter of an attainment in a moral tension which is itself the result of sin and the fall. We cannot thus get outside of our own personalities any more than we can rise above the ground by lifting ourselves up by the hair! The evolution or development of our humility *per se* is the development of sin! To cultivate human personality and goodness is thus apparently to come very near the Kingdom of God in form, but in reality to get farther way from it.

Perhaps we are now in a position to see the bearing of this discussion on the sinlessness of Christ and on the nature of his freedom before temptation. To suppose that his freedom was the freedom or ability to sin or not to sin, is to suppose that he had only a relative goodness, and therefore a personality achieved in a world of sin; it is to presuppose that he was not spontaneously good, for it presupposes that he did not have a good nature to begin with. If there is one thing more evident than another it is that in all his temptations Jesus was bound to win, but that does not make his temptations any less real; they were real and more real than we can ever know precisely because they were assaults upon a nature that was itself holy. The fact that his nature was such as it was does not in any way invalidate the temptations as real and genuine — to assert that is absurd, for it is to assert that for the temptations to be real or genuine Jesus had to have either a neutral or an evil nature! The nature that controls the freedom has nothing whatsoever to do with the validity of the temptation. That error arises only when we think of the ability or power of Christ as mechanical force or as omnipotence conceived of as natural power raised to the nth degree. But as we have seen we cannot *so* think of Christ's ability or omnipotence. It was personal always and therefore always capable of being confronted with a decision with a challenge. The fact that he was bound to make a decision one way does not mean that his personal Character was invalidated!

3) And so thirdly, we must assert of Jesus Christ that he was unable to sin not only because he did not sin but because he was of such a nature, in being One with the Word, that he would not have sinned. The question is often put: Could Jesus have sinned if he had liked to? The question is irrelevant and absurd, for the whole point of the matter is that he would not have liked to. It was just because sin was

so loathsome to him that he could not have sinned. There is no freedom apart from character; there is no "can" apart from "like". Christ could not have sinned because he loved God. He loved God and did what he liked; but what he liked, he did, and what he liked was to love God. He could not sin against what he was, the very Love of God incarnate. The fact that Christ is one with God in Will and Purpose and Love means that he could not have sinned any more than God could have sinned; though by the very fact that he became man he was subjected to temptation in a way that God is not in himself, for God cannot be tempted. To sin is to sin against God. To sin is to move against and away from God. But as one with the Word, as Word of God moving from God into time, Christ could not have moved against God; that is an absurdity. Christ could not be what he was not. He was the Word of God and could not be anything else than the Word of God become man; thus even in temptations which were so fearfully real, he was always the Word of God, the Son, the Express Image of God; for him to have sinned would have meant that he was not the Christ; it is a contradiction not only of terms but of thought to think of Christ's freedom as anything else than as *non potuit peccare*.

When we think of the possibility of sin in Christ we must remember that the word "possibility" has two meanings which are difficult to distinguish. The possible means on the one hand a possible alternative which is impossible; that is to say, it refers to an occasion. In this sense there was for Christ the possibility of sin. On the other hand "possibility" may mean an alternative which is on the road to actuality, a possibility which is not improbable. This possibility for sin cannot be applied to Christ — the distinction is the same as we have already made in repudiating the *potuit peccare* or *potuit non peccare* of Christ and in affirming the *potuit peccare*.

All this means that real freedom is freedom which cannot sin. Christ had such freedom. I think that is essentially what St. John means when he says that he that is born of God cannot sin. Now such freedom is actually the freedom that the Christian receives from Christ, and is only obtainable in Christ. That is to say, the freedom that Augustine spoke of in those Words: "Love God and do what you like." It is thus a freedom that has the suspicion of antinomianism about it; it is a freedom that is from behind the law and the ethical imperative; it is a freedom that is identical to bondage to Love; the freedom that we have toward God and the good under the constraint of the Love of Christ which is shed abroad in our hearts by the Holy Spirit. In this experience the Christian has a changed nature and his actions flow from that nature; his personality is here grounded in God and not in himself or society. As grounded in God through Christ it is grounded in love, and acts of love flow spontaneously from it. Thus the "philosophy of the Christian's life is to become what he is", to be what he is in Christ. His life is an outworking of that which God has worked in him. He is now free to do good because he is one with the Good. He is thus temptable in the sense that temptation may assail him, but he is not temptable in the sense that he may be overcome by temptations so long as he abides in Christ. This means that perfect freedom means perfect bondage to Love, to God in Christ. The more adjusted we are to Christ, the more that our characters are overgrown with holy habits as with the habit of Christ thrown over us like a garment the less are we temptable, that is, liable to fall in the face of temptation. The perfectly good man cannot sin. He may be tempted but he cannot be anything else than what he is. After all our acts are just what we are in certain incidents; and these incidental acts show us what we are in reality. If the tree is good it bears good fruit, if bad it bears bad fruit. We must think of Jesus as the Tree planted perfectly in

God, as the Man made One with God, and therefore as one bound to bear good fruit, and only good fruit.

Let me end this chapter with a citation from F.W. Camfield: "But the moral struggle of Jesus is not made thereby unreal. We may remind ourselves that very often the temptations which give us the most trouble and occasion us the bitterest struggles, are those to which our nature will not let us succumb. We could do these evil things, but then we simply could not. We are here terribly temptable but we cannot fall. And the achievements which cost us the most are not seldom the very ones which we are bound to realise. We cannot leave a certain task alone, maybe we wish we could, but we simply cannot. There are many experiences known to us in which constraint and freedom are one. And the intensity of Christ's struggles, the bitterness of the cup which he had to drink, what is all this but an indication of the passion of love which lies behind God's deed of renunciation and sacrifice? What is it but the earthly human counterpart of the sacrifice in the heavenly places?" (*op. cit.* p. 275)

CHAPTER 9

The Significance of the Humanity of Christ

In Jesus Christ our Lord we have One whom we confess to be Truly God and Truly Man. For the first time in Divine relations with men a Mediator has come from God to Man who is both God himself, and is a fellow-man, one with God and one with us. In him a bridge between God and Man has been established. If you build a bridge over a canyon you have to get on both sides of the canyon first. Christ is the Mediator who certainly by his very coming reveals to us the canyon between man and God, but who bridges that canyon in his own divine-human Person. In virtue of his Godhead he is the *Via quo itur*, in virtue of his Humanity he is the *Via qua itur*, as St Augustine expressed it. The humanity of Christ is thus an essential part of the divine work of Salvation, and it is our business now to trace something of its significance or importance in this regard, and in so doing to gather up much that we have discussed sporadically hitherto on this subject.

Looking back over the event of the Incarnation and seeing its significance and the great pain it cost even God, the cost his Love bore so gladly for us, we may say reverently that God had to become flesh in order to save us, for what he has actually done has shown us that there was no other way for us to be saved. When we say he had to, we are not arguing from any metaphysical premise at all. We are rather reflecting on what God has freely and actually done. Here we learn that God can and does reveal himself and has come himself to save men and women; we learn that God has actually revealed himself and does actually save men and women. We know no other can do this, and that there is in fact no other way of salvation than this. We do not bring our ideas of what God "can" or "must" do to save mankind, but it is from what God has actually done for us in the Incarnation of his only-begotten Son through which alone we know anything of God, that we learn what "can" with God means at all. And so by reflecting in this way on the actuality of revelation now already taken place we may say that there was no other way, and say, with reverence that God had to do what he did do to save us; but that "had to do" which we may in our language ascribe to God is a "had to do" of his wonderful Grace - and of Grace only, although it was certainly necessary for our salvation.

We shall have to explore these two sides a little more, namely, the "does do" and the "can do" of God in Christ.

1. The Humanity of Jesus Christ signifies the *objective actuality* of God's coming into the world in revelation and redemption, that is to say, in reconciling the world to himself. The fact that Christ God's only begotten Son became incarnate and is really and truly man, or to put it the other way round, that this Man Jesus of Nazareth is really and truly God, means that *God himself* has really and truly come

among us as one of us, without of course ceasing to be who he is, and is eternally. The manhood or human nature of Jesus Christ means that the Incarnation is no mere theophany, no docetic appearance of the Divine, no phantasmal and unsubstantial protraction with which we cannot have anything to do, and with which there is and could be no actual point of contact   *Anknüpfungspunkt*, to use Karl Barth's term again. Jesus was no dream of God on earth, but God himself, very God, actually incarnate on earth and in time in a way that does not override but is consonant with earthly forms and historical existence. Had God not become Incarnate he would not really be here with us as the God whom we Christians worship, for in Jesus he would not really be historically real for us and have to do with a historical people in definite historical acts and events. Certainly the supremely important fact about Jesus Christ was his Divine Person, but that Divine Nature, that Eternal side of him, "is something which secured its foot-hold in the world through its actualisation as a real element in the time-series, a perfect earthly medium of grace. Had Jesus' manhood been fictitious or abridged, no fully saving power could pass forth from him to win mankind, and God were still far away." (H. R. Mackintosh, *The Person and Place of Jesus Christ*, p. 385)

Nor must we think on the other hand that the humanity of Christ was some sort of general humanity, humanity in some universal sense. Certainly it was that also, but it was that in virtue of the fact that it was joined uniquely and hypostatically to the Son and Word of God; nevertheless, we cannot let go of the idea that the Word became united to a particular man, the man Jesus of Nazareth, the historical son of Mary, who was crucified under the governorship of Pontius Pilatus in Judaea, a man of definite historical record and definite historical existence. The Word became flesh, became united to an individual human being, Jesus of Nazareth. We do not know any other humanity after all than that which we find in individual persons. The humanity of Jesus Christ was just such humanity, that of an historical and individual person, in fact just such humanity that it could easily be passed by without there being the perception that there was anything more than humanity there!

There is no sense in universalising or deifying the humanity of Christ in itself apart from the fact that it is united to the eternal Word or Son of God. Thus today we hear often of the "divine humanity" of Christ in words which speak of his infinite human capabilities. People point out his great mental agility unsurpassed in history and among men; they go so far as to assert that had he wished he might have been the greatest painter or scientist or musician or mathematician! There may be something in this idea, for we cannot underplay the abilities of the human Jesus, but that is really quite beside the point. What is science but the attempt of man to construct in thought a universe something like the real one under the limitations of his own knowledge, that is to say while cast entirely upon a his own human exertions and resources? What is music or art but the attempt in refracted conditions of our temporal existence and appreciation to express something which after all cannot be expressed? The *raison d'être* of these arts and sciences is simply the pursuit of an object entirely within the compass of human limitations and on the sole power of human resources. But what Jesus came to do, and do as man, was to do the will of God on earth; he came to confine himself to the task of mediatorship in order that he might carry out the reconciliation between man and God. Thus his task in becoming man was precisely so far as that aspect of it is concerned that he might be called his becoming "flesh". But nevertheless his life in the flesh was marked by the fullness of manhood and was no mutilated humanity — rather would it be mutilated if in any sense it were thought of after the fashion we have just been referring to. Jesus comes as bone of our bone, flesh of our flesh; he speaks a human voice, is brought up in a human family, eats, drinks, thirsts and is hungry, grows weary and is pained, rejoices, sleeps, sheds tears, encompassed within real humanity. That is to say the significance of this is that the Eternal has drawn so near that he is one with us, a fellow human being, a *Mitmensch*, a Brother (here we use the word correctly!); the eternal has actually come among us in such a way that he exists in a medium with which we are familiar; that he has *actually* come among us human beings as one of *us*; that the reality of God is an actuality, an actuality to *us*! The Humanity of the Lord Jesus Christ guarantees a veritable Incarnation, guarantees that we do really have God, God incarnate, among us. "If the manhood of Christ is unreal, at any remotest point, God has not stooped to unity with man." (H.R. Mackintosh, *op. cit.* p. 404) "The measure of Christ's humanity is the measure of God's Love." (*ibid.*) Just so far as Christ has stooped to be one of and with us, so far does he love us. And that he has gone all the way he could go with us, even to the point of dying among men, means that his love is to the uttermost, absolutely unlimited. But notice the idea that Christ's actual humanity is the measure of the love of God is quite incompatible with the idea that Christ was not really divine, for if Christ were not really divine the love of Christ to men would be but human love, martyr-love.

Modern liberalism has portrayed much and often wonderfully the love of Christ for men, and teaches that therein we may see a glimpse of the Love of God. But that is not really the love of which we are concerned in the Christian faith; for to deny that Christ is Divine is to say that God's love was not great enough to stoop down to us and take human flesh, to be one with us! Thus both these truths, the Divinity and the Humanity of Christ, must be held inseparably together; and you only can speak rightly of the humiliation of Christ as the love of God when you see that it means that *God himself* came right among us and took flesh. "Forasmuch as the children are sharers of flesh and blood, he also in like manner partook of the same." If Jesus Christ is not God, then God has not reached us, but has stopped short of humanity; then God does not love us to the uttermost. But the fact that Christ is God, really God, that Christ is perfectly human, flesh of our flesh, bone of our bone, means that God has stopped short of nothing; in his love to the poor needy beggar he has donned the beggar's rags in order to embrace him and love him. Thus the humanity of Christ Jesus is the objective actuality of God to us in revelation and redemption; it guarantees a veritable Incarnation of God "in all points made like unto his brethren", as the writer of the Epistle to the Hebrews expressed it. The humanity of Christ means that God loves us sinners to the very uttermost, that he has actually come to us in reconciliation.

This actuality of God's actual coming in the humanity of Jesus Christ has significance for both revelation and atonement.

a) The actuality of revelation is grounded in the actual humanity of Christ. What is revelation, the revelation of God? It is *Jesus* Christ himself. Jesus Christ is the Truth himself. In him all the Truth of God revealed to mankind is now actual among us men and women. Thus St. Paul says in I Cor. ch. 1 that Jesus was made to us Wisdom from God, Righteousness, and Sanctification and Redemption. The humanity of Christ, that is to say, is not simply an act of God, but an act of God in which his act and Person are one in *Jesus*. We do not have such actuality in the Old Testament. There we have the proleptic shadows of the coming reality; they were real as such, but by their very nature pointed beyond themselves toward saving acts of God that were yet to take place. Thus in the Old Testament we have really the Word of God, but it is a Word in promissory form, not one which is itself actualised in humanity or among actual human beings in history. It is a Word which has not yet become a deed; or it is a Word which has not become fully personal and actual. In Jesus Christ, however, we do have not only the Word but the Word made flesh, not only revelation of God but such a complete and final revelation that it is itself actually God himself.

Thus, you remember, Prof.T W. Manson pointed out to us in a lecture the other day that Christ according to the writer to the Hebrews is the effulgence of God's glory and the facsimile of his Person. That is to say this revelation of God's glory was at the same time such a revelation that it was actually God in Person; a revelation that carried with it the actuality of God to men. This is not only because Jesus Christ was divine but because Jesus of Nazareth was the historical actuality of God in the actuality of his self-revelation to mankind. Joined to the humanity of Christ the Divine Effulgence was actualised among men. As St Paul wrote, it is *Jesus* who is the "mystery of God in whom all the treasures of wisdom and knowledge are hid." (Col. 2:3)

b) It is a severe misunderstanding of the whole of revelation in the Bible if it is thought that the revelation consists of certain principles, ideas or propositions, which are given there. We have already thought of this in relation to the Person of Christ and seen how Hegelian or Schleiermacherian approaches made Christ into symbol dissolvable in the idea that is symbolised — in other words again even the Ebionite Christology passes over into the Docetic! The fact is that we do not have in Christ a symbol that is separable from the actuality symbolized. It may well be said perhaps with justice that Jesus is a symbol, but in no ordinary sense of the Word. He is such a symbol as is completely one with the reality symbolised; thus the important things in the Christian revelation are most emphatically *not* what is commonly spoken of as "the Fatherhood of God and the brotherhood of man and good neighbourly love". *The* really important thing is just the Person of Jesus Christ, *God-Man*, and it is in him that these ideas or truths have any actuality at all. Without the humanity of Christ they are not actual and without the Divinity of Christ they are not real. But without the hypostatic union of both humanity and divinity in the One Person of Christ they are meaningless so far as revelation and salvation are concerned. While the hypostatic union between the Word and Christ means that there is no access to the Word apart from the Man Jesus Christ, the real humanity of Christ is the guarantee that in him we have been given the actual objective Self-Revelation of God in Word and Person. In fact it can be said that it is the humanity of Christ and only it which is the revelation of the eternal Word. (Cf. Karl Barth, *Kirchliche Dogmatik*, 1.2, p. 162) It means that the Word of God is not only the Word which creates but that the Word — incomprehensibly! — becomes creature itself, that is to say *man*, the Man Jesus. Did he not become creature, the Word had not come, or become actual to us. But in that he came and became flesh we know that *God* is behind it — that here in Jesus we really have to do with *God himself*; that we are not left hopeless or in ignorance, but that God has revealed his very Self in Jesus and guaranteed that to us which we could not guarantee ourselves. Just because Jesus is Man, because in him the Eternal Son of God really and actually became Man, revelation means the assumption of the temporal by the Eternal; and therefore the assumption in him of creaturely finite man into relations with God. That is to say again: it is the Humanity of the Lord Jesus Christ that guarantees us participation in the revelation of God.

c) The Humanity of the Lord Jesus Christ has to do with redemption as well; it provides the actual ground in our human historical existence and the essential basis in human reality for atonement. That Jesus the God-Man is he who atones means that atonement is made for us who are men and women. "If he who lived and died for all men had himself been man only in seeming, or in part, no expiation were after all made in our name; for only he can act with God for man who speaks from man's side. It is as Christ became our fellow, moving in a true manhood through obedience, conflict, and death, that he entered into our condition fully and what he did availed on our behalf to receive from God's hand the suffering in which is expressed the Divine judgement upon sin. Jesus' manhood is the cornerstone of reconciliation." (H. R. Mackintosh, *op. cit.* p. 405) How could Christ have died *for us*, how could he have borne *our* guilt and *our* sin and carried it away had he not *really and actually been Man*? To allow here the Manhood of Christ to be mutilated by docetic apologetic against naturalism is to disrupt the Atonement, and to make the act of Christ in life and death and resurrection meaningless for us, beyond the example of a heroic martyrdom — and even that is not of sound sense for who would put himself in the way of death for us in order to show his love for us, if there was nothing to save us from in death? That Jesus Christ really identified himself with men and with sinful men is something that is of absolute religious significance; that he is man and died *as man* while being at the same time God, means that the death he died is a death *for* men, that it is an act of God for men.

Further, that Christ is man means that he is our great High Priest, as the Epistle to the Hebrews declares, High Priest praying and interceding for us at the right hand of God; and not only that he is God's Son or Word to us, but that he is also *our* word, as it were, to God, our response to him. Jesus takes *our* sin and represents *us* before God the Father offering up for us the perfect sacrifice of a perfect Man. As such he is touched with the feeling of all our infirmities and is able to succour us all. Once more, that in Jesus the Eternal has actually assumed our humanity, that the Word of God has actually become Man, means that in Jesus Christ the destiny of man is actually assured, and brought back to its true relation to and place in God from which it had fallen; but this time bound to him by an indissoluble relation. Jesus Christ is not only the example as Man for all believers, he is the archetype of them all. Our lives are hid with Christ in God, and in Christ we have given to us the objective actuality of the salvation of those who believe in him; that the eternal destiny of the Christian is one with the eternal destiny of Christ — but that would not be so, were Christ not really and truly man.

2. The Humanity of Jesus Christ signifies the *objective possibility* of God for us in revelation and redemption, that is, in reconciliation. Here we repeat to a certain extent what we have already said in the last section only from another angle, or in another respect. Just because the Humanity of the Lord Jesus Christ means the objective actuality of God for us, it means also the objective possibility of God for us. That does not mean only, however, that because what God does do, he can do; it means also that because God does do and therefore can do, that we "can do" also in his "can do": "I can do all things through Christ who strengthens me (πάντα ἰσχύω ἐν τῷ ἐνδυναμοῦντί με)", said St Paul in his Epistle to the Philippians, 4.13. Because the actuality of God for us is guaranteed in the humanity of Christ, that means too that God is free for us and we have in that very freedom of God the possibility of his divine revelation to us and divine salvation for us. That the Word of God Eternal and Transcendent in himself has become man means that God is revealed to be free, actually to be free to become Man, and be what he is in Love

and Grace for us. Therefore in that freedom we have the objective possibility of God. In Jesus Christ we have the real objective *Anknüpfungspunkt* (to use again Barth's often repeated term !), between God and man! The fact that the Word has seized hold of the Man Jesus Christ and united itself (or rather himself) to him, means that we too may be united to the eternal Word of God in him.

As he in himself God is not free for us, not free for us to reach and to have, either in revelation or in redemption, or reconciliation. In other words, looking back from the actuality of revelation, we may say that God could not and did not reveal himself to us as he is in himself, or in such way that we would be capable of apprehending him: *finitum non capax infiniti*! But the fact that the Word has become flesh, that God has assumed human form, means that he can be and is actually free for us; therefore free in such a way for us and all human beings that it is now possible, possible for the first time, for *us* to know God! For God to reveal himself to us he must reveal himself in actual human form, for we human beings cannot get outside our human forms without ceasing to be human and therefore without ceasing to exist! The Humanity of Christ thus means not only the actuality of God's Being for us, but the possibility of *our* knowing God. If God does not assume flesh, then our faith is vain and empty. If God would reveal himself to us, he must become our "fellow", as it were; if he would reconcile us to himself, he must himself be the Mediator uniting in himself both human and Divine reality. There are several points I would have you note here:-

This actuality of God's coming to us objectively in the humanity of Jesus Christ has significance for both revelation and atonement.

a) The actuality of revelation is grounded in the actual humanity of the Lord Jesus Christ. What is revelation, the revelation of God himself to *us* human beings but one that entails the possibility of *our* knowing God and of *our* having to do with him, and also that in his assuming humanity God himself assumes *likeness with us*? That is rather a wonderful event. It is not that we as lost are remade in the Image of God and are only thus saved, but that the remaking of us in the Image of God, means that God himself takes on the image of man for our sake, that God the Word takes on human *Gestalt*, our human form; for only in and through that human form, perfect and united to God in Jesus Christ, may we through Christ be imprinted over again in the image of God - in our hearts. That is of course not subjectively possible except through the descent of the Holy Spirit who transforms us through the Word into the Image of Christ; but the fact that the Word of God assumes human form is the objective possibility for that; that is to say: now that the Word of God has become flesh it is possible for all men to be saved through Jesus Christ and be restored to the image and likeness of God for which we were created by him. Now here we have to note also that this very assertion of the possibility of salvation in Christ, implies the contrary also, namely, that outside this interrelation between us and God in Christ there is no Salvation; for there is no Incarnation of God apart from or outside of Christ, and therefore nowhere else is there an actual relation between men and God which betokens at the same time the possibility of Salvation for them. Only in and through God incarnate in Christ, God become man in Christ, may we, or anyone, really come to know God and be saved by him. The Humanity of Christ is thus crucially significant for the saving knowledge of God by man. God would not be creating the possibility of Salvation did he assume a form unknown to us or unknowable by us. In short were Christ anything other than Human there would be no possibility of knowing God and experiencing salvation. It is the human form and reality of Jesus of Nazareth which is the necessary "point of contact" or *Anknüpfungspunkt* for our Salvation, the necessary the bridge between God and man, and man and God.

b) It is precisely this actual Humanity of Christ which makes faith possible for us, and reconciliation possible as well. Jesus Christ can reveal God to us just because, while being God he is also visible and knowable as man. This means that the Eternal Word enters our world within its earthly conditions and is veiled thereby, even to the extent of humiliation and death. It is just this veiling that is our salvation for the naked Majesty of the Lord God in his Self-revelation and Word would slay us. It is sometimes asked if God cannot reveal himself to us without Christ, without this form known to us which he assumed. The answer to that is that if the revelation of God were to take place apart from this veiling in human being or in the form of another being whose form was unknown to us in our world, it would mean the disruption of the conditions of this world and of mankind — it would mean the end of all things. It would mean impossibility! It is the authentic Humanity of the Lord Jesus Christ which betokens real possibility in our world of human being and space and time. To say that the Word veils himself and so makes faith a possibility means also that the objective possibility lies in the human reality and historical nature of Christ. This is why as the Christ he remains concealed in history. Were he to unveil himself directly he would make history disappear. Where he to unveil himself directly he would no longer be a historical personality, accessible to human beings, but would but still be the Son of God he was in himself from everlasting to everlasting.

It is the fact of sin which complicates the matter, for in sin we are all clothed with insincerity, with a mask of hypocrisy. Now a complete unveiling and disclosure of the Son of God to us, would mean the penetration of this mask of ours in such a way that there would be left no room for faith; it would be sight, and death following. For no man can see God and live. That is why in his mercy God does not let man see him directly unveiled in his majesty, for that would result at once in the final judgment of man with no possibility or time for repentance. It is only when God confronts man not openly or in his unveiled Majesty, but in and through the mediation of his incarnate Reality and Love, where faith can take place and God's Love casts out fear, that it is possible for the sinner, man or woman, to cast himself or herself wholly upon the Love and Grace of God and be saved. God in the Lord Jesus Christ does not manipulate people, but he treats with them gently and personally where the answering faith of the sinner may respond in love. Thus in order not to manipulate human people, but to confront them in such a way that they will be given the freedom and the possibility to decide for him and to surrender to him, God has become incarnate in Jesus Christ veiled in his divine Majesty.

All this means that in his saving Love God determined to become man, and has taken such a human form among men that he could pass for a man, that men and women, could pass him by and not know him as Lord and Saviour, as very God! It is precisely as such in the humanity of the Lord Jesus that God confronts us in a way that he delivers his assault of love upon our sin, and calls us either to unmask ourselves before him in confession, repentance, and faith, or to reject him, God incarnate. It is here that, so to speak, the pinch comes in: it hurts us to surrender our masks, for to surrender our masks is nothing else than to surrender our whole personalities which consist largely in these masks of insincerity that we wear! It should be clear, then, that unless God were really known *as Man*, in Jesus, there would be no room for faith; for direct and immediate revelation of God would leave no room for repentance. Thus for the incarnate Lord God to reveal himself directly to us in such a way as to infringe the chosen limitations of his humanity in Jesus, as well as our own, would be abolish any possibility of faith on our part and for our salvation.

This is why faith is so deeply concerned to preserve the complete *humanity* of the Mediator as well as the truth of his transcendent albeit veiled Deity, and in each case for exactly the same reason — space for us to confess the Lord Jesus Christ as our Saviour, true Man and True God. It is in and through the Humanity of Christ that God incarnate confronts us and reveals himself to us so that we may be free to surrender to his love and put our trust him as our God and Saviour; that is, to provide for us the possibility for personal decision in faith, instead of being overwhelmed by his Transcendent Majesty. Where God approaches man directly there is no room or possibility for faith, for were God would confront him directly in his unveiled Majesty there would be no room for faith, for repentance and confession, and for love. It is thus a part of God's Grace that he veils himself in the humanity of Jesus, and approaches us Incognito, as it were, knocking at the door of our hearts like a stranger. The humanity of Jesus is thus an utterly essential part of the Christian faith; and without it there can be no experience of faith in Jesus Christ at all. Through the humanity of the Lord Jesus, his incarnate Son, God does not force himself upon people, but always acts with them gently and personally, and in his unmitigated love calls and invites them to put their trust in him. It is thus in the humanity of Jesus Christ, his vicarious humanity, that we sinful men and women my take shelter and really know and Love God the Father, and love him as his children, praying to him as the Lord Jesus taught us: "Our Father who art in heaven, hallowed be thy Name. Forgive us our sins as we forgive those who sin against us".

c) This possibility and freedom to know and love God as our heavenly Father, however, of which we have been thinking is not something that is ours as our own possession. It is itself a gift; and lies in the Grace-Act of God in taking upon himself membership with us in our race. Apart from that act there is no possibility for men and women to know him, and no possibility for their salvation. In themselves men and women are not free toward God, to know him, believe in him and love him. Nor does the fact that Christ is Man mean that because we too are human we may find in his very humanity the one saving point-of-contact with God. That point of contact lies not in our humanity but in this particular Man Jesus, who comes to us in the humanity he has assumed from us, his vicarious Humanity in and through which he has allied himself with us and takes out place before God in his judgment and mercy. God in Christ really comes to us in his love and grace, with whom as our God-given Mediator therefore we can and may really have contact and saving relations with the Eternal God, without fear. Jesus is in himself the objective ground and the possibility for human faith in God. In faith man is wholly dependent on what he receives, and must surrender himself in which no room act for any self-justification is left, that is, no room for one's assertion of freedom. But this abandonment itself cannot be achieved by man in his own strength; it is not even a human possibility at all, that is subjectively speaking — and here we have to do with the reality and presence of the Holy Spirit who makes valid this objective actuality and objective possibility provided for us in the saving Humanity of Christ which is united to the Eternal Word of God. But now both these, the objective actuality of God among men and with it the objective possibility of God for men, proclaim an objective reconciliation for *all* people, men, women and children. For this saving purpose of his love, Christ calls us who believe in him to be ambassadors for him to persuade people everywhere that God in his love has come among us reconciling the world for himself. He is the propitiation for our sins only but for the sins of the whole world.

CHAPTER 10

The Significance of the Divinity of Christ

In the last chapter we considered the significance of the humanity of Christ, the fact that it is in Jesus Christ as Man that course of God's action towards us is actualised and made free for us. The humanity of Christ is the objective guarantee of God's action among men and women for their salvation; we have to think of the obverse of that significance here. If the humanity of Christ is the guarantee that God's Salvation actually reaches men; the divinity of Christ is the guarantee that the action of Redemption in Jesus Christ is actually of God. Of course we do not start out in this way; what we say now presupposes the foregoing discussion, in which we came to think of Christ as truly Divine made known to us in and because of his self-presenting to us as the Saving Word of God himself. We are to turn this round now and investigate something of the true significance of the Deity of Christ thus apprehended; this, we must assert, is the guarantee that the Salvation which we experience in Jesus Christ is *really* Salvation; that is to say, it is a Salvation from sin against God which only *God* himself who is sinned against can effect. Thus the significance of the Deity of Christ lies in the fact that "The course of action which God adopts towards man is identical with the existence of Jesus Christ." (Karl Barth: *Gifford Lectures*, p. 70)

We may begin our discussion here by expressing this in the negative: Christ is significantly Divine in that he is not a derivative of God. In other words the whole significance of Christ lies in the fact that in Christ we do not have just something divine, but *God himself*. There is really too much loose talk today about the "divine", as though anything could be divine which is not God himself. It seems trite to say it, but it is nevertheless something which our generation has to learn: namely, only God can be divine. We hear talk about humanity as divine, and of all men as somewhat divine, and of the humanity of Christ as especially divine. That betokens, it seems to me, a serious mental as well as a religious disease! In fact much like the disease of the mad Roman Emperor Caligula! Honesty must agree to the statement that nothing can be called divine which is not actually Divine! Divinity cannot be a predicate in a sentence in which the Subject is not also Divine! Thus you cannot say that man is divine without making sheer havoc of your words, amounting to nonsense. Man is human and cannot be divine. To say that man is divine is a contradiction in terms. It would be a different thing when you say that man is also divine; that is wrong too, but it does not involve a contradiction of terms. It simply states the falsehood that man while being man is also God. On the other hand, we can say that God is also Man in Jesus Christ, but we cannot say that God is human without violating language and thought together as well as theology.

Strictly speaking therefore we cannot have a sentence in which God is in the predicate, or where Divinity is in the predicate. *God is always Subject* — Divinity only can be the predicate where Divinity is also the Subject or where the verb is copulative in which the Subject and Predicate are equal, such as, "The Word was God". This brings us back to the point that Christ is not a derivative of God, is not a predicate of God, but is *himself God, but God incarnate.* That is the significance of the Divinity of Christ — a relation of identity between God and the Divinity of Christ; and therefore that the action of Salvation in Jesus Christ is God's own action — that the presence of Christ is God's very own Presence; or rather, to put it the other way round, "God was in Christ reconciling the world unto himself." Christ is not somehow God, not simply "divine" in the loose modern sense, but truly God and perfectly Divine. The New Testament never calls Jesus Divine; it is nearly always the other way round; that *God* became man, that is, the subject is God, and the persistent Subject. Thus if the humanity of Christ means that God reaches man in actuality, the Divinity of Christ means that it is precisely and always *God himself* who is the Subject of action and revelation in Jesus Christ our Lord. The Church has consistently rejected the idea that Christ is in any sense less than fully God; no divine something will suffice for salvation, no Arian Christ can be the object of our faith, which is faith in very God himself.

This is then the fact with which we start out: that Christ is the fullorbed Object of faith. We Worship Christ as God, and none other than God himself can be the full and proper Object of faith, as Professor Lamont used to say to us in Edinburgh. The dogma of the divinity of Christ has the significance of guaranteeing that basic assertion of faith which puts Christ in the central place. "We are not called to believe like him merely, but to believe in him." (H.R. Mackintosh, *The Person of Jesus Christ*, p. 345) It is true that faith in God is conveyed through Christ, but it is a faith that is not separable in its object, from his Person; and the fact that it is not separable from his Person is, as we have seen, the guarantee that it is open or free to us, actually possible for us. Christ Jesus obtrudes himself in front of us and he himself takes the Place of God; the significance of the Divinity of Christ means that relationship which we have with Jesus is itself *relation to God.* We cannot but believe in Christ as we are everywhere called to do in the New Testament: "Believe on the Lord Jesus Christ and thou salt be saved", with the implicit, indeed, explicit implication, that this Christ is the Lord God himself present to us. In still other words, the dogma of the Divinity of Christ means that what Christ is to us all in Person, in word and deed, what he is in all our knowledge of him through the New Testament record, in Grace and Forgiveness, he *is* antecedently and eternally in God. Thus the Divinity of Christ is the guarantee that these actions of his are real not only for us in time but real, eternally real, in God himself: that Christ is the presentation of God in such a way that he is not simply from God but God himself - he is the self-presentation of God. Therefore we do not simply believe something about God through Christ as we might venture to believe about God through a prophet, but that we believe *in God himself* directly because we believe *in Christ himself*, because he is the Object of immediate faith. That Christ is the Object of faith for salvation and that he is Divine as only God is divine are equivalent. Were that not so there would be no guarantee that our salvation is really from or of God himself. This means of course that the Divinity of Christ is itself not a derivative but a fundamental statement of faith; it is the first statement of faith from which all other statements of faith must begin and end. Faith starts with the fact that in laying hold of Christ by faith we are laying hold of God himself — for faith means that this One whom we see and hear in the Lord Jesus has eternal content and eternal validity; that God is what Christ is, and that Christ is what God is. Apart from this God is not immediately present to men; and men are not brought into an immediate and new relation with God in which they find and actually receive reconciliation and forgiveness.

If Christ is not God, if God is not fully and wholly in Christ, then God is not reconciling the world unto himself in and through Christ, then the work of Jesus is not valid antecedently in the Eternal God. If Christ is not God, then the love of Christ is not divine love, and we do not know that God is Love; we may know that Christ is love, but if he is man and not divine in the only real and proper sense, then all that we have is a revelation of man at his highest reaching up into the heavens. If Christ is not God, then we do not have a real coming of God to men; just as Christ's real humanity means that God has really come to *us men and women* and to dwell among us, so Christ's Deity means that GOD, very God, himself has come to save us. The dogma of the humanity of Christ makes actual in our world what we believe to be from God, but that is held alongside of the dogma of the Deity of Christ which makes the complementary link to the eternal: neither can really be held without the other — and the statement that must arise from true faith is always: "Very God and Very Man". The dogma of the Divinity of Christ means, therefore, that our salvation is anchored within Eternity, that it is more sure than the very heavens. Without this faith we are but adrift upon an open sea at the mercy of all the winds of cold and bleak logic which bring the black clouds of doubt and scepticism and despair. Strike away this dogma and you have struck away Christianity, for strike away this dogma and all you are left with is only a lovely man, but one who is a madman suffering from megalomania.

The discussion thus far we can gather up in two points:

1) The first significance of the Deity of Christ lies in the real and actual Presence of God in Christ. We assert here again what we asserted in the significance of the humanity of Christ, only with differing emphasis: God is present, actually present in Christ. That is to say, we are emphasising here not the actuality of the presence, but the nature of the presence, not its human side but its divine side. Christianity is pre-eminently the religion of the *Parousia of God*, of an actual coming of God and of a real presence of God held together in the same thought: in Jesus Christ the Son of God. The denial of the humanity of Christ turns Christ into a Byzantine figure, unreal and non-actual for men; the denial of the Divinity of Christ turns him into a Renaissance Christ in which the eternal is shut out by the rounded forms of humanism. It is the latter we are to think about here, and yet it involves with it the former, for, as we have seen more than once, Ebionitism always turns into its opposite Docetism! Thus the denial of the Divinity of Christ not only reduces the Person of Jesus into a figure of Romanticism as in modern liberalism, but it removes God far away into the distance. If God is not really present in Christ, then God still dwells in some dark place, completely hidden, unapproachable in an infinitely far-away region, and all we can do is to spend our time in empty philosophical speculation about his existence or reality on the one hand trying to find out something about him, and on the other hand following in practical life as far as we may the best Man that ever lived, Jesus of Nazareth who spoke about God, but going one better than he with every step in the advance of science and civilisation which faith in him nevertheless set on foot in the western world. That seems largely to be a picture of modern Christianity and what people are doing even today — because they do not seem to have, or have not realised the affirmation of

faith: God is actually and immediately present in the Lord Jesus Christ and perfectly *One* with him so that we know with solid assurance that there is nothing in God essential to his Nature, Being and Character which is hid from men. The removal of God from men resulting from the denial of the Divinity of Christ results always in indecision and uncertainty. That is also characteristic of modern times as well as of older times.

In the Medieval age, it might be said that God was held to be the God of the future and not of the present, the overarching eternity of the Christian faith was recognised but it was not one with which people had actually much to do in this life — they worked toward it. Uncertainty was rife, therefore, and men and women were feverishly working out their own salvation; never sure whether they would ever manage to get through purgatory or not; and so they spent their lives in anxiety heaping up deeds or merit which might in the end weigh up against their misdeeds; fear pervaded the world and the mercy and judgement of God belonged to the future.

A parallel situation has arisen in modern times. Because the Deity of Christ is denied, people are not sure of what they believe. How do you know you are right and not wrong? How do you know they are not right and you may be wrong? Such is the uncertainty engendered through relativism so characteristic of the modern mind, because the one rock of certainty which anchors the faith of men and women, the Deity of Christ, the actual presence of God among us is struck out of their faith. When that goes the bottom has drops out of Christianity. Hence we see today the enormous emphasis on ethical and human values, on personality and social relations, in which man tries to find a foundation for his feet. But he is building his house on the sands; and the winds now descending on the world with the rain of doubt it always brings will soon wash it all away, and great will be the fall thereof: the fall of humanism and humanistic Christianity.

Against all this the Church sticks to its solid affirmation in the real Divinity of Christ as its rock foundation. It alone holds along with the humanity of Christ to the presence of God in the world. If Christ is not God then God has not come to us from the far country but has sent someone who is not he God we have only his word for it that he is of God; but he makes himself to be more than that, therefore we cannot even trust his word to the effect that he is from God! For his "from God" is based on some claim of his that he is "one with God". Thus the denial of the Deity of Christ cuts two ways; it spoils belief in the Man Jesus and makes him a liar, as well as cuts him adrift, and with him cuts us all adrift, from God. With the denial of his Divinity Jesus becomes but a human teacher involved in the peccabilities and errors of humanity. The God of such a religion is essentially deistic, detached from God and out of immediate touch with the world. However, the Incarnation of God in Jesus Christ means the end of all Deism, and the end of all doubt and darkness about God, for it is the coming of God in Person'; it is the revealing of God through God; it is the joining of heaven to earth and not their separation which could and would mean darkness and disaster, sin and rampant evil.

2) The affirmation of the Deity of Christ signifies that in Christ Jesus we have the very presence and action of the Lord God himself. This affirmation has to do with a different aspect things. It means that man's salvation is an act of God himself, that his redemption rests on God's decision. How can man have a part in God and in the realm of Glory, how can time come to share in eternity? That is the question of man, the great question mark put to human life. It is answered only by the act of God in the Incarnation, an act which is identical with God himself. That identity

means the real and active presence of God to mankind, the act of God behind that identity is the decision which we are now thinking of. How can man have a share in or a real relation to the eternal God ? The answer comes in the words of God: "You have not chosen Me, but I have chosen you." That is, the Deity of Christ is the decisive act of God himself in the world in which he decides to save mankind — the act of his reconciling love.

It is not too much to say then, that the doctrine of the Deity of Christ is basically and really the same as the doctrine of election — for the fact that the eternal God himself has chosen to become Man in the Lord Jesus Christ means that the salvation of man rests on that *divine* choice or decision. Election is what it ultimately is, and means therefore, because God has chosen and willed to become man in the Lord Jesus Christ. By the power of God's action a person becomes what he cannot become and cannot be by his own strength. By the act of God when he became man in Jesus, mankind was brought into relation with to God, earth was brought into the presence of heaven, and time began its share with eternity which could not possibly have originated from earth or by man through some upward movement from below or in time. The descent of God in Jesus Christ to earth accomplishes what the ascent of man could not. Thus "the doctrine of the divinity of Christ snaps the connection of mutuality between divine revelation and human faith." (Barth *Church Dogmatics*, 1.1, p. 483) Election means that *God* acts, that *God* executes his decision; and our election means that it is executed for us.

The doctrine of election has been much misunderstood because it has not been thought of *IN CHRIST*. Even the Reformers and their followers who insisted that it should only be thought of thus were often led aside into vain philosophical speculations regarding election or predestination into some form of determinism. An other way of expressing the real truth of election is to say that the Deity of Christ is equivalent to the miracle of Grace, the miracle of God's action toward and with men; that in spite of sin and evil, God actually came to save, and to seek and save those for whom he offered himself in Christ. He unites man to God in Christ which man could not possibly do and does not even co-operate in doing. Thus in a basic and all-important sense we are all elected in Christ — but as a matter of fact in Christ too we are all damned, for he received on himself the sentence of death for every man!

However, with that we are not now concerned, for what we are concerned to say at this point is : that the Deity of Christ means that God himself is actually and actively present in the Person of the historical Jesus Christ; that the death of Christ on the Cross and his Resurrection were personal acts of the eternal God himself; that therefore our salvation in Christ is a salvation by the very hand of God. We may put this clearly when we say that the course of action which God adopts toward mankind is identical with the existence of Jesus Christ. The existence of Jesus Christ *is* God's decision and man's election. Jesus Christ is God, that is to say, the God who is eternal and who chooses to deal with men and women and who therefore, eternal God though he is, acts in time. It is thus that the *Scottish Confession* identified the Coming of Christ, or rather the Coming of God in Christ, as the sum of the doctrine of predestination. And without that doctrine we are of all men the most miserable — for otherwise salvation is made to depend on man and on his feeble sinful efforts, or his attempt to climb the steep ascent of heaven and conjure with the stars! Thank God Salvation is not of ourselves; it is the gracious unmerited gift of God. We do not need to reconcile heaven to earth and earth to heaven - that is done already in the mighty act of God which *is* Jesus Christ, for

God, the one eternal God, was in Christ reconciling the world to himself. The work of God is finished; we have but to enter into our inheritance in him through the Gospel; but really to enter in; and part of that entering in is just what we are discussing, the recognition and affirmation of the Deity of Christ! Salvation is thus of Grace and not of works — no works of ours can bring us to God. It is the work of God in Christ alone which brings us to God and God to us. As the humanity of Christ signifies the objective actuality of God in the world on the one hand, and therefore the objective possibility of God for men on the other hand, so the Deity of Christ signifies objective activity of God in reconciliation for all men and women in Christ who is the propitiation for the sins of the whole world, and correspondingly the objective presence of God in Christ possible for all people. On one side, in the humanity of Christ we have the great *Anknüpfungspunkt*, or the all-important point of contact, between man and God, and on the other side, in the Deity of Christ we have the great *Anknüpfungspunkt* between God and man: both are bound up together in the act of God in which the Word assumed flesh and united himself hypostatically for ever with Jesus Christ.

These two points, we have been discussing correspond to two others: the revelation of God and reconciliation, both of which we must now look at in the light of the Divinity of Christ.

a) "The essence of the divinity ascribed to Jesus is to make clear, impart, and carry out who God the Father, God in the proper sense is, and what he wills and does for men, to represent this God the Father." (Karl Barth, *op.cit.*, 1.1 p. 443) The whole of the Christian faith turns on the conception that men see in Christ very God and worship him as such. The permanent relation of Christ to the world is dependent on his permanent and essential relation to the Father. He is the only begotten Son of the Father who *is* himself the revelation that he brings. For only God can reveal God. In Christ God reveals himself in the mighty Act which is identical with his Person. That revelation would not be complete and real were Christ not very God. Were he not man it would not be actual to us, but were he not also God at the same time it would not be valid, for no exalted man can reveal God, since exalted man is but a creature; nor may any "descended idea" reveal God, for a descended idea is but a creature too. We tend to forget that, and theologians of the extreme right and left both err in the same forgetfulness or ignorance as the case may be. God's thoughts are not our thoughts, and our language about God is creaturely, and quite distinct from God's language. God's language must become human before it can be understood by us. Our language as such cannot convey God; it is only when there has come about that union in which God's language takes on human form that it can be revelation of God. Unless at the back of this language we use, even if it is Biblical language, there is God in Person conveying himself to us through language which in itself cannot convey God, the Words of the Bible would be mere guess-work, and we would have no knowledge of God. To reveal God the revealer must take the place of God and only God can take his own place. Now that is just what the dogma of the Divinity of Christ asserts, namely that Christ takes the very place of God in our faith which corresponds to his revelation. Christ is also a creature, but were he only a creature he could neither reveal God nor take the place of God. *He who actually and really reveals God in Person is God in Person, the Lord Jesus, God and Man in his one Person*; but that belief in all-important connection between Christ and God is precisely just what we conserve in our confession by including in it the acknowledgement of the Godhead of Christ Jesus. It is expresses the certainty that what we have in Christ came from the very bosom of the Father, and nothing but the very heart of the Father can convey what that heart is like. That heart we find in Jesus of Nazareth. "The unheard-of nature of the love of God for the world of fallen man, the power of reconciliation would be underestimated, were the true divinity of the Reconciler called in question. A superhuman or semi-divine event, one which strictly speaking is not miraculous but in the last resort self-evident, within the universe and so creaturely, does not answer to the seriousness of the problem to be solved, does not answer to the character of almighty grace actually inherent in the event which Holy Scriptures describes as the event of reconciliation or revelation. The character of almighty grace which this event possesses, in the light of which the problem to which it is the answer becomes a problem of infinite seriousness, demands the acknowledgement that its Subject is identical with God in the full sense of the word." (Karl Barth, *Church Dogmatics*, 1.1 p. 470)

b) And so we come to think of the second point upon which ultimately the whole of the Christian doctrine of salvation depends, the fact that it is *God*, really *God in Christ*, who suffers and bears the sin of the world - that is the particle of truth, the *particula veri*, as Karl Barth once said, in the Patripassian heresy. The Christian doctrine of the Holy Trinity does not assert that there are three Gods but that God is one Being, three Persons; that the Father, the Son and the Holy Spirit are distinctly three yet One indivisible Being as God. That is why the Christian Church has always rejected completely the heresy of Tritheism, that there Gods: and resolutely held without any hesitation that the Father, the Son and the Holy Spirit are One Eternal Being, yet distinctively Three in One: the Son even as incarnate, and the Holy Spirit and the Father are eternally and absolutely One. This means that we cannot but think of the suffering or passion of the incarnate Son as in a completely inexplicable way as grounded in and upheld by the Father and the one Eternal Spirit of the Father and of the Son. Let me repeat the wonderful truth of the eternal inexplicable Oneness in Being of the Father, of the Son and of the Holy Spirit, who as such in their threeness and oneness share in their distinctive ways in the redeeming Passion of the incarnate Son, yet in such a way that it was neither the Father nor the Spirit who was crucified at Golgotha in Judaea.

There is indeed, then, a *particle of truth,* in the heresy of Patripassionism, in the suffering of the God the Father, for it was *God* in Christ crucified who reconciles the world unto himself, no other. This means that the ultimate reality of our redemption and salvation from sin is anchored on the divine side of reality - the vicarious suffering of Jesus on the cross reveals and points to the pain in the eternal heart of God the Father himself. No wonder St Paul wrote in his Epistle to the Romans: "If God be for us, who can be against us? He who spared not his own Son, but delivered him up for us all, how shall he not with him also freely give us all things? (Rom.8.31-2) There is a Cross, the Cross, in the very Heart of God the Father.

The Christian doctrine of salvation is no pagan doctrine of placation or propitiation. Man cannot propitiate God or in any way make amends for the sin he has committed against the infinite Majesty of God. All that man can do is finite and sinful in itself. To represent God the Father and carry out the Father's own will, Christ Jesus must himself be God, one with God the Father in Being and Act, different from him only in the fact of his incarnate existence and the mode, not the nature, of his redeeming activity. What Christ did and suffered for us God himself did and suffers as the Father of the Son. In plain blunt language, only God can bear the wrath of God, and if the Atonement really means anything at all it must mean that it is God who suffers there in Jesus Christ — if the divinity of Christ is denied the Christian doctrine of atonement becomes immoral — that is why spurious ideas of atonement go along with weak faith in the Deity of Christ; and the reason is perfectly clear, and the logic perfectly lucid. No one can act as a substitute for sinful humanity in face of the divine reaction against sin, but God himself. The God and Father of our Lord Jesus Christ who is in his Majesty the Law itself, the eternal law of God's eternal Being, and who as such pronounces the verdict of the law against sin, is the only One who has the right to forgive because he is the only One who has the power to bear in himself the consequences of his judgement on sin.

And at the very heart of God's self-revelation in Christ Jesus, and at the very heart of the Gospel, we learn that in the incarnation of his Beloved Son, and in the humiliation of his Beloved Son, in the agony of Christ Jesus, very God himself was present in and with him throughout, when he was made of no reputation and took on himself the form of a servant under the curse of the Law and the judgment of God, when he became obedient unto death, even the death of the Cross, the Lamb of God bearing in himself the sins of the world, very God, God *himself* was present throughout his beloved Son's atoning humiliation and passion. But if this "himself" were cut out of that atoning humiliation and passion, the Gospel would be empty of any saving and redeeming reality, empty of the very Love of God. Empty the Gospel of God, "God with us" and it would become little more than immoral paganism, an attempt on the part of man through human sacrifice to appease God, and to justify himself before God, even if the man Jesus represents man in that action of martyrdom or sacrifice. The pivot of the whole work of reconciliation and atonement rests on the fact that *God himself* is the Subject of the Christian Gospel, in the whole incarnate life, work, death and passion of Christ. God became Man, the Word became flesh; it was God in Christ who came to reconcile the world; and while Christ suffered it was God who in him and with him who suffered in and for the sins of the world. Luther asserts in a sermon on Hebrews 1:1 f.: "There must be here as great a payment for sin as God himself is, who is outraged by sin." That is substantially the same thought as that of Anselm who thought of sin as infinite because it is sin against the infinite Majesty of God; and therefore it can he purged only by an act of a infinite kind and nature. In other words, it is only *God* who is outraged by sin who can forgive sin. Who can forgive sins but God only? And so the fact that Jesus forgave and really forgave, is evidenced by the actuality of the salvation: that Christ is God, that it was God himself is in Christ reconciling the world unto himself.

The relation between the revelation and the act both on the part of Christ is well illustrated in the evangelical account of the paralysed man who was let down through the roof of a house in Capernaum to our Lord. First Jesus pronounced forgiveness, thereby revealing the forgiveness of God, and then, in face of the question "Who can forgive sins but God only?" Jesus replied that you may know that the Son of Man has power on earth to forgive sins, he said to the sick of the palsy: "Take up your bed and walk". That is the act of Power, both Jesus' word pronouncing forgiveness and his act of healing act were his answer to the question: Who can forgive sins but God only? The same is true of the Cross and the Resurrection. The resurrection shows us that it was very God himself who had been suffering in and with his beloved Son on the Cross and it was God himself who had come in the Lord Jesus to break through sin and death. In dogmatic language the significance of the Cross lay in the Deity of the One who died there. Without that Divinity and so without the resurrection the Cross would have meant defeat and shame alone; it would have meant not the defeat of sin but the defeat of love. It is the Deity of Christ that gave significance to all that he did and was, all that he still does and is, through the Cross and Reconciliation. It is that fact which gives Jesus significance, which itself constitutes the significance of the Deity of Christ.

The course of action which God adopts towards us all, men and women and children, is identical with the existence of Jesus Christ. That word "identical" is dogmatically the same as the dogma of the Deity of Christ; and without that "identical" all is hopeless chaos and darkness. Just because God and Christ are one in being and essence, though different in personal modes of existence, do we *know* God and are sure that our salvation is OF GOD; just because Christ is Divine as only God is, do we have to do directly with God and are able to worship him. What Christ is, God is; what Christ is to us he is antecedently in himself, eternally so in God. Thus the love and grace of Christ, the forgiveness of Christ and all his will and work, rest for their validity on the very Deity of Christ alone. The significance of his Deity, the Divinity of Christ, has nowhere been better stated than in the famous *Nicaeano-Constantinopolitanum* and in the second article. The Latin form of it runs thus:

> Credo in unum Dominum Jesus Christum
> filium Dei unigenitum
> et ex Patre natum ante omnia saecula
> Deum de Deo, lumen de lumine,
> Deum verum de Deo vero,
> genitum non factum
> consubstantialem Patri
> per quem omnia facta sunt.

CHAPTER 11

The Person and Work of Christ

We noted in the last Chapter that the course of God's action towards man is identical with the existence of Jesus Christ, for he was God incarnate; that God's act is to be thought of in terms of a Person. We are to discuss now the relation of the Person of Christ himself to the Work he carried out — that relation has been put finely by H.R. Mackintosh when he says of Christ: "His work is but his Person in movement." (*The Person of Jesus Christ.* p. 326). "With a true instinct" , he remarked, "early religious art invariably represents Jesus as acting." "The Person and Work of Christ are not to be thought of separately or without the light each casts on the other. The understanding of both proceeds *pari passu*, and we cannot understand the work of Christ without understanding who it is who works. And so we cannot understand *Who* it is who works without understanding what it is that he does." Professor Mackintosh also added in a note: "With a true instinct, early religious art invariably represents Jesus Christ as acting."

In *The Death of Christ* Denney wrote: "It is the doctrine of the Atonement which secures for Christ his Place in the Gospel, and which makes it inevitable that we should have a Christology or a doctrine about his Person." (p. 318) The same thought is put incisively by Luther: "Christ is not called Christ because he has two natures. What does that signify to me? He bears this glorious and consoling name because of the office and the work he has undertaken." (*Werke*, vol. XII, p 244 - *Erlangen Edit.*) That thought is put even more succinctly by the words of Melanchthon which we have already discussed: *Hoc est Christum cognoscere, beneficia ejus congoscere.* That, however, can lead to a one-sided view of Christ and also of his work as it was expounded in Lutheran thought later. Thus according to Albrecht Ritschl Christ's Person was understood and known because of the value of his work for men and women in redemption — that means, Christ is pragmatically thought of, and that turns religion into a anthropocentric affair. This aspect of the doctrine of Christ must not be allowed to stray in this way; we must bring all our thoughts of Christ's work into direct relation with our apprehension of his Person. Undue emphasis or abstraction on either hand leads to confusion. Christ's Doing and Being are indissolubly One. He was what he did and did what he was, and that can be said only of him, only of Jesus of Nazareth. There is no cleft in his Person; there is no mask which is not his real self. His actions are not different from his innermost heart. He is transparently divine in word and deed. His natures are united together in One such that he is truly Divine and truly Human, perfectly Divine, and perfectly Human.

In our discussion of the Being of God we noted that for us the Being of God is known only through his acts. The Being of God is God being Father, Son, and Holy Spirit to us; and what he is to us he was and is antecedently in himself to all eternity. God may not be known as he ultimately is in himself but only as he reveals himself in action. His action means that *he* issues forth, that *he* comes, that *he* works. Thus the most important element in his action is his presence-in-act. His reality is his reality-in-act; apart from his acts we do not know God at all. But we know God not through any act, not for example through the act of Creation for there God does not communicate himself but creates a reality distinct from himself. God may really and actually be known in an act which is identical with his Person, that is, an act in which God himself is present in the Act which issues from his Being. That act we found to be Jesus Christ himself, the act in which the act of God and his Person were identical. There in Christ Jesus God communicates not something but *himself*. That is to say, the work of God is not simply an instrument but a self-end. Thus we cannot say that God's Being is something other or wholly other than the act of self-communication in Jesus Christ. What God is in Christ he is wholly in himself; and what God is in himself, he is also in his acts. And so when we think of the Being of God we think of Christ; we think, that is, of God's Being, as being Father, Son, and Holy Spirit to men. Certainly these cannot be thought of in abstraction from the God who is and becomes Father, Son and Holy Spirit to us thus in Christ. While Christ is, is the act of God identical with God the Actor; Christ is yet distinct as the Revelation from the Revealer. This distinction gives him meaning. The point I wish to emphasise is that apart from this Act of God, apart from his Being Father Son and Spirit, we do not know really God but have only an empty idea of God floating about in our minds. It is only on the ground of this identity between the act of God in the incarnation and God as he is eternally in himself that we have anything more — that is a positive knowledge of God as Father, Son, and Holy Spirit.

Now this means that we are to think of Christ as the act of God identical with God's reality in the incarnate Person of his only Begotten and Beloved Son. Christ himself is identical in his existence and life with the operation of God for men's salvation — we are therefore to think of the Person and the work of Christ as one, that is, of the Act of God in him for men's salvation as one with the Person of the Eternal or Son or Word who became flesh in Jesus Christ. Christ is what he does, and does what he is. Too often has the activity of Christ in his teaching or in Atonement unfortunately been thought of in abstraction from his Person; but his activity or work issues from his Person and what Christ is in his acts on the Cross he is in his own Person. He is perfectly what he does. He is in himself what he reveals of God the Father. "Only he can reveal perfectly who is what he reveals. The words of Jesus are the voice of God. The tears of Jesus are the pity of God. The wrath of Jesus *is* the judgment of God." (see again H.R. Mackintosh, *op. cit.* p. 341) Indeed a large part of Jesus' work was to confront people with his own Person. "He lived out the transcendent life which constituted his personality, confronting men as his Divine self, and letting the fact of his being tell on their minds as a revelation." (*ibid.*) What Christ does therefore in the flesh, what he speaks in words, what he does in his life and his death, from the cradle to the grave, is what he *is* in Person, what God is and does for us. Thus in part the question about the Person and Work of Christ is to be understood in accordance with the hypostatic union of the humanity and divinity in Christ; as the union of two natures in One, in one Mediator between Man and God who is both God and Man truly and perfectly in himself. Thus the work of reconciliation which he accomplishes, he is in his Nature and Person as the Mediator; what he reveals to men of God he is himself; and it is precisely because he is who he is that his work is a work of reconciliation; and it is precisely because he is who he is that his word is a word of revelation. If it is through the work of Jesus and through the word of Jesus that we are confronted with him in such a way that we know who he is; it is also true that it is because we know who he is that we know too what his work as work and atoning reconciliation really mean. Each aspect of his work and word is to be interpreted in and through the other. Christ's Person consists in just this, that *he is our God*; that is to say: Emmanuel, God with Us. But God with us involves in the "with us" both the elements and ideas of revelation and reconciliation. Thus just as we know the Being of God only through his acts and his acts only in the light of his Being, his Being Father, Son, and Holy Spirit, to us, which he is antecedently in himself in eternity; so also we are to think of our knowledge of the Being of Christ as his being Mediator to us, and that what he is to us he is eternally with God and in God. His manward side represented in his humanity has validity and significance only because of his Godward side, represented in his Divinity. The Humanity of Christ has *no* significance apart from his Divinity, and the Divinity of Christ has *no* significance for us apart from his humanity — the two are involved in a relation of reciprocity so far as our apprehension of them is concerned.

Now when we think more specifically of the actual work and the actual person of Christ, we cannot think of his work of reconciliation or atonement as a kind of transaction apart from or objective to Christ; it is not simply an act done by Christ — it is first and foremost the Person of Christ himself in activity; and just because it is the Person of Christ does it that his work has the significance it does have on the Cross. In other words, the significance of the Cross does not lie in the death or the shed blood of Christ in his sacrifice simply, but it lies in the fact that the Person of Christ is the One who shed his own life for us and who bore our sins. The Redemption is the Person of Christ in action; not the action by itself thought of in an objectivist impersonal way, as for example it was apt to be the case in the thinking of St. Anselm. This relation of the Person and the Word of Christ can be thought of in terms of the relation of the Incarnation to the Cross of Christ. What Christ is in his Person as the Incarnate Word in whom God and Man are united and united even in the humble form of a servant which he assumed, Christ is on the Cross; that is to say, in the meeting of God and man over human sin. The Cross is the outworking of a decision that constitutes the Person of the Mediator himself in the incarnation. The atoning reconciliation wrought out on the Cross is already anticipated in effect in the incarnate Person of the God-Man. The Cross is the visible working and working out in human flesh what had already taken place in the decision of God the eternal Son to descend into the human sphere to redeem and reconcile humankind to himself. That is to say, the act of redemption carried out on the Cross is identical in essence with the act of election — both of which are Christ Jesus himself. Thus it is not too much to say that "his Being is itself Redemption." (Brunner, *The Mediator*,. p. 402)

It is this aspect of the Christian Gospel which is stressed in St John's Gospel so much. In the Synoptic Gospels Jesus calls men to his side to follow him, and he leads them. In John's Gospel he speaks of himself as the Way. In the Synoptics he teaches them truth, in John, he says: "I am the Truth". In the Synoptics he is recorded as saving peoples' souls and lives, in John's words Jesus says : "I am the Life". That is to say, the Act of Christ IS Christ; the Work of Christ IS his Person. He himself is the Way, the Truth, the Life. His being is itself Redemption — and it is because that is so that all his works of healing and words of forgiveness, his vicarious life and his and his atoning deed on the Cross, have their true significance, and validity. Christ Jesus is perfectly what he does and proclaims —

it is the Person and the Presence of God in him that constitute Salvation. The Cross is rather the Instrument which serves that Presence, a presence possible only in an act of reconciliation — therefore Emmanuel, God with us, is his name. That is why he is a Mediator, because in his own Person God is reconciling the world with himself, in the actual existence and life of Christ Jesus the God-Man. Is this not a part of the meaning of the prologue of John's Gospel: What Christ has to say to us, he is in himself, the Word; what he has to do for us; he is in himself the Son. (Vide Brunner, *op. cit.* pp. 428 & 402 f.)

Christianity means that God was in Christ: for us to know and have God is to receive forgiveness, to have life and grace. The revelation of God in Christ and the reconciliation with God, are both mediated by Christ who incarnates and mediates the presence of God to the sinner — and that act is already living in his Person. For in his Person he is what he reveals, and in his Person he brings what he does for us on the Cross. God has actually come among us in him and can come to each of us; indeed God now seeks us, makes himself the friend of the publicans and sinners, in and through the Lord Jesus. The importance of this lies in the fact that one cannot have to do with the Cross of Christ without having Christ himself; one cannot think properly of atonement without thinking of the Person of Christ. Too often is the work of Christ thought of separately from his Person and that leads to a dead abstract or formalistic orthodoxy. The Person of Christ must never be subordinated to his Work. Christ's self-bestowal *for* us is his self-bestowal *to* us. To have the one without the other is to think of the death of Christ in purely forensic and objectivist terms — it is after all to deal in ideas even if those ideas appear formally correct. It is the realisation that the crucifixion of Jesus Cross is in order that God may be reconciled to us, that he may be present himself to us, and precisely in Jesus Christ, that we arrive at a correct standpoint from which to view both the Cross and the Person of Christ. The Cross removes the great obstacle from the way of union of God with man. Salvation in St. Paul is summed up in the doctrine of *Union with Christ*: that means everything, for it means the experience of all the riches and bounties of God; but in order to be joined with Christ and share the power of his exaltation we must go to the Cross — the Cross is the road to that end, and that end is Christ the Son of the Father, the end in God incarnate himself. Christ Jesus is the Action and Person of God together. He is the Gift of God to the world, but the Gift entails the Cross.

In the Person of Christ we have to do with the fulfilment of all the acts and words of God such that in him God has established a firm and actual footing in time and human affairs. This being so we are to think of Jesus' work and act on the Cross as beginning immediately he was born and as increasing with his growth into Manhood, deepening in intensity as he entered the public Ministry. *Jesus' whole life is his vicarious Passion*; for his life represents the coming of The Son of God in the form a servant and under the curse of the Law. The Passion begins when he identifies himself with our sinful race and bears in himself the assaults of evil. We can never fully understand what that means, for the Holy One to descend into this world of sin and foulness and actually to identify himself with it; Jesus' very purity increases and intensifies his Passion — his whole vicarious life is Suffering, and he drinks the cup of the suffering-servant who identifies himself with the world to the very utmost frontiers of humanity, that is, to the point of death on the Cross. Christ's whole work lies in the fact of his Sonship existing here under these human conditions subjected to the pain, temptation, evil, suffering and death of a fallen world under the ban of the Law of God. Thus in it is in his *vicarious humanity* which Jesus lived out in the realm of humanity's alienation from God that he is our Redeemer and Saviour. He entered vicariously the realm which is under the wrath of God - he the incarnate Son of God did that; he very God himself did that, for the Lord Jesus was and is God! That is why Jesus' Message breathed his own Sonship; the consciousness of his own Person in these conditions. "His whole message is simply his action determined by his consciousness of Sonship." (Emil Brunner, *The Mediator*, p. 425) His work and action lie in the fact that *he* as very God is present in the world of humanity, present vicariously and in identification of himself with the world in its condition. He does not proclaim the action of God or of another; he points to himself and acts in his own Person: he himself is the Kingdom of God and the King. In him is God present with the World, and in him takes place the battle of God with the World of darkness. His Person is the arena of the Great Struggle and by bearing sin in himself he defeats it by carrying it to death on the Cross where sin and evil are vanquished and slain.

Thus when we think and speak of the Person and Work of Christ we mean or ought to mean fundamentally the same thing. It is the Cross which discloses to us the secret of the Person of Christ — namely, that he is in Person the Mediator between God and Man, Mediator who is God and who is Man in his own self. It is the Cross which shows us in dreadful colours what his Person really means his identification with our race and sin, all for our sake. There at the Cross there becomes very clear what he suffered in becoming flesh for our sake, for the sake of sinners. On the other hand the Cross takes on intense personal significance when we realise the nature of the One who died there. The Crucifixion was not simply an objective sacrifice for the sins of the world much like the sacrifice of a lamb in the Old Testament liturgy. He himself and his sacrifice are one in his vicarious humanity. The Priest had to offer under the old order a lamb for the sins of the people; but it was an impersonal and objectivist transaction. Here we do not have that, for *the Lamb of God Is Jesus Christ who himself Is the High Priest.* By virtue of his humanity he represents man, and by virtue of his Deity he represents God, though his humanity has no independent existence apart from his divine Person. The atoning act is fundamentally an act of God on our behalf who himself provides the Lamb for atoning sacrifice, the incarnate Person of the only-begotten Son of God who freely surrenders himself as that atoning sacrifice for us. It is the Person of Christ that gives meaning to the Cross, in showing us that is God in him who is at Calvary. It is *God himself* who suffers in Christ for us there; it is *God himself* who bears our burden in Jesus and who forgives us in and for Jesus' sake, forgives us in and through him. We must not, therefore, think simply of Christ as someone sent by God and who at the command of God carried out the work of redemption alone and on his own. No! God himself present in Person, in the Person of his only-begotten and beloved Son, carries it out, and carries it out in the Person of the Lord Jesus Christ in whom humanity and Deity are perfectly united for ever; and the Cross of Christ is thereby revealed to be eternal in the heart of God, without in any way being diminished in its once and for all reality and actuality in the historical crucifixion of the Lord Jesus under Pontius Pilate in Jerusalem. Thus we are to think of the Lord Jesus as in his own divine-human Person dyeing for us on the Cross in such a way that he is and was and ever will be he in *himself* divine Revelation and Atonement. The Cross is, so to speak, a cross-section of the life and work of the Mediator at the most intense moment of his vicarious passion, in his death for us.

Fundamentally, therefore, when we study the doctrine of the Person and Work of Christ, we are concerned with the activity of God in which he aligns himself in

Jesus Christ with the world of sinful men for their redemption and reconciliation, in order that he may reveal himself to them and bestow himself richly upon them in Life, Light, and Love. As such the Lord Jesus Christ, the incarnate Son of God, his only begotten and beloved Son, is the very heart of the Gospel. In his incarnate Person he unites the activity of divine and human natures, and of divine and human activity in revelation and reconciliation, in fulfilment of the eternal love and decision of God to redeem and save mankind. The Lord Jesus' Person is to be understood from the eternal purpose for which he came. In him we learn that the Incarnation is supremely the mighty act of God's grace for sinful men; and takes place just because God in his boundless mercy wills to save men. Had there been no sin, would there have been an Incarnation? We cannot really think or say that! The Incarnation is a *new* act of God which he wondrously and in his infinite mercy elected to undertake for the sake of and on behalf of men, women and children for their redemption and recreation. Thus in the incarnation of his only begotten Son, it is very God himself, not a substitute for him, engaged in the fulfilment of his eternal purpose. The Person Jesus Christ is therefore is to be understood from the purpose which brought him here, as the embodiment of God's unconditional Grace and will to redeem and to forgive us sinners.

However, we cannot assert that the Son of God came among us and to be one of us simply to die and to carry out a transaction for men. We cannot rest content just with a substitutionary view of the work and Person of Christ. In our understanding of Christ, we cannot divorce the Person and the Work of Christ. He came to give *himself* to us, he came that God in him might give *himself* to us. He is the end of the Incarnation, in his own Person; he is the Revelation who is in himself what he reveals. It is God himself whom we have in Christ, God giving himself to us; and so his purpose in coming into the world cannot be abstracted from his Person who has become and ever remains the be-all and end-all of the Gospel and Christian belief, the Alpha and Omega of our faith. He is God, God Manifest and all we shall know of God: there is no God behind his back, no other God than Christ our Lord; he is the only-begotten Son who only has declared the Father to mankind in and through himself as God as well as Man. Between the Father and the Son there is an exclusive and reciprocal relation. We cannot have the one without the other, and so Christ's Person, dynamic and not static Person, is both God for us and God to us, both Person and Word, act which is identical with the very Person of God.

In his incarnation, the vicarious work of Christ coincides with his Person; his being with his vicarious life and passion. "The whole existence of the Mediator consists in making himself one with humanity in its sin and sorrow. The Incarnation is no mere gesture; it is reality, stark and painful. Jesus drinks the cup of human existence in all its alienation from God, to the very dregs. Nothing is spared him; he is not the Royal Son of God who visits man wearing a disguise which he throws off when things become too hot for him, so that at the critical moment he may reveal himself to the amazed multitude as the Son of God. He rejects the idea that when his position is most desperate he might be saved by legions of his Father's angels. Everything must be fulfilled. He will have no privileges.

"Christ's identification with humanity does not only involve suffering in the usual sense. Primarily it is a simple direct proof of his solidarity with us. He does not separate himself from humanity. It is this which is his sign-manual, that he does not separate himself from us. He is the friend of publicans and sinners...He thus expressed his identification, in principle, with everything human. And he did this at the point that matters most: at the central point, at the point where man is alienated from God by his sin...The final proof of his identification with humanity was given in is sufferings on the Cross. The Cross is no mere act of endurance, as one might bear a disease or a stroke of destiny. This feeling that the Son of Man `*must* suffer' means something both exterior and interior. He bears it willingly, he takes it upon himself deliberately, he gives himself up...The suffering of Christ means both surrender for man and unreserved solidarity with the whole human race; but, above all, it means solidarity with that which separates humanity from God, with that therefore which from the point of view of God is a necessity, with the divine wrath, which works death.

"The Mediator gives himself up completely to this suffering of the wrath which comes to man from God. In this self-sacrifice his identification with humanity rises to its greatest height, in this vicarious giving of himself to the real endurance of the divine judgement, the divine wrath. The mere achievement of death is not the main thing, as though we were here concerned with a human `sacrificial animal'. `He was obedient unto death, even the death of the Cross.'" (Emil Brunner, *The Mediator*, pp.493 ff)

This obedience is just as important as the actual event. Here it is the idea of vicarious sacrifice offered under the righteous judgment of God in contrast to the forensic idea of penalty which is expressed; it is a personal act. The trembling and horror of Gethsemane form part of this sacrifice, and, above all, that last cry on the Cross: "My God, my God, why hast thou forsaken me?" Those words on the lips of Jesus at Calvary, were not just a repetition of the words of the twenty-second Psalm. It was real suffering; there was nothing make-belief about it; it was a real surrender, not a drama which had already been prepared in the heavenly world. The way in which Christ suffered from his connection with God is only possible *to him*, because he does not act as a human being in his own interest, but for God, as God's representative. "The depth of Christ's suffering is due to the cause for which he suffers; because Christ knows that he is wholly identified with the cause of God, therefore he is in a position to identify himself so completely with man, to give himself unceasingly to man, really to feel `the whole misery of man' — a phrase which on the lips of anyone else would be a mere phrase — to suffer and to die *for* humanity and not merely with humanity." (Cf. Emil Brunner, *op. cit.* p. 493 ff.)

CHAPTER 12
The Background of the Cross

The central message of the Christian Gospel is that Jesus Christ bore our sins on his own Body on the Tree. It is there that we penetrate into the depths of our understanding of the Nature and Person of Christ, and gain our understanding of his vicarious humanity. His suffering cleaves his Person open, as it were, and in him we see into the very heart of God. It is at the Cross that we see the Person of Christ in the most important act of his ministry in the world, the point to which all his public ministry had led. The importance of this is indicated by the relative space the Evangelists give to the passion of Jesus. Thus for example in St. Mark ten chapters are taken to speak of the three years or so of our Lord's ministry, indeed of his whole life, and the remaining six are devoted to the last week in his life. Similar proportions are to be found in the other three Gospels, showing the significance of the Cross in our understanding of the Person of Christ. The Cross is, as I have expressed it, a cross-section in the Life of Jesus Christ, of his Person in action at the crucial point of his life on earth. And it is this cross-section that gives us the clue to the constitution of his Person as the Mediator, as the Son of God who stoops to identify himself with a world of sinful people under divine judgment. "He hath made him who knew no sin to made sin for us, that we might be made the righteousness of God in him." (2 Cor.5.21) That at once indicates to us the purpose of his Life, the *telos* of it, and we are able to understand something of our Lord's true nature and work.

Before we proceed any further, however, it behoves us to understand something of the background of the Cross, of the world into which Christ entered in the Incarnation. He came to die for our sins, to redeem us; he entered into the situation of our estrangement and alienation from God in order to reconcile us to the Father. Just what is this estrangement? What is this world that he entered to save or redeem us, and why should he do it and do it in this way? What was the necessity for his Incarnation, for the Cross and the reconciliation he thereby effected? If we are to understand Christ, and if it is true that what took place on the Cross reveals the redeeming import of his life and work, and enables us to discern the character and purpose of his vicarious life, then we must think first of the actual situation to which the Lord Jesus, as the incarnate Son of God, addressed himself.

I say we must think "first" of this situation. But it is true that we do not really understand what it is all about until we actually face the Cross and see there in true colours the situation as it is unmasked by Christ in its stark and dark reality. To understand the Cross we need to understand what it means that Christ died there for us and our sins, to reconcile a fallen world; but to understand that, we need to understand what sin and the fallen world mean into which Christ descended to fulfil his substitutionary, vicarious and redemptive purpose. We must thus proceed within the circle of theological thought in which both sides of what took place the crucifixion of Jesus are to be discerned in the light of each other, the judgment of God upon the sin of the world, and the passion of Christ in bearing it in our place and for our sakes.

It is a very significant fact that neither in the Old Testament nor in the New Testament was there do deliberate attempt to formulate a doctrine of sin first in a general way and then to show against that background the grace and love of God in redemption. Nevertheless it is the whole tenor of the Biblical message that the Grace of God and the purpose of Redemption by God are in answer to the desperate need and sinfulness of mankind. The point is this: it is the answer which they give to the desperate need and sin of human beings, men and women, which itself speaks most illuminatingly and most effectively about sin itself. This means therefore that we must be very careful in speaking of a background for the Cross, a dark background of sin and despair which are met by God in atonement. Rather is the Cross itself the background in which sin is shown up and the despair of man is exposed to which the Cross is the answer and the remedy. Nevertheless, unless we do see the shadow that the Cross casts on this background we do not understand the Cross; and therefore while we cannot speak effectively and finally of sin except in the light of the Cross we must understand something of it for our very apprehension of the forgiveness that comes from the lips of Jesus as he dies on Golgotha: "Father forgive them, for they know not what they do".

This fact warns us that we must not bring to our Christian understanding any preconceived notions of sin and evil, or if we do they must all undergo correction by the Cross. We can say, with Karl Barth: "There is, so to speak, an unfruitful knowledge of sin, of evil, of death and the devil, that succeeds in making it hard for a man to have happy and confident faith in the Almighty Father and Creator, but without making possible for him, or even bringing nearer, faith in Jesus Christ as reconciler. To gaze down into that abyss, as far as it is possible for us to do ourselves, does not in itself help us in the least, so frightful is the abyss! How frightful it is no man has ever yet fathomed of himself. What man has in this respect fathomed of himself has been nothing but relatively puppet sins and puppet distresses, that are far removed from the actual problem of Theodicy in its awfulness. Grace must come first, in order that sin may be manifest to us as sin, and death as death; in order that, with the *Heidelberg Catechism* (Q. 5), we may confess that we are by nature prone to hate God and our neighbour, and therefore, with Luther, that we are lost and damned men. We cannot in ourselves know what our misery and despair, our guilt and punishment really are; that becomes manifest to us in the fact that Christ has taken them upon himself and borne them." (Karl Barth, *Credo*, p.43f)

Hence, in dealing with the background of the Cross, the background of sin, we are to beware of a misanthropic and unfruitful view of man and sin which does not arise from the revelation of God but rather from the devil in his distortion of the Law of God. The knowledge that "I have sinned...and am no more worthy to be called thy son" (Luke 15.18f), is not the discovery of an introspective or abstract anthropology. In Jesus' parable of the prodigal, only the son who has already recalled to mind the father's house is aware that he is a lost son. We are first and only really aware of being God's enemies, because God has actually established reconciling relations between himself and us. (Cf. also Karl Barth, *Church Dogmatics*, 1.1 p. 465 f.)

Our discussion of the background of the Cross will thus be the background that is uncovered by the Cross itself, the darkness that terrible deed casts up on humanity. The Cross alone exposes for the first time the real condition of mankind; it strips a person of the external mask that covers his wretchedness and exposes him to view. It is at the Cross that we see the shadow cast on the world, but it is the shadow cast by the Cross itself upon men — that is why men dislike Golgotha, especially those of the Romantic-idealist type for they refuse to see the reality of things as it is laid bare on Calvary; they hate the shadow it casts on humanity and try to sublimate it by works of art; but the grim reality shines through it all and tells honest people that the Cross is the supreme judgement on mankind, pronounced by themselves in this dastardly act of crucifixion as well as by God who submits to that fearful act in Christ.

We have already discussed the fact that the very coming of God to the world means that the world is fallen away from God; the offer of grace and forgiveness in Christ means a devastating disqualification of the world and all its values, even of all that it counts so dear and noble. That disqualification and judgement reach their height at the Cross; but it is because it has already been manifested by the spotless Life and Person of Jesus Christ who is in himself what he does, that we can now proceed to draw a sketch of the background of darkness in which the Cross stands up like a grim sentinel of judgement as well as of hope. The Cross reveals to us the fact of the world's sin. The very fact that Christ had to die for the world, the fact that High Heaven had to stoop to such ignominy and shame, that the very Son of God had to stoop down to the lowest level of reproach and death, being crucified as a criminal, betokens the depth to which man has fallen. The Cross is the supreme revelation of the sin of mankind. Man is so utterly sinful that nothing will suffice, but that the very Son of God must be plucked from his bosom to sacrifice himself for mankind. The darkness of the Cross is the most terrible and scorching judgement on man that could possibly be made: man is so bad that he rose up and slew the very Son of God. Man is so foul that God had to stoop down in humiliation to Golgotha, a mound of rotten skulls and refuse outside the precincts of the city, a dunghill, the habitation of dogs and scavenger pariahs, in order to reach him. Let no one man draw up his hypocritical skirts and disassociate himself from the race of men who slew Christ; for we are all part of it; and if Christ came today, we would do the same, only no doubt with a greater refinement of cruelty than even the Romans were able to devise and adopt. The crucifixion of Jesus Christ is itself the most devastating judgement on our race and on each of us that could possibly be imagined. There we see our sin in its utter blackness, in its stark reality. There all masks and all mental-dishonesty are stripped away from us; we look with open eyes on our naked souls and see ourselves as we really and actually are. The gulf between man and God is so complete that Christ on the Cross had to cry "My God! My God! Why has Thou forsaken me?"

Let us now try to understand what this sin is and what its disclosure actually involves that we may understand something of the Holy Person on the Cross who mediates forgiveness to us the better.

The Cross is the acme of sin's achievement where it assails God and slays the Christ. Sin is revealed in its own act to be an attack upon God. And so sin is revealed to be something from which God turns way his face in judgement. "My God, my God, why have you forsaken me?" These words let us know what constitutes the dire nature of sin and guilt. Sin means guilt before God, and guilt means, in the words of St. Paul, "The handwriting of God against us" (Col. 2.21), to which God has attached his own signature. As Alexander Maclaren put it: "There is a double veil, if I may so say, between man and God; the side turned outward is woven by our own sins; the other side turned inwards is made of the necessary antagonism of the divine nature to man,s sin." (*Expository Comm. on St. Matt.* p. 349, Vol. III) This veil, which we see in the flesh of Christ bearing our sin woven through the judgement of God against the sin of man, is rent in two at the Cross from the top to the bottom; woven through the wrath of God against the sin of man; and in the rending of the veil we see what it truly is, at the Cross of Calvary.

Let us consider this more carefully. We start out with the revelation given through and by the Incarnation that man is far away from God. The very fact that God had to come to man, means that man is cut off from God. But this distance between man and God is not to be construed as a metaphysical distance or merely as the distance between the Creator and the creature great and real as the latter is. The distance between man and God is due to the nearness of God! That distance is a moral one; and is to be seen in the clash of wills, God's righteous will and our rebellious will, rather than any ontological difference between God and the creature. It is just because God is near him that man feels himself cut off from God, for when God comes near, the *Holy God* comes near, man cries out: "Depart from me O Lord, for I am a sinful man. I am not worthy that Thou shouldest come under my roof." These words are only spoken at the approach of God in Jesus Christ. The fact of God's immediate presence judges man and condemns him. The difference between man and God, which is evidently minimised when God is thought of as at a distance, is brought out into bold relief by his *advent* or the *parousia* of God in his incarnate Son. Man is thereby revealed to be in the very inner slant of his mind and in the twisted texture of his human being originally created by God in his image to be at enmity to God and to God's Nature.

It is this fact that is so revealing: namely that the sin of man, sin of and in the creature, presupposes the nearness of God his Creator. Thus we may say that sin is not only rebellion against God, but as such that it threatens the very relation of man's being to God, the fundamental relation in which his being as God's creature created in his image consists. Sin as a severance from God pre-supposes a life-unity with the Creator, given and maintained by his Spirit. The Spirit of God is God in his freedom to be present to the creature he has made and to realise the relation of the creature to himself. Sin is what happens between the human creature and God. The creature in order to be a creature requires relation to the Creator. That relation is given by the Holy Spirit who upholds the existence of the creature, but of the creature as an entity distinct from God himself. There is thus between the Creator and the creature a double relation, in which the Creator gives existence and life to the creature and in which the creature depends on the Creator for life — and that relation is a moment-to-moment relation — it is a relation of continuous creation, as it were. (For the above see Karl Barth, *Church Dogmatics* 1.1, pp. 516f & 539f.)

The human creature is made not only to have existence but to have fellowship with God, a relation filled with the rich content of God's Light, Life and Love. Hence sin is rightly understood only when it is seen to be the fatal contradiction introduced into that relation of being between the creature with the Creator. Sin means that the creature who depends on the Creator for existence and life rebels against the Creator; and so sin inevitably and always takes on also the character of suicide; by rebelling against the Creator and asserting his independence the creature is acting against the innermost relation which constitutes his very being and existence; and so sin is such, it has been said, an impossible possibility! The fact that we are to note particularly here is that sin involves at its heart this double relation between the creature and God into which it introduces a fatal contradiction. The central point in every human being is his relation to God. Sin means that central point has been violated. Man has introduced discord or contradiction into the innermost centre of his existence. As a sinner he has violated the very core of his creaturely existence before his Creator, or otherwise expressed, he has fallen away the essential core, the central thing in his life, and has become literally and actually eccentric. But just because the creature as creature exists in and through a relation to the Creator, and it is as such that he sins against the Creator, his sin is inevitably characterised by a double relation: the creature against the Creator and the Creator against the creature. It is only the creature created for personal relation to and lives in relation to with God who can sin, in taking his own way in rebellion against his Creator, but that change in his relation to God the creative source of his being cannot but be qualified by a corresponding change in the attitude of God towards the sinner. That is to say, the attitude of the Creator who gives the creature existence *and* life is changed so that the Creator is now against the creature while as Creator he nevertheless continues to give existence to the creature! That contradictory state of affairs between the creature and the Creator results in a drastically changed relation of the creature to God, a change from *life* to *death*. To be sure in God's mercy the creature's existence continues to be maintained by God as Creator; but the creature as such does not have real life, a life positively related to God and in living fellowship with him. As a sinning creature, instead of being positively related to God, becomes negatively related to God. That is a negative relation which will bear fruit in the disruption of his existence as well. And so while sin means that man is negatively related to God the very source of his existence and being, it inevitably means that man whose very existence depends on relation to God, will suffer and does suffer physical death.

It is wrong to think that in the event of sin the change has come about only in the relation of man to God and not also in the relation of God to man — in fact it is less than half the truth, for it is the relation of God to man that is the all-important factor in a man's life even as a sinner. Therefore we must think of sin as objectively real from the point of view of God as well as existentially or subjectively real from the point of view of man. Sin is not simply the perversion of man's mind and attitude toward God but affects man in the ontological depth of his being; and it also entails a real "change", as it were, in God's mind and attitude towards his disobedient and rebellious creatures or children; and it is that which constitutes the innermost nature and therefore gravity of sin, the guilt of man before God.

Let us approach the subject of sin more narrowly still.

Sin is essentially rebellion against God; it is movement in a direction directly counter to the self-assertion, the "I am that I am", of God's very Nature as God. God as God, the Universal and Absolute Being, the Creator, asserts his nature to be universal and absolute; asserts his divine Nature and Holiness or Character as God to be binding on all his creatures as his creatures. In being who he eternally is, God affirms his Holiness to be the universal norm of life. That is his very Godness or Godhead, his Majesty in virtue of which he is God; his Honour and Deity. This means that sin is a contradiction of that in virtue of which God is thus God; it is a counter to God's self-assertion in Holiness and his self-bestowal in his Creative Love. We must realise, then, as P.T. Forsyth expressed it, that it is the "Love of the Holy God that is the consuming fire." (P. T. Forsyth, *The Work of Christ*, p. 85) Sin is thus an attack upon the very Godness of God and God to be God must and does in his Being, precisely by his Being God, reject and resist sin. To be God is to be counter to the private self-assertion of man. There can be only one God who affirms or asserts his Nature to be supreme. When man asserts his own nature in opposition to God he is asserting himself, as it were, to be "God". And God precisely in virtue of his very Being God resists sin with the full force of the Godhead. In plain Biblical language sin is countered by "the wrath of God". This is the negative aspect of the holiness of God. And God would cease to be God if he were to condone sin or overlook it. To say "God is", therefore, in his relation to and before the sinner is to say "divine Judgement".

This must be clearly understood if we are to understand the Cross and the Person of the Mediator aright, if we are to appreciate the fearful gravity of the whole situation. Sin is not simply an act in itself done by man; it is *sin against God*. That is why the Psalmist said: "Against Thee, Thee only have I sinned"! The fact that sin is against God means that sin is an act which takes its real colour and character from its being against God — it is not sin just because it is against love or goodness, but because it is against God himself. Now that means that sin is a twofold event. It has two sides attached to it. On the one hand, it is the act of man's rebellion against God. If God did not resist sin there would be no such thing as a distinction between good and evil. But on the other hand, sin is qualified as sin, named "sin" precisely by the act of God in resisting it. It is this act of what the Bible call the "wrath" of God that gives the constitution of sin as sin its deepest nature and dire gravity. We read in the Book of Exodus, that Pharaoh hardened his own heart in resisting the Will of God; but we also read that God himself hardened Pharaoh's heart. The act of evil becomes sin against God as God names it sin and as such becomes guilt; that is, in Pauline language, sin is registered by the handwriting of God against us, the handwriting to which God appends his own signature, as it were. Thus in the innermost constitution of sin and its characterisation as sin we have to think of the negative assertion of man against God on the top of his positive self-assertion against God; and think of negative assertion of God against the sinner on the top of the positive self-affirmation of God's own nature or Holiness and Love toward the sinner. Thus we must think of the innermost constitution of sin as double: characterised by an act of human rebellion and an act of Divine wrath against sin. And in both cases is it a personal act. God personally resists sin; that is why it is called his "wrath"; for sin is a personal act against the very Person of God. It can be met only in a personal fashion. There is nothing in God lower than the personal and he always acts Personally, even here in countering sin.

We can now go one step further. Sin is not simply an isolated act; it is not something incidental or accidental; it is constitutive and has to do with the actual existence of man as such. We noted that sin is the contradiction introduced into the very nature of man as essentially dependent on God. Sin is only possible in the presence of God, in the relation of the creature to the Creator. In sin there is brought about a perversion of the attitude of man to God with a corresponding "change", as it were, in the attitude of God toward man. Thus the central point in man's existence and life is altered. Indeed the existence of man as a *whole* is altered in its relations with God. The theological terms "radical will", "original sin", "total depravity" simply express this fact. Each of the terms involves something different, and therefore there are these three terms; but the central point in each of them is this constitutional change in man in which he *is* committed and wholly involved.

Evil is an activity of the very personality of man, and this cannot be exhausted in any single move on his part; the whole personality in each human being, in each of its constituent elements is responsible for evil, and is therefore never free from evil (See Brunner, *The Mediator*,. p. 127 f.) Sin is a contradiction in the heart and at the basis of human existence as a personal being before God, his/her Creator, a fundamental state of disharmony between a human being and God. We have to do here not with isolated acts of will which are but the outward manifestation of this inward disharmony, but have to do with a radical enmity in man which amounts to a corruption of his *whole* existence and a disintegration of his very *self* in its relation to God. "Whatsoever is not of faith is sin", said St. Paul. The correlative of sin is faith: that is, the correlative of sin is a relation of trust and surrender to God which works by love and spells fellowship with God. Sin is the contradiction or perversion introduced into that inner relation of human being to his/her Creator. "Sin, interpreted in the Christian sense, is certainly not only a determination of the will — in the sense in which we use the word 'will' nowadays. Sin is equally a determination of existence, of the being of humanity itself, as it now is, of human 'nature'. Sin from the Christian point of view, is primarily something which affects the nature of man as a whole. Evil has not been understood if we think: 'Now, at this moment I have done something wrong, but previously before the actual decision, I was either good or neutral.' Whoever takes a view of sin of that sort this kind is not merely lacking in a theologico-scientific impulse to explain the existence of evil, but he is lacking in moral earnestness. We take sin seriously when to some extent we become aware of the depth of its roots. For I need to see that evil has its root in the very depths of my nature in order to realise that "I" am really evil, a sinner. Until I see this I regard evil as something accidental, like a splash of mud, not like something which belongs to "the essence of my nature". "A man who has not yet seen that evil is entwined with the roots of his personality is a superficial person; this means that where man is a unity, a whole, where the individual has the one foundation of the mental and spiritual life, evil is poisoning his existence. This is expressed in harmony with the thought of the Bible — when we say: man does not only *do* wrong, he does not only commit sinful acts, but he *is* bad, he is a sinner. A sinner is not a human being who has sinned a certain number of times; he is a human being who sins whatever he is doing. So long as this is not perceived the gravity of sin is ignored, and the point of view remains superficial." (Emil Brunner, *op.cit.*, p. 141 f)

The Christian doctrine of sin is not that just man sins but that he *is* a sinner; this state of alienation from God is the determination of his existence. You cannot have any such thing as a half-sin; likewise you cannot have any such things as a half-sinner. The reaction of God in the Law does not say that this act is wrong or that but that the *person* who does these things is wrong. Sins are simply the visible manifestation of an invisible corruption of one's whole relation to God, that one is torn away from his/her origin in God.

We can now take the final step in our understanding of sin. Just because sin is thus of the nature of man and determines his whole existence in relation to God, sin is something that he cannot change; for all that he does or determines in regard to himself is done within the self-determination of his existence in and by sin. In other words what man does for himself is done in his autonomy which is now itself rooted in sin; so that the more a man strives to save himself by himself, the more he sins! This means that sin belongs irrevocably to man as man, and that he cannot change it. This element in sin which cannot be changed is known as *guilt*; that feature or element which belongs unalterably to the past and which determines the existence of each man or woman in the present. Guilt means that our past constitutes a powerful element in our present. Therefore we can conceive our life as a whole only when we see it in this dark shadow of guilt. (Emil Brunner, *op.cit.* p. 443) It is this unalterable nature of man, this guilt which lies between man and God. Thus Rudolf Otto says "A transcendental guilty fall from grace, from association with God into estrangement from him, from faith into disbelief, is what now constitutes *original guilt*". (*Religious Essays*, p. 27 f)

This in-turned nature of man lies between man and God as an immovable obstacle between their fellowship. God can no longer admit man to his presence without ceasing to be God. His eyes are too pure to look on evil without consuming it. Man's nature as such, as guilty, is thus a nature determined not only by his inclination away from God due to sin, but is also characterised by the divine reaction from it in the way of criticism and judgement. Now just as sin is a two-sided affair, so now man's nature as sin-determined is a two-sided affair. There is the divine reaction to man on the one hand and there is man's prior movement in a direction against and away from God, on the other hand. This is the guilty tension in which human personality is now caught and built and is characterised. The tragedy and the amazing thing is that man can be so audacious and bold in his self-righteousness and self-assertion, that he dares to claim that this divine reaction of which he is aware in himself in his conscience, is actually his own better self; and so while trying to cover up his sin, he is in fact masking his sin with a personality that is sin-born and sin-determined! This hypocrisy is exposed at the Cross where man sees himself for the first time in the true light, in stark actuality. However, what I wish to emphasise at this point is that guilt as belonging to man and his nature is that side of sin which shows us that man's nature is doubly determined: by his own autonomy or sin and by the divine wrath against his sin. Man's nature is just as two-fold as every act of sin. It represents broken fellowship, and it is on the ground that he lives in a relation of existence maintained by God himself.

What we cannot understand is why God does not cause that relation of existence between him and the creature, in virtue of which the creature is a creature, to cease to be. But it is God's patience and persistent un-flagging love to the sinner that maintains that relation of his to the creature even when the creature sins against him, and God by being who he is as God does and must maintain his Holiness or Godness over against the creature's sin by resistance to it. This point must be carefully grasped before we can understand the deep meaning of the Son of God's entering into this world and assuming our nature in order as *Mediator* to die for us and so save us from sin and from our sinful natures. Those for whom Christ died on the Cross precisely as creatures, that is to say beings whose existence is maintained by relation to God, and yet whose natures as sinful are determined both their own rebellion and by the divine reaction or criticism against them.

It is in this fallen and twisted humanity that God's Creator Word, his beloved Son the Lord Jesus Christ, became incarnate and in and through his Incarnate being and life penetrated and endured the contradiction of sinners against their Creator, in order to break the bonds of sin and death. This is why the Cross is so terrible, because guilt is so terrible. And guilt is so terrible because at the back of it there is the full force of the divine resistance to sin. The gulf which separates man and God in the very nature of fallen man is a black abyss, a gulf whose reality has been produced by man and is under the divine judgment upon sin — that is the meaning of hell. And Christ must descend into that hell in order to save and redeem man. He the Mediator must descend into the blackness of man's alienation from God to save him; he must unite in his own Person man and God and bear the guilt of man before the presence of God. It is because the righteousness or law of God stands inexorable in the path between man and God that the gravity of the situation is so fearful. It is such that only God can deal with it at great cost to himself.

It is the Cross itself which shows us all this; but without looking down into the Abyss which the Cross spans we cannot understand the Cross itself. I say "the Cross"; but it is the Lord Jesus, the Man on the Cross who spans the gulf of hell in his own incarnate Life and Person. "He placed himself beside the guilty; conscious of the gulf between God and sinners, he crossed in spirit to our side of the breach and numbered himself with the transgressors." (H.R. Mackintosh: *The Christian Experience of Forgiveness*, p. 189) That is the point we must grasp as best as we may. While sin is the double reality of man's opposition to God and God's opposition to man, Christ comes, as St Paul tells us in the concrete likeness of sinful flesh (ἐν ὁμοιώματι σαρκὸς ἁμαρτίας, Rom.8.3), numbering himself with the transgressors. He was "made sin" for us who knew no sin (2 Cor.5. 21)! He became a curse for us (Gal.3. 13) who was not cursed! The depths of that are quite incomprehensible, especially when we realise that sin contains in its very constitution as sin the judgment and condemnation and wrath of God upon it. By taking upon himself, in himself, the guilt of men, Christ Jesus placed himself at the very point where the Holiness of God resists sin. Christ's saving work is of such a kind that it must express the reality of guilt and expose it in its truest colours, must expose it in terms of the wrath of God, and yet at the same time manifest in the midst of it all the overwhelming Love of God. In the forgiveness Christ Jesus mediates the gulf is indeed spanned but in such a way that the very act of throwing a bridge over the abyss the depth and breadth of the gulf are made still more evident. "My God, my God, why hast thou forsaken me", cried Jesus on the Cross, echoing the Second Psalm and thereby revealing in that cry his utter and complete identification with lost mankind under the holiness and judgment of God. That is why Golgotha casts such a dark shadow over the world. That is why the Cross creates its own background; tearing away the superficial crust, exposing our sin and guilt and dealing with it at its worst; in its attack on God in Jesus Christ; and in God's attack upon it: *Eli, Eli! Lama sabachthani?*

CHAPTER 13

The Mediation and Intercession of Christ

In our discussion of the Person and work of Christ we learned that Christ is to be understood functionally and not metaphysically, dynamically rather than ontologically; his Person is one with his Act, his Act with his Person. It is his dynamic Being that is his supreme activity: all his saving acts are to be understood from his primary activity in the Incarnation when he the eternal Son of God became man in order to be the Saviour of the world. As such Jesus was one the historical people of Israel in Judaea, then under Roman rule. He was born of the Virgin Mary at Bethlehem, and lived as one of the family of Joseph, the Carpenter, and Mary his wife in Nazareth. After thirty years he entered public life and was baptised in the river Jordan by John the Baptist who hailed him as the Lamb of God who takes away the sin of the world. Then for three years Jesus proclaimed the Gospel of the Kingdom, teaching and healing people in Judaea, Samaria, and Galilee, and in Jerusalem, Son of God though he was, as a historical Person on earth. He was the only begotten Son of God, who came not to condemn the world, but that the world through him might be saved.

His work was thus his *Person in action.* That Person-in-saving-action, we see most truly at the Cross where the Lord Jesus Christ is to be understood in fulfilment of his supreme work: dying for the sins of the world. It was his crucifixion at Golgotha that provides us with our deepest insight into the divine significance of Jesus in his vicarious life and vicarious death as the Redeemer of mankind. It is there in his sacrificial passion that the holy divine-human nature of Jesus' Person as the incarnate Son of God is revealed to the understanding of saving faith. It is there at the cross that the meaning and purpose of his incarnation really become revealed to us and we are given to understand most deeply the nature of the incarnate Person and Sacrifice of the Saviour, for us and for all mankind, especially when we see it all in the light of Jesus' resurrection from the dead.

Then we went on to think of the background of the Cross itself, the shadow cast by the Cross as it revealed the sin of the human race for which Christ Jesus died sacrificially in atonement. In our discussion of the nature of sin we saw that it had a double constitution. On the one hand it was an act of man in rebellion against the will and nature of God; on the other hand it was met by the act of divine resistance or wrath. That was an ultimate factor in the nature and reality of sin, because if God did not resist sin, there would be no difference between good and evil or between obedience and disobedience, between faith and sin - in which case there would be no sin at all. We further saw that sin is closely connected with death, for sin goes back not simply to an act by man but to the fallen nature of man and to his human existence in its rebellion against God in the fall of mankind from God. Sin as the perversion of that nature is moral suicide, and results in death.

Now both of these pairs of facts must be considered in a proper understanding of the Person of Christ on the Cross. When these two aspects are not clearly seen the right significance of the work of Christ is not properly apprehended. In modern theology there have been two notable and significant attempts to understand the Atonement of Christ: we may let them to be represented by the views of R. W. Dale and John McLeod Campbell. In Dale's view we find stressed the substitutionary work of Christ in his submission to divine judgment and in satisfaction for sin offered on the Cross, rather than the vicarious life and obedience of Christ in the Incarnation — though it is not without some account of that aspect of atonement. In McLeod Campbell's teaching, on the other hand, we find stress on Christ's vicarious life of obedience to the Father and his atoning suffering in life and death in fulfilment of the love of the Father without a major place being given to the conception of forensic satisfaction of divine justice in the sacrificial death of Christ on the Cross. The suffering and death of Christ on the Cross, it might be claimed, is somewhat subordinated to emphasis on the vicarious obedience Christ in his mind and life to the Father. McLeod Campbell sought to think through the inner relation of Christ's incarnate Person to the Father in respect of his atoning life as well as his atoning death.

We shall have to take both these aspects or views of the atonement fully into account. It is not so much a matter of drawing a balance between the two as to reach a real understanding of the atoning mediation and intercession of Christ in his obedient life and vicarious death. On the whole reaction to them both has been said to be this: Dale's concept of the substitutionary import of the death of Christ was sometimes regarded by many to be nearer to traditional Anselmic concept of atonement with a stress on the aspect of penal judgment and satisfaction before the wrath and righteousness of God; Mcleod Campbell's stress, on the other hand, was on the atoning obedience and love of the incarnate Person of Christ, with primary emphasis on his vicarious life and passion as the incarnate Son in fulfilling the holy and forgiving love of the Father, with relatively little attention given to the idea of satisfaction.

We do well to take both these stresses into our understanding because of the double nature of sin already discussed. I believe we must seek to understand the work of Christ in terms of a *Mediation* in which both the divine and human aspects in propitiation and reconciliation are given full place in the vicarious life and substitutionary death of Christ. God himself is always the Agent in propitiation. The Bible does not speak of God as being Propitiated, but of God himself as providing in his love propitiation for the sins of the world. If sin is qualified as sin by the attitude of God, then it is relation to the Holy God that must be taken into full account, in the atoning life and death of the Lord Jesus, the only begotten Son of God the Father. If sin is the action of man rooted in his fallen nature, bringing death — sin being the contradiction into which the creature has become entrapped in respect of his own fallen being — then the work of Christ from the side of the creature must be stressed. These two sides are maintained and fulfilled in Christ's incarnate Person and vicarious Life and sacrificial Death on the Cross - but as such they derive from and refer back to the gracious will and loving act of God the Son of the Father to assume human existence in the flesh, the flesh of sin which the Son of God vicariously assumed throughout his incarnate life to his death on the Cross as the Lamb of God bearing and bearing away the sins of the world. That is to say, we are to see in Christ Jesus in his vicarious life and death, the Person of the *Mediator*, whose life and saving activity are one in reconciling the world to God. His work is inseparable from his Person whose work it was to bring about that Oneness of mind between Man and God which constitutes the act and state of reconciliation. And it is just because his saving or redeeming activity is one with his Divine-Human Person as Mediator between God and mankind and between mankind and God, that the Lord Jesus Christ crucified for us and risen again, ever lives at the right hand of God the Father as our Intercessor or High Priest for ever acting on our behalf. Our understanding of Christ's atoning mediation and intercession should, I believe, be more in line with the teaching of the Epistle to the Hebrews than it usually is in Protestant dogmatics.

The Cross of Christ may be looked at as man's supreme attack upon God, as sin at its worst and deadliest in attacking God and actually slaying his beloved and only begotten Son, Jesus Christ. But, as Kierkegaard said, there we see that Christianity means God's attack upon man. There was in the third century a story or a interpretation of the Cross which pictured it, rather crudely, as the hook which God bated with the Person of Christ. The devil was beguiled to attack Christ and was hooked. And now God has the devil on a chain. Such an interpretation of Christ on the Cross is crass and must certainly be rejected but it might well be said that it reflects a real truth in which the Cross of Christ represents God's defeat of evil and of the author of it. There is a double factor visible at the Cross: the enmity of man against God, and the judgment of God against man. This must be resolved and God must triumph not simply in defeating sin — that he must do in any case — but in reconciling man and defeating the enmity of the sinner's mind. There must come about the loving communion between God and man which was broken by sin and the fall; the very existence of man into which was introduced the double contradiction must be transformed so that there is life, light, and love between man and God as well as the reconciliation in being between man and God, and indeed a oneness of mind. We shall see that in such a healing of the breach between man and God the breach is itself exposed and widened; at least widened to view. The Father in the far country sends his own Son at last to the vineyard and the householders; but they conspire and slay him adding that to all their crimes. Thus as McLeod Campbell says of Christ: "His honouring of the Father caused men to dishonour Him — His manifestation of brotherly love was repaid with hatred — His perfect work in the sight of man failed to commend either His Father or Himself — His professed trust in the Father was cast up to him, not being believed, and the bitter complaint was wrung from him —'reproach has broken my heart.'" (*The Nature of the Atonement*, sixth edit. p. 112)

We are, I believe, thus to think of Christ in terms of his incarnate mission in restoring and actualising real mediation between God and man and man and God, in and through the vicarious life and death of the Lord Jesus, considered from both sides. He is able to do this because he is the Mediator who is both very God and very man. In this saving and redeeming activity God and man are one, and the fellowship between man and God is restored in and through Christ.

1) We are to think of Christ as the act of God, dealing with man on behalf of God. In the Person of Jesus Christ on the Cross there took place God's supreme act of judgment on man's sin, and the Father's supreme act of love in the reconciling of man to himself. At the same time it is the supreme act of God in vindication of his own mind toward sin in judgment or wrath, but in and with that the act of forgiveness and restoration.

2) We are to think of Christ as dealing with God on behalf of men - he is our High Priest, bone of our bone and flesh of our flesh, made in all points as we are and touched with the feeling of our infirmities, yet without sin. Here we are to think of him both as offering atoning sacrifice for sin and as victoriously fulfilling from man's side the obedience which brings about the reconciliation between God and man and man and God. Thus the atonement is to be understood, not only as the vindication of the Divine honour and revealing the Mind of God the Father in his grace and forgiveness toward sinners, but also as the reconciling life and activity of Christ as offering in himself the perfect obedience of man to God in confession of the sin of the world and a vicarious bearing of it before God. He confesses our sin: and in so doing he restores our minds to unity with God. Can two walk together except they be agreed? asked a prophet in the Old Testament. Man too must be brought to agree with God in what took place at the Cross when agreement and a oneness of mind with God were established in the life and death of Jesus on the Cross in which he acquiesced with God in the judgment of sin and accepted the forgiveness offered there.

This two-sided work of his Christ achieved on the Cross and restored the fellowship with God for which man was created. He was able to do this because he was the Mediator who is both God and very God: man and very man. In it this act in which God and man came together and both God's judgment and man's sin were laid bare so that we are given there the deepest insight into the Person of Christ as Lord and Saviour and into the very Heart of God our heavenly Father. The Cross is not only the medium of God's love but the measure and revelation of it.

1. The act of God in Christ for God.

The Act of God in Christ on the Cross must be thought of in accordance with his Being which is itself God's reality in action, for it is in the Cross that there was manifested his supreme self-assertion as Holy God and God's supreme self-bestowal as Holy Love. In other words we think here specifically of God's attributes of Holiness and Love. Holiness is very Godness of God, his self-affirmation as the I Am, of God toward and for us, of what he is in his unapproachable Majesty. Love is the self-bestowal of God is his will not to be for himself alone but for mankind, so that all the riches of his Love may be made freely available for them. Thus in the Holiness and Love of Christ, God incarnate, we are to think of the Dominion and Communion of God — and that is precisely the message of Jesus, his message of the Kingdom of God interpreted in terms of the Fatherhood of God; that is to say, the act of God's Dominion as bound up with the act of his Communion, or, to use other words, the holy I Am-ness of God and the holy Love of God. In both God is sovereign; his act is the establishment of the Kingdom of God. It is in this light that we must look at the divine activity in Jesus on behalf of God on the Cross, and for mankind. There we see the Love and Holiness of God in operation. God is not simply remote and aloof in his own Being but personally and lovingly present in Jesus, affirming that his Nature and Being shall be recognised by all as the one Lord God: "I am the Lord thy God, thou shalt have no other gods before." That is fundamental to our understanding of the Cross of Christ. If God is God, then he is the only God. If God is God, if Jesus Christ as his Only-begotten Son is God incarnate, then God's Nature and Majesty revealed in him, remain sovereign and exclusive in their claim. There in the Lord Jesus on the Cross, the Lord God himself, precisely as the eternal I am who I am, is present, in vindicating his divine Nature, in affirming himself in his own Holy Being, and in summoning all mankind to love him as he loves them. There in the Lord Jesus on the Cross God's very Being God summons all human beings really to be and live as those whom he has created in his own image, for relation to him and communion with him. There at the Cross, the God and Father of the Lord Jesus, reveals his innermost heart in his holy judgment on sin and in his holy mercy for sinners, and calls all people without exception to come to him and be saved. That is only possible as God by being God, in his very self-affirmation as God, opposes the self-assertion of his creatures over against him, and rejects it as sin. That is precisely what sin is, and is judged as sin, which as such falls under the judgment and condemnation of God. That is precisely the state of the world into which God the Son became incarnate, as Jesus born of Mary to be Immanuel, *God with us* in our fallen world, come to be with us, to redeem us and deliver us from our bondage to sin and its condemnation under God's holy Will, the very Will of him who has created us and loves us, and to be healed and restored to relationship with himself.

We do well to pause again here before the Cross to consider the fact that in this reconciliation of sinners with God in Christ, in which God gives himself unconditionally to us, is possible with the act of God's forgiveness - but what does that really mean?

Let us pause consider further what it means that here at the Cross the God who is inviolable and unchangeable in his own Nature asserts by being God that the world he created is and shall be his own; that the world shall belong to him the Holy God, and that the Holy God shall be the Sovereign of the world. It is here in the fact that God both gives himself in his Holiness *to* men and asserts himself in his Holy Love to be *for* mankind, that we may discern the depth of the God's Love and the reality or his self-giving to mankind in which God wills to have fellowship with us and wills to be *Emmanuel*, God with us. Here God in unlocking himself and imparting himself to us, also affirms the bond between us and himself and which we may not transgress. Love is God's holy self-bestowal to man in the affirmation that God is and ever will be his God in his holiness and love, who summons all those for whom Christ died to surrender themselves to him in the obedience of faith. They are thus claimed by God and called to conform to this Nature and as Holy Love. Thus in the very act of God's self-giving in his holy Love to man bounds are set within which man is called to have holy fellowship with God. God's Love means the giving of God himself to us in fellowship, the *Holy* God to us in fellowship, the *Self-*giving of God who in his absolute and exclusive will to be God, the Holy One. Here his will *for* us, which is Love, precisely as such calls us to be holy as he is Holy. His Self-giving in his Love to us as Holy God, calls us to be holy in our fellowship with him. It is the holy God who loves and it is the loving God who is holy. It is one and the same God in his Self-affirming Holiness and in his Self-giving Love, the one and only God behind both acts.

Thus in the act of God in relation to God on the Cross we are to see in the self-revelation of God as Holy Love, and thus the self-affirmation of *this* God to be sovereign and opposed to all counter claims and assertions, and at the same time the self-bestowal of this God of Holy Love freely to all mankind. The Cross is thus to be understood in such a way that these two acts of God are not impaired in reality or vigour and in such a way that they are really manifest fully for the first time toward men. And the Cross is to be understood in such a way that fulfilment of both these mighty Acts on the part of God are possible together! That means therefore that it is in his Love that God must and does affirm himself in the face of sin against sin; that God reveals himself in his innermost heart; that God gives himself in his love unconditionally to man. That is only possible with the act of forgiveness; or rather forgiveness is only possible as all these "natural" acts of God's Being have been fulfilled and are carried out. They are acts of God's very Being as God. We are not yet thinking precisely of the act of God's forgiveness but of the two acts of God at the Cross countering sin in its double form as act of man against and God and in its qualification as sin by God — and so here we must think of the act of God apart for the moment from the act of forgiveness in which all are ultimately bound together.

Now the Cross means that God *himself* stooped to bear the sin of the world and to slay it in the resistance of his holy love against it. We are not to think at all of a contradiction in the heart of God between his love and his justice; those rightly understood as I have tried to show mean that they are not in opposition but belong to one another and there can be no true Love without Holiness and no true Holiness without Love. However, both mean divine resistance against sin; else love were not love, and holiness were not holiness. Both are opposed to sinful man; as a sinner, not to man as such. Both act together in condemning sin, but both are present in bearing sin in and for the salvation of mankind.

In the mediation of Christ, then, we are to see the exhibition of the divine Mind at enmity to sin, and the execution of the Will of the divine Mind on sin; but, in and through that execution and beyond it, the reconciliation of the divine Mind is such that there may be on the part of God an atonement or "at-one-ment" between God and man. That is to say, the divine Mind at enmity to sin is to be brought to look in Grace on mankind in such way that their sins have been judged already. God can look on man only with resistance against sin; but God himself absorbs the divine resistance against sin in himself and at cost to himself. But precisely in all that   this he must and does vindicate his own nature in opposing sin while saving man. That is what we see in Jesus Christ who came among us in his divine-human Person as God to vindicate the divine Name; to bear-witness for God, as McLeod Campbell puts it. Paul sees the Cross as the justification of the statement that God is Just. If God is God, is Just, why have sins been allowed such a loose reign in the world? Does that mean that sin is not so important to God after all? Does that mean that God is after all of such a nature that human beings may assert themselves and their own natures against God with impunity, without divine resistance? That would mean that God was not God, that God was not Just; or that God was not such that he asserted himself to be the Universal and Absolute Lord of all mankind. And so we are to think of the Cross as the supreme act of God in Christ in respect to his own holy Nature in which sin, hitherto winked at as or overlooked, as it were, at the Cross is finally condemned and God is vindicated in his Name as Holy Love. In order to carry that out Christ came as *God himself* at Calvary. It is *God,* the Eternal Lord God of Holy Love, who acted in Christ in his self-assertion and self-bestowal to mankind.

The mystery of the Cross is that these two acts of God are combined in one. On the one hand, we have the act of God condemning sin — which we have learned from the Bible to call the wrath of God — and on the other hand we have the act of God in which in Christ he identifies himself with our sin. He, Christ Jesus, God incarnate, as St Paul expressed it, was made sin for us and was numbered among the transgressors. Luther in very bold, unacceptable language, but well meant, actually spoke of Christ as a "sinner". "Because in the self-same Person which is the highest, the greatest and the only sinner, there is also an everlasting and invincible righteousness; therefore these two do encounter together the highest, the greatest and the only sin, and the highest, the greatest and the righteousness. Here one of them must needs be overcome and give place to the other...righteousness is everlasting, immortal, invincible... therefore in this contest sin must needs be vanquished and killed, and righteousness must overcome and reign. So in Christ all sin is vanquished, killed and buried, and righteousness remaineth a conqueror and reigneth for ever." (Cf. McLeod Campbell in this respect)

We are not to think of this identification of Christ with us in our sin as a legal fiction; or merely as a forensic matter, although it is that also, but as an actual fact, as an accomplished reality, which precisely is what it is, the "justification of the ungodly"; just as it is and will be an actual fact that we are made righteous in Christ Jesus. The amazing thing fact, then, is that in the crucifixion of the Lord Jesus God absorbs in himself his own wrath, but yet really vents it. He does really resist sin and resist it where it must be resisted — namely, in man. But in Christ he became a man in order to absorb the divine resistance; and in doing it Christ died for all mankind. Looking at it from another point of view we must think of Christ as having gone down to the very depth of our sin and guilt in order to break their bonds; but to go down to the depth of sin he had to go to the point where he was made conformable with us sinners in death. To be made conformable to us in death is the uttermost point of his identification with our sin - in doing so he destroyed death and sin together.

We cannot, it is sometimes thought, really get away from a some aspect the so-called "penal" view of the death of Christ, but nowhere in the New Testament is the death of Christ spoken of as punishment. McLeod Campbell rightly was always trying to ward off any kind of interpretation of the death of Christ like that, but he maintained with real vigour the wrath of God in his judgment upon sin. What else is the wrath of God but the resistance of Holy God towards sin? And what else is the resistance of Holy God toward sin but his retribution or judgement upon sin? Campbell was quite right in pointing out that there is a suffering in God which is not to be penally interpreted. Thus for example God is represented in the Old Testament as saying through a Psalmist: "Rivers of water run down mine eyes, because men keep not thy law." There is *suffering* in God caused by the act of sin before there is judgment in a vicarious sense. We must always think of this suffering of God's love for sin as itself vicarious; as giving birth to the Cross. The Psalmist wrote those words because he suffered in sympathy with God; but God's feeling or suffering is the sign that sin wounds his heart. What McLeod Campbell perhaps did not seem sufficiently realise was that it is just this wounded Love that must react, if it is to be Love, in affliction, but not in punishment as such, and certainly *not for the sake of punishment* but for the sake of God. We must remember the words of Isaiah: "By his stripes we are healed"; and think of the death and suffering of Christ accordingly. Of course there was a wound in the heart of Christ, such as he manifested when he wept over Jerusalem in sorrow which was not penal; but that does not exclude the fact that there is some penal-like suffering in the death of Christ i.e. in voluntary suffering, his coming voluntarily to die at the Cross. The point is that it is God himself who stoops to endure and bear that suffering in Christ. And his beloved Son absorbs it as he alone could and live through it all.

Thus against the act of God's wrath which constitutes the obverse side of our sin, its judgment, God comes himself to absorb that wrath in his Son; to bear the judgement of God himself and the sentence of death. He reacts here against sin as he had never done before; and for that reason alone the sin in crucifying the Son of God is the greatest sin every committed by mankind — infinite in its blackness and guilt. But here also right in that divine judgement there is a divine meeting of that judgement; and therefore both a vindication of God and the judgement of sin in the flesh. Now that sin has been judged and really judged, God may bestow himself freely to man. The "hostility" (so speak) in the mind of God has been fully carried out against sin. When we speak of hostility in the mind of God we do not mean hatred. We can never speak of God like that. Hostility here means God's opposition to sin, means his Holy Self-assertion against sin; and a self-assertion which will continue to be hostile so long as there is sin in mankind. Hence arises the doctrine of satisfaction; for God's wrath is thought to be satisfied with the judgement of sin on the Cross. That word may in some respects be unfortunate but it represents a truth that we cannot let go.

2. In the Mediator we have an act of Christ with God on behalf of man.

It is Maurice that makes this representative act of Christ the main element in his interpretation of the Atonement. But while it is an essential part it cannot stand alone at all, for the act of Christ here on behalf of man is ultimately an act of God from the human side; for it is the Word who assumes human form in order so to act. Thus the divine side is bound up with the representative side of the Cross and cannot be separated from it.

To understand this side we have to remember again that the relations between God and man are two-fold. Man was created in dependence on the Word of the Creator and has fellowship with God. He is given a relation to God which he must exercise; and his being consists precisely in the exercise of that relation in fellowship with God. Man is made for fellowship with God; and that fellowship is one through the Word incarnate, who is Christ. In the book of Genesis we read that Epoch walked and talked with God, and was not, for God took him. That expresses the real relation of man with God. This relation has been broken by the Fall and the Word has come to restore that relation. The two-sided relation between God and man, and man and God, can be expressed in the terms of Glory and Image.

In fellowship with God man is in the Image of God; for it is in fellowship that he conforms to God; that is the meaning of fellowship; and the characteristic relation is that of faith which always conforms in love to the Divine Author and Partner in the fellowship. This relation to the Father is to be understood in terms of a relation with God in and through Christ the Creator Word of God made flesh. Thus we may say, as St Paul has taught us, that it was through Christ the Word that we were all created; it is in Christ that all creatures consist and have their being; it is in the image of Christ that all human beings, all men and women, were created. Christ is himself the very effulgence and express Image of God; he is the only-begotten Son; we are sons of God in him, and in Christ we may have the image of God. But our Sonship or our being in the image of God is not the same relation that Christ has with God.

Between Christ and the Father there is a relation in being which is quite unique and private; but our relation to the Father is one mediated through that relation which Christ has transcendently between himself and the Father. We are sons in a secondary sense; we are in the image of God properly speaking only when we are in the image of Christ (who is both the Image and Reality of God) and conform to him in love and fellowship. That of course was not at all clear in the Old Testament; but it became evident especially in the Wisdom literature that relation to God was through *Wisdom*, spelt with a capital "W". Again it was evident earlier and more later that the relation of the Old Testament saint to God through the *Torah* - not the written Law but the Law of the Lord God alive in the heart. The Wisdom and the Torah we see fulfilled in Christ who is the Law alive and the Word Incarnate, and knowing whom we become like him; to whom we conform in faith and love.

All this is to say, our very being as human creatures, as men and women, is bound up with the Word or Son of God. Now in the fullness of time this Son of God through whom we were all created has come into the world and taken upon himself the form of man whom he created. Our existence as persons consists properly in him; and in his incarnation he comes to us now in our own form in order to restore the form which has been lost in us; I speak here, of course, of the essential form in which humanity consists the Image of God, not of the outward form which is the visible mark of man, though certainly, Jesus Christ did assume that form too. But he comes as a brother; that is as a fellow-man, or fellow human being, although as God. He comes as the Head and Creator of our race in whom we all consist. He comes, therefore, in virtue of the fact that he has become man, as one of us; and not simply as one man among others, but as *the only one* who can actually represent all men and women for all men and women consist in him. Thus he comes as "the proper Man", as Luther called him, and as the Head of our race, as our Representative before God and mankind. It is thus that Christ takes upon himself in a voluntary act our human being, that is the personal being of us men and women, and bears them before God; it is thus that he becomes our High-Priest, and makes a sacrifice to God which is none other than himself, in an expiation which satisfies the Majesty of God; in an act which represents all humanity and covers each individual case in an objective atonement.

On this side of the work of Mediation we can see other depths in the doctrine of atonement; in the relation of Christ's death to the remission of sins. It is McLeod Campbell who stresses here the act of Confession, which we must think of for a little. R. W. Dale writes: "On any theory of human redemption it is morally necessary that, on the part of those who have sinned, there should be a real and frank consent to the Justice of the penalties from which redemption and forgiveness release them. While there is any resentment on our part against the righteousness of the law by which we are condemned, our antagonism to God, whose will is inseparable from that Law, remains....We are conscious that this consent and submission ought to be given, and that so long as we shrink from it the controversy between God and us cannot be closed. It is an offence to resent the penalties of the eternal law of Righteousness, as well as to transgress its precepts." (*The Theory of the Atonement*, p. 479f.) A very good example of this is to be found in the 51st Psalm, ver. 4: in the confession: "Against Thee, Thee only have I sinned, and done this evil in Thy sight: That Thou mightest be justified when Thou speakest, and be clear when Thou judgest..Behold Thou desirest truth in the inward parts: and in the hidden part Thou shalt make me to know wisdom."

The noble words of McLeod Campbell are: "That oneness of mind with the Father, which towards man took the form of condemnation of sin, would in the Son's dealing with the Father in relation to our sins, take the form of a perfect confession of our sins. This, confession as to its own nature, must have been a perfect Amen in humanity to the judgement of God on the sin of man. Such an Amen was due in the truth of things. He who was the truth could not be in humanity and not utter it, — and it was necessarily a first step in dealing with confession of our sins." (*The Nature of the Atonement*, p. 116 f.) Campbell then goes on to ask: "What is it in relation to God's wrath against sin? What place has it in Christ's dealing with that wrath?" To this he answers: "He who so responds to the divine wrath against sin, saying, 'Thou art righteous, O Lord, who judgest so', is necessarily receiving the full apprehension and realisation of that wrath, as well as of that sin against which it comes forth into his soul and spirit, into the bosom of the divine humanity, and, so receiving it, he responds to it with a perfect response, a response from the depths of that divine humanity, and *in that perfect response absorbs it.* For that response, has all the elements of a perfect repentance in humanity for all the sin of man, a perfect sorrow, a perfect contrition, all the elements of such a repentance, and that in absolute perfection, all—excepting the personal consciousness of sin — and by that perfect response in Amen to the mind of God in relation to sin is the wrath of God rightly met, and that is accorded to divine justice which is its due, and could alone satisfy it." (*op.cit.* p. 117 f.)

This is a very important emphasis in McLeod Campbell but does it lack a deep enough view of sin? For "confession" is not enough for the remission of sin; not even a vicarious penitence and confession by Christ. The point is as Athanasius expressed it that sin has become part of us in corruption and no confession will disturb that. Our beings while in relation to God for existence are in contradiction to him which results in a real death. Just because our persons are tied up also with our bodies, our sin issues into physical death as well; but the important thing is the fact that death means separation from God. If then Christ is really to submit as our representative to the mind of God on sin he must submit to the point of death: it is not a matter of attitude only but of actual physical work, and death on a Cross that lies at the bottom of the atonement. In his correction of Campbell Dale writes: "Had he simply made a confession of sin in our name, he would still have remained at a distance from the actual relation to God in which we were involved by sin. He has done more than this. By submitting to the awful experience which forced from him the Cry, 'My God, My God, why has thou forsaken me?', and by the death which followed he made our real relation to God his own, while retaining — and in the very act of submitting to the penalty of sin, revealing in the highest form - the absolute perfection of his moral life and the steadfastness of his eternal union with the Father." (*op. cit.* p. 482 f.) But by confession, as McLeod Campbell thought and wrote of it, is far more than that: it was the *real* confession by the Lord Jesus acknowledged and enacted in his acceptance of divine judgment on sin - that is, as his actual submission to the divine affliction upon him, which cannot, however, be construed as "punishment".

It has to be said that Christ did not really confess our sin unless he submitted to the deepest depth of our sin and submitted to the Divine opposition to it or the penalty attached to it — namely, separation from God, hell, call it what you will: At any rate the "Eli, Eli, Lama sabachthani?" Perhaps that aspect was omitted by Campbell because, it has been argued, that he did not seem to understand the depths of sin. He did not seem to understand sufficiently that the idea of sacrifice depends on the actuality of it . We find in the death of Christ, however, as Campbell reveals, not only perfect confession but perfect submission to and acceptance of the affliction by God upon us guilty sinners, with the acknowledgement that we deserved to die and suffer for sin. Jesus' very submission was his actual confession of our sin and the acceptance of God's judgment on it and of that divine infliction on him, in God's judgment on our sin and guilt. It is this vicarious submission of Christ in his Incarnate oneness with us, which makes our submission possible. His submission is the ground on which our sins may be forgiven. We can anticipate the question of forgiveness at this point to say that God could not condone sin even with repentance for it unless he were to introduce into his Being a contradiction or "fiction" as Dale calls it — but in God that can have no place. "If therefore we are still to be related to God through Christ, it would seem to be necessary that there should be included in his actual relation to the Father an expression of the truth of that relation into which we had come through sin. That expression is found in his death." (R.W. Dale, *The Atonement*, 24th edit.,p.482) This means that in the crucifixion and affliction of Christ on the Cross for the sin of mankind, God himself in his oneness with Christ endured the ultimate "penalty", call it what you may, while inflicting it.

Anselm was fond of thinking of sin as debt toward God. From this debt man cannot simply be exonerated by mere mercy or the mere will of God. For such a remission would be a mere pretermission of punishment, which, if satisfaction otherwise be not made, it would be to let sin go on without being brought into orderly relations with the righteous nature of God. And if sin be unpunished there is no objective distinction between the good man and the sinner. Man is thus under the obligation to render God satisfaction, and yet he cannot do that. It must be a complete satisfaction. Only God can make such a complete satisfaction. But since no one ought to make this satisfaction except men, it must be a God-Man who makes it — hence his answer to the question: *Cur Deus Homo?* The point which we must note in Anselm's argument there is that Christ in his relation to men as their representative makes that perfect satisfaction before God as only he can do it. As Man by his perfect obedience toward God he breaks through the hermetically closed relations between God and man, and opens up the way to the Father through the sacrifice of himself.

In this aspect we are to think of the work of Christ for men in yet another way — that is the way of the *Priesthood of Jesus*. Christ is here regarded as our *High Priest* who offered in himself atonement for us, in sacrificing himself in holy expiation for our sins. As such the Lord Jesus is constituted before God as our High Priest, who on the ground of sacrifice and expiation through his blood enters the very Holy Place and pleads for us in intercession with the Father. The language of Leviticus may help us here to understand the work of Christ on our behalf. On the great day of Atonement in Israel two animals without blemish or spot were brought to the Tabernacle and upon both the high priest laid his hands and confessed the sins of the people. One of them was taken and slain and the priest by the gesture of sprinkling some of the blood of the slain animal upon himself and the people indicated the identification of himself and the people with the death of the lamb or ram. Then in virtue of the sacrifice he entered into the Holy of the Holies and sprinkled some of this sacrificial blood upon the mercy-seat between the Cherubim, and the glory of God descended in response: a response of grace and favour. God lifted up as it were the light of his countenance upon his worshipping people and gave them peace. In the same way the Lord Jesus has made peace for us, through the eternal Spirit, and is now set down at the right hand of God. Only Jesus sacrificed himself the just for the unjust — what the blood of bulls and goats could not do, Jesus could do and did by virtue of his perfect submission and by virtue of his Incarnation. The sprinkling of the blood on the priest and people in the Old Testament ceremony was but a gesture of the truth. Jesus Christ, however, has really become one with us and in virtue of that oneness with us, and also in virtue of his oneness with the Father, he made peace for us bringing us salvation and reconciliation. On the other hand, in the old Levitical ritual the second lamb was not slain until after the gesture had been made in which the sins of the people were laid upon it, and was then led without the camp and driven out into the wilderness - the eternal scapegoat bearing away from Israel their burden of sin and guilt. Christ himself was led away and taken without the city walls to the `wilderness' of Golgotha, made a curse for us the Lamb of God bearing and bearing away the sins of the world. But it was as man that he bore our sins, nay as more, as the incarnate Son of God, the divinely anointed One, and who alone as himself the Lamb of God, as well as his anointed Son, could bear our sins as no sacrificial lamb or scapegoat of the Old Testament rite could do except in symbol, and no lamb sacrificed in the ancient Tabernacle could do except in symbol.

But here we think of Jesus the Son of God incarnate acting on behalf of men in such a way that way that in being crucified on the Cross, he died *for* them. He died for our sins, in our stead, on our behalf. He suffered separation from God and tasted of the wages of sin that we might not; he descended into hell that we might not do so. His death was thus a representative death; a substitutionary death. In this sense it may be described as a ransom by which we are delivered or freed from the slavery of sin and judgement on it, and are restored to the freedom of God. It was the actual confession, not in word only, but in his incarnate being and life and his vicarious death in submission to the Father on behalf of our being and life which was forfeit because of our guilt. It was the propitiation for our sins, the propitiation originated by God himself and carried out by him in the Person and Work of the Incarnate Word, through which we are brought into such relations to and with God that all moral reasons disappear for withholding from us remission of sins and restoration to fellowship with God. Christ dies *FOR* our sins, *FOR* us. The depth of that *FOR* we can never hope to fathom. St. Paul was ever reaching out after new analogies to help him bring it within the grasp of human comprehension and always he had to stop breathless in speechless wonder, without grammatical completion of his sentences before the ineffable love and wonder at the height and depth, the length and breadth and depth of that *FOR* of God's love. Whatever else it may mean it means that what Christ did there once and for all he did for us and on our behalf that we might *NOT* suffer as he did that dark and dread "Eli, Eli Lama Sabachthani". The principle that we deserve to suffer and die and be cut off from God was asserted on the Cross, but also that because of the vicarious life and substitutionary death of the Lord Jesus, it might not have to be asserted in our death. He was forsaken by God that we might not be forsaken. He did not suffer simply that he might share the infliction of God's righteous judgment on our sin, but that God's judgment on our sin might actually be exhausted and remitted. *"Thanks be unto God for his unspeakable gift."*

CHAPTER 14

Forgiveness and Reconciliation

We have been thinking of the Atonement as the act of God Christ in which he brings about our Salvation and restoration. The act of Atonement in which God procures for us forgiveness may be viewed as the basic element in reconciliation. The Atonement is not an end in itself; the Atonement means in part at least the transcending of the ethical and legal relation into a deeper relation with God in which the forensic and condemnatory aspect of the Law is removed, precisely because sin is removed. This whole act of restoration to communion with God we call "reconciliation". It is a divine transaction of such a kind that guilt is not only cancelled but one in which we sinful people can be certain of forgiveness even when faced with the Holiness of God. In other words, Reconciliation means the abolition of the enmity between man and God. and God and man. It is an act of God in his love and mercy who approaches us as we actually are, and not an act in which operates with a fiction; namely, that we were not such bad sinners after all. Forgiveness and reconciliation are not certain on any other ground than on the ground of God's absolute Holiness. Unless from the very Holiness of God there comes the word of pardon, a word from God in which he recognises our guilt, judges it as well as forgives it, we do not really have any reconciliation because we cannot have assurance of our forgiveness otherwise. In the words of McLeod Campbell: "In one view the holiness of God repels the sinner, and would banish him into outer darkness, because of its repugnance to sin. In another it is pained by the continued existence of sin and unholiness, and must desire that the sinner should cease to be sinful. So that the sinner, conceived as awakening to the consciousness of his own evil state, and saying to himself, `By my sin I have destroyed myself. Is there yet hope for me in God?', should hear an encouraging answer, not only from the love and mercy of God, but also from his very Holiness." (*The Nature of Atonement*, p. 26) The point to be noted, however, is that this assurance can never be taken for granted; not even from the Love of God. The Cross alone, or rather God's action in and through it, can give us this assurance from the very heart of God's Holiness. Fellowship with God is costly: but the Cross means that God himself bears the cost of restoring the conditions of fellowship (Emil Brunner, *The Mediator*, p. 453), a cost which man could not undertake.

Reconciliation means the renewal of an "at-one-ment"; the restoration of an original relation between man and God which had been disrupted by sin. Reconciliation with God presupposes that the present state of affairs between man and God is not one of friendship but one of hostility or enmity. In fact it presupposes a serious state of affairs on both sides, God's wrath and our sin — and therefore as something objectively real which we cannot change. It is not simply a matter of one being at enmity with another human being, a state which can be remedied by both coming to an understanding and mutual forgiveness. When the enmity is on one side of the relationship, that of another human being only, the enmity is really a subjective affair and due to a misinterpretation by one of the other. And that can be cleared by a frank revelation; by an open disclosure of the situation between the two parties. Such an understanding of divine forgiveness has often been held in modern times; it was in fact the view of Albrecht Ritschl for whom guilt was an unfortunate distortion of the mind of man which made him see God as he ought not to see him. Therefore the message must be simply that God Loves. Assure the sinner that God loves, and all is right again. This shallow and superficial view of forgiveness has entrenched itself firmly in much of modernity — until it has become difficult to understand that we sinners cannot take God's forgiveness for granted. To say the least this betokens a very serious moral disease. The honest sinner knows that God is opposed to his sin; and that reconciliation if it is to be achieved will not be a merely matter of coming to an amicable understanding, as though the factor which had crept in between God and man did not matter very much after all to either God or man. The plain fact is that man lives at dispeace with his Lord, and God has a quarrel with man; the obstacle to forgiveness is on both sides, and it is real for both sides. In fact we can say it is much more real for God than it is for man, because sin for man is after all something held to be just human and unreasonable; but to God sin is a personal attack upon his holy Being and is fearfully real.

We have already discussed the fact that man's original relations with his Creator which were positive and meant that his life as well as existence had been disrupted. While dependent on God for his very existence man has introduced contradiction into his relations with him in which he becomes and is negatively related to God. His relations to God as a sinner are determined precisely by the fact that he has become disobedient and inimical toward to God; man is still God's creature, but he becomes God's enemy in virtue of his sin. Of course man's relation to God does not cease for he continues to exist and live before God, and as such a two-sided relation is involved in which each counters the other. That does not mean of course that God ceases to love the sinner, but his very love to and for the sinner intensifies the relation between them. Now when we think of it, what else is religion, what else is man's religion but the life of man in his relationship with God, so to speak his having traffic with God? True religion is fellowship or communion with God which is the supreme end of man's life. As the Westminster *Shorter Catechism* expresses it: "Man's chief end is glorify God and enjoy him forever." He was made for that purpose; made in the image of God to have communion with him and is lost when he is cut off from God, like a fish out of water. And it is not simply a matter of environment but a mater of a person's inner relation, for one's religion is not simply an existential matter like his relation to the environment, but has to do with a person's essential inner relation to his Creator; it has to do communion with God for which man was created. The disruption of that relation means the disruption of life; it means that the centre of man's being is destroyed — namely, his relation to God. Man is at variance with God in his innermost being, as his conscience whispers silently to him. And in a real sense God's attitude and relations with man are correspondingly changed, although God never ceases to love him or remove his presence from him. God is there, and there for him, but it is because God is there that the situation is fraught with tension and can become rather terrible, for in his love for man God will not let him go. If God were to disown man altogether and cast him off then the variance between them would be at an end, if that is conceivable, for in that case man would simply cease to exist.

The "dreadful" thing (cf. Kierkegaard's book *In Fear and Trembling*) is that God holds on to us in spite of our sin - he will not let us go. He is near us and his presence is felt in the reflex of a bad conscience. Thus man is conscious of being a sinner because of God's presence to him, and the obstacle between man and God remains in that God in his love for man still holds on to him and will not let him go. *But* his very presence to man means that God is, so to speak, withdrawn from him, not of course that God is absent from him; it means that God is critically present to him; that before God man faced with his judgement. The Presence of the Holy God reveals to man that there is a breach between him and God. It is this holy Presence of God that makes the breach so impossibly wide or rather deep, that makes the quarrel so serious and so trenchant. It is a state of affairs produced by sin in one way and in another way affected by God's very love which will not let man go.

This situation is desperately tragic, however, because having sinned, and sinned against God, man cannot go back and undo the sin. He cannot forgive himself even if he wanted to. The sin that caused the breach is sin *against God*, and therefore only God can deal with it; but deal with it, of course in such a way, that man must acquiesce in it if he is really to be forgiven and be reconciled to God. A prisoner may be released from confinement or be remitted a penalty by the state on grounds that the state may consider just; but whether the prisoner is released or not he is not forgiven. Only the offended person can do that — the person from whom he stole or the one whom he defamed. Sin is a personal affair and only can be personally dealt with. But sin against God is supremely personal and can be forgiven only by a personal act on the part of God himself.

We must note that forgiveness, real forgiveness, is thus the only thing that can heal the breach, that can restore man back to God. It is not simply a misunderstanding between them that must be cleared up; for what is needed is an act of actual cancellation of guilt and restoration to fellowship; and that must be shared by both parties, though it is only the one sinned against who can take the initiative. Only if God himself intervenes, God against whom we have sinned, who alone can forgive us, really forgive us, cancel the guilt an undo the sin, can we recover our communion with God, with the gulf which lies between us bridged or done away. God must, so to speak, stride over the abyss of hell and lift us across. Such forgiveness must be a real personal act. No mere proffer of friendship will suffice. Forgiveness is not a necessity or a general truth that we can reach anyhow. It can be grasped and understood only as an accomplished act and as an actual fact; it is real only as such an accomplished act.

Properly speaking we human beings can never really forgive one another for we can never undo the wrong, even if we could forget it, far less cancel the guilt. Only God can really forgive sins, because fundamentally sin is against God and against his Nature as God, and he alone can forgive it, blot it out, undo it, putting it behind his back, as it were, and, *mirabile dictu*, forget it! Let me repeat: only God can really forgive sin, for he alone can cancel its guilt and undo it. Our sin is sin *against God*, against his very Nature as Holy Love, in conformity to which we have been created as human beings, made in the image of God. When we sin against God, however, even though we are made in the image of God, we cannot on that ground forgive one another's sins, for we cannot act as God to one another. Our Lord Jesus taught his disciples to forgive the sins of others against them, even if they sinned against them seventy times seven, but he also taught that only God can forgive sins. When we forgive others who sin against us, as God has forgiven us, all we can really we do, really do, as far as it possible for us, is to put away our resentment against them. However, what we do in forgiving another is something quite different from what God does in his acts of forgiveness. We can never undo the guilt of a sin when it is committed against us; for we cannot undo it or even forget it, try as hard as we can. We cannot undo what has actually been done, nor can we put the clock back, as it were, and thus forget it as if it had never been done. But God can do both, because sin is stamped or qualified as sin in that he judges it as sin, but unlike God we cannot do so, even when forgiving it. We cannot therefore argue from the fact of human forgiveness to divine forgiveness, and simply assume that God will forgive because we do. That is to come dangerously near to thinking that all God does in forgiveness is simply to remove his "wrath", or lift his judgment against. We must forgive someone out of dislike or hate because we hate; but God can never hate. He may be, and indeed must be angry and judge sin, but he cannot hate; for hate is sin. Remember, however, that the Lord Jesus did teach us in prayer to forgive others as we are forgiven, although it is ultimately only God himself who can forgive sins.

In this light we begin to see further into the fact that forgiveness cannot be taken for granted. We may or take human forgiveness for granted. We expect it in kind and good people, but actually it is often rather a courtesy than real forgiveness. For we are quite unable to translate our word of forgiveness into action, by undoing sin. Forgiveness is not real even between sinners like ourselves unless it is actual. We say we forgive, but we cannot justify a man — if for no other reason, because we are not the moral law. We cannot undo the past. It is only one like the Lord Jesus who can actually forgive, for he really can undo the past. He can say to the paralysed man: "thy sins be forgiven thee", because he can also say: "take up thy bed and walk". It is thus the resurrection, if I may say so, that makes the Cross really substitutionary — and the word of forgiveness the word of power.

The question arises: Can God really forgive? Jesus came all the way to tell us so. God can actually forget and undo our guilt! He can justify us and blot out the past. We would never have known that apart from the word and act of Christ. It is a sheer miracle, and the more we think of it the more the wonder grows that God can actually do it and does do it. Jesus can speak the word of actual downright forgiveness because he also actually can and does forgive. It is a bad mistake to think that Christianity consists just in the teaching of Jesus that we should love and forgive one another as children of our heavenly Father. Christian truth is not some sort of general truth but actualised truth. Certainly Jesus says: "You shall know the truth and the truth shall make you free"! But that does not mean that if you realise that God is love that love will cast fear out of your conscience or heart and set you free: You need not worry, God will forgive; after all he is Love!! That has nothing in common with the Christian Gospel. You and I cannot take God's forgiveness for granted!

The Christian view of the facts is that truth is not something that can ever be taken for granted; it only can be expected and received when it can and does become actual. Thus we are to understand Truth in the same sense as the "Word". For the Word of God is the Person of Christ. And the Truth of God is the Person of Christ. Jesus said: "I am the Truth"! That means that Christian understanding of truth is utterly different. Thus as St John wrote "Grace and Truth became in Jesus Christ." Our English versions are wrong when they say that truth came! The meaning is that Truth *became,* that is, truth came in becoming or having become what it really is in the Person of Christ. In other words, Christ himself IS what he says. Christ is actually in his Person the truth of God's forgiveness. The truth of his forgiveness is not just something spoken; it becomes or rather became a person, a living reality. It is intensely personal, and as such becomes actualised in personal relationships. Thus the incarnation of the personal reality of the Son of God among human beings means and involves reconciliation. The incarnation of God's truth is the Lord Jesus Christ, which means that Divine Forgiveness has become actual — that is the glad tidings. Christ is God's own merciful action toward men. He acts out in reality, translates into real being on earth, the astounding fact of God's forgiveness. It was because he did that, because he kept company with publicans and sinners, because in that way he turned things upside down in a reversal of the moral order of things, upturned the whole standard of values, because he actually forgave sins and justified sinners, that the Jews took and slew Jesus as one who infringed the Law.

Thus in the life and activity of the Lord Jesus, the Son of God, as himself the Truth, as well as the Way and the Life, the Truth of God has become and is personally incarnate. It thereby became clear that forgiveness is not simply a general truth but truth that becomes personally real. Thus the incarnate Person of the Lord Jesus in the midst of sinners meant and means that real divine forgiveness, forgiveness as God's truth, always costs, and as we shall see, costs in person. It costed a "voyage of anguish" for Christ to forgive, as became clear when he drank the cup in Gethsemane and sweated blood; it cost him in personal agony and suffering on the Cross. The humanity of Christ suffering agony and suffering on the Cross revealed what divine forgiveness means in cost to become man in Jesus, and indeed to God himself in the humanity of his incarnate Son, suffering agony and shedding blood in *the actualization of divine forgiveness*. That was the truth of forgiveness "becoming" real and actual to us in the Divine-human Person of the suffering Jesus Christ. "Father, forgive them", Jesus cried as they condemned and crucified him, for they did not know what they were doing.

The suffering of Christ on the Cross is the reflex of the suffering eternal in the heart of God — the cost of forgiveness. How can we, or ever could we, take divine God's forgiveness for granted? The Cross means that forgiveness was indescribably real for God himself, and it is as such that it is and becomes true and real to us and for us in Christ.

Unless forgiveness carries with it a holy or sacramental pledge there is actually no real forgiveness and no reconciliation. That is why Forgiveness is itself a "Word" of God; it is a word that is at the same time effective; it carries with it its own actualization. The Cross announces itself as Forgiveness. It strikes us as the Word of God always does; it cannot be legitimised outside of itself; it is an ultimate fact like the Love of God or the Grace of God with which it is really identical. It is an astounding miracle. What rational connection is there between the death of one man on a cross and the forgiveness of the sins of the world? There is no rational connection. The connection is an altogether divine transcendental one — it is the resurrection again which makes the Cross really and actually and savingly substitutionary, and therefore invests it with its wonderful meaning — the Cross announces itself as Forgiveness, and that comes to us as a creative act. It is a direct act of God. No act of creation can be understood properly or explained. Creation is something that comes to us out of nothing and therefore cannot be expected; it is sheer unadulterated miracle. Forgiveness is such an act. Of course forgiveness is not creation but recreation; it presupposes the creation; and presupposes something wrong that has happened to human creatures which it changes, and restores what sin has done to them. But it is yet the act which in restoration corresponds to the original act of creation; for it is itself creative.

Let us pause to note that it is simply because truth is thus creative, as forgiveness is creative, in other words because Christian truth is not the kind that just *is,* but the kind that is true only as it *"becomes"*. Thus, incidentally, there can be no "true" natural theology — for natural theology deals only with the realm of abstract ideas, with fancies that are not actual truth. Thus natural theology, if true, means that there are other Incarnations!

It is just because of this nature of forgiveness as a creative Word that actually effects what it declares that this so hard to understand; and that really baffles any explanation. Let me quote from H.R. Mackintosh. "The reality of pardon, imparted by such a God, can never be demonstrated to any one who has not know it from within, nor can it be shown to follow necessarily, as X follows from Y, from any rational notion of God that might figure in a metaphysical argumentation. But though not to be explained, it can none the less be experienced as something irresistibly borne in upon the mind that submits itself, with candour, to the impression of Jesus Christ. The point, however, is that it *is* experienced as that which passes all understanding. It is the breaking of eternity into time, the intervention of a love beyond all measures, a supernatural event not deducible by an human calculus from the nature of the universe but rather the spontaneous and unanalysable deed of God. We do not reach this by hard thinking, we are confronted by it. It emerges from pure love as an inexplicable gift to the unworthy which conveys the solution of our sorest problems, in the sense that we can now endure their weight unmurmuringly and perhaps even with joy, since God has forgiven us and is our Friend. He has done all; the love and the glory are His alone." (*The Christian Experience of Forgiveness*, p. 33 f.) (Cf also Bultmann, *Jesus and The Word*, p. 202)

Forgiveness, however, is even more difficult to understand than a creative act. In Creation we understand God to bring into being something out of non-being, *creatio ex nihilo*. But that is the freedom of God the Lord, the only self-existing creating Being. There is nothing there contradictory to his Being. But is it so in forgiveness? When we understand the Holiness of God aright; his aseity and integrity, his self-consistency, we begin to wonder if after all forgiveness is actually possible. Can God forgive and be God? Can the Moral Law forgive and still be the Moral Law? Many people have declared roundly that this is impossible and inconceivable. It may appear that way to us — and indeed unless it does appear that way to us there is something severely wrong with us! Here we reach the heart of the problem of forgiveness. In the face of this we must start from the fact that *in the Cross we do have a Word of God which announces itself to us as Forgiveness*. The Cross is the answer to the problem of Forgiveness. That is, in Pauline language, the Cross is the Wisdom of God and the Power of God. It is both the reason why? and the reason how? we are forgiven. It is the Divine *Logos*, the rationale of Forgiveness. Thus the Cross or death of Christ on the Cross is the reason why we are forgiven. It is for Christ's sake that we are forgiven — and here we encounter again the miracle of substitution.

We must try to understand forgiveness a little more closely. Forgiveness is by God the self-bestowing and self-asserting God, and the forgiving of the sinner; that is to say, it is forgiveness of the one that God precisely *as* God condemns. Forgiveness contains in it an implicit and explicit judgement, an exposure of sin, of the sinner. At the same time forgiveness means justification, a verdict of acquittal, in fact a verdict of "not guilty", for it means the justification of the ungodly. How can these things be held together? We have already discussed how they are held together in Atonement, the act of expiation of our guilt by the death of Christ. But we can now enter somewhat more into its significance in relation to the question of forgiveness and reconciliation.

There is no doubt about the fact that sin must receive the full reaction of the Lord God — God would not be God did it not. Therefore forgiveness cannot be imparted in such a way as to violate the inviolability of God. God cannot bestow himself on man in such away as not to bestow himself in his self-asserting holy nature. Forgiveness cannot therefore be bestowed without judgement or penalty. To quote Emil Brunner: "Forgiveness...would mean the contravention of the logical result of world law; therefore it would mean a process more vast and profound than we could ever imagine, a change far more vast than the suspension of the laws of nature. For the laws of nature are the laws of the divine creation, external laws. But the law of penalty is the expression of the personal will of God, of the Divine Holiness itself. Forgiveness, therefore, would be the declaration of the non-validity of the unconditioned order of righteousness which requires penalty." (*The Mediator*, p. 446 f.). If therefore forgiveness comes to us from the Cross, it must mean as we have seen already, that at the Cross the divine reaction against sin is made and met, and really met; for perfect forgiveness can be carried out only where the reality of guilt is fully expressed, and the reality of judgment, but where at the same time there is a real acquittal. That only can mean that the Cross is the resolution of the paradox or problem: that in the death of Christ Jesus on the Cross punishment was meted out to the guilt of man, and yet the great act of divine self-bestowal which bridges the gulf created by sin.

This fact is brought out by Horace Bushnell in his point that forgiveness always costs. It is only a bad man that forgives easily. The good man cannot forgive without a struggle, for it means the contravention of his goodness. But as we saw no man really forgives, though we have a reflection in human experience of real forgiveness just as our human fatherhood is named after the divine. But we cannot argue from one to the other. The Cross is the supreme indication that it *costs God to forgive*. The Cross means labour or travail for God; the act of giving birth to a new relation between man and God. We cannot take forgiveness even on the part of God for granted (see Brunner, *ibid.* p. 453 f.), for even by him it can be achieved only through agony and pain, inasmuch as sin always causes him pain. If the committing of sin causes him pain; how much more the forgiving of it where he must judge it?

When we think thus of forgiveness as enacted through the death of Christ we must be careful to note a number of further points. The first of these is that forgiveness is not simply equivalent to remission of penalty. Penalty may well be remitted but there is not necessarily there any forgiveness. On the other hand, forgiveness does not automatically carry with it the remission of penalties. In fact very often we only can think of forgiveness and the requital of penalty as going together! "Over a certain area of experience pardon and retribution invariably go together, because the holy love that constitutes the Father's very Being makes anything else impossible...If God did not chastise sin in the very act of forgiveness, and in the persons of the forgiven as a sequel to forgiving them, he would not be more loving than he is; he would cease to be God." (H.R. Mackintosh, *The Christian Experience of Forgiveness*, p. 25)

St. Paul has an interesting word in I Cor. 11.32 which will throw some light on the discussion at this point. He says: "When we are judged, we are chastened of the Lord, that we should not be condemned." The same thought is voiced by Paul when he speaks of delivering a couple of wayward Christians on Corinth over to Satan, and again in the exhortation to judge ourselves lest we be judged! I think too this was the experience of David who was smitten with guilt after numbering the Army, and requested that he might fall into the hands of the living *God*, for it is precisely in *God's* judgement that there is mercy. To make this clear we must remember that the supreme punishment of sin is guilt; that is the heart of hell. That is to say, divine judgment is there the divine withdrawal; the forsaking of people by God; it was of this that the Old Testament saints were most afraid, that God should turn his face away from them. They could endure anything else but that, and endure it gladly if only they would be granted the presence of God through it all. The greatest judgement on sin is its being countering by God, the divine displeasure and the separation from the fellowship with God — that really IS death and hell, in effect. Now it is with this that the Cross has to do — with our guilt and divine judgement on it. God interposes himself on our behalf between his own wrath and our destruction. Thus Christ is to be thought of as God in the act of expiation — apart from the Deity of Christ, let me repeat, the whole matter is nonsense. The death of Christ must not be thought of as the cruel sacrifice of the Son for us. The Life and Person of Christ Jesus is the divine decision to suffer himself vicariously for men. We do not first know who the Person of Christ is and then understand his work. It is the case that we have in our study of Christology advanced first from the Person of Christ to his work, but I have maintained all along that it is only in the acts or work of Christ that we really know and understand him. It is at the Cross that we see Christ to be God, to be the Mediator who is very God and very Man. This must be kept in mind whenever we think of the Atonement: Christ as Person depends on his function. He is the *Redeemer*-God; and apart from his Redemption we know really nothing of him.

To return, then, the Cross has to do with the expiation of guilt in which guilt meets its penal or just deserts. And that Christ has met and done away with in that he has triumphantly interposed himself in our place has broken the power of guilt. Just because it is a finished work is it a substitutionary work. At the same time he has declared the ultimate non-validity of the penal Law *for us*! But a point I think we must make is this, that this judgement on guilt does not necessarily absolve us from all the penalties we have incurred by our sins. For though our past has been severed from us in the sight of God — that, though he forgets our sins and casts them behind his back as the Old Testament puts it — we are still sinners, and sin is itself penalty. That is to say, we live in a world bound up with sin and enmeshed in a network of sin and penalty. That is the order of things. While guilt is pardoned and there is untroubled fellowship with God in Love and Grace, nevertheless we are still in this world of sin and suffer the results of sin, others' sin as well as our own. That is part of the solidarity of the race and the interpenetration of our human personalities in a social-network of life and existence. Thus the act of forgiveness which carries with it condemnation of sin does not automatically lift us out of this world which it would have to do did it mean that we were remitted of all our chastisements or penalties. Indeed as H. R. Mackintosh pointed out in the passage quoted above, forgiveness actually includes this judgement on sin; it includes a real chastisement. It may be fair therefore to draw a distinction between what I shall call for the moment "chastisement" and the moment of "condemnation" with the words chastisement and judgement applying to both. Thus we think of Christ as suffering judgment or chastisement in our stead, as being judged for us inasmuch as he met and satisfied the reaction of the Divine Honour against sin and guilt; but we do not think that Christ was disciplined, or `punished' in that sense for us (actually the New Testament never speaks of Christ as being "punished" for us), that he was "chastised" for us as the Prophet said. (Cf. Isaiah 53.6 :"The Chastisement of our peace was upon him".) In other words retributive judgement fell upon him; but do we think that corrective and disciplinary punishment was meted out to him as well? It seems to me that forgiveness carries these with it. For it does not mean that because Christ suffered for us that we can escape scot-free with immunity! In fact we cannot accept forgiveness without at the same time taking up the Cross — nor does any really penitent sinner want to. The really penitent sinner is the one who welcomes judgement on his sin. He suffers gladly. Did he still wish to escape it he would not really be penitent. Thus the acceptance of forgiveness means the acceptance of condemnation or judgement or death — to submit to the Cross means that we are crucified with Christ. Yes, primarily, that means that when he died, we died, but it means also the daily act of submission and the daily death in forgiveness and humiliation. In this spiritual experience we do suffer judgement and do die that we might live.

This brings us to the more positive side of forgiveness and reconciliation: that of restored fellowship with God through Christ, in fact through union with Christ. He came to assume our Lot, said Irenaeus, that he might raise us to his lot. He came in the form of a servant made under the Law that he might transform us into the likeness of his own Image and Person. That is to say through the act of expiation accomplished and finished for ever on the Cross Christ Jesus makes possible the sinner's free communion with the Father. He has abolished the enmity and has established harmony. He has forgiven all our trespasses and blotted out the registry of sins that were against us, the handwriting of the ordinances, as Paul called it. He does not act as if there were no charge against us; but he takes that charge and nails it to the Cross. Now! Who shall lay anything to the charge of God's elect? It is Christ that died, yea, rather that is risen again! Christ has made peace through his blood; and brought the peace of reconciliation. This is the peace that the angel choirs sang about at the birth of Jesus: this is the peace and this is the good news that the prophet prophesied about in the glorious 61st Chapter of Isaiah. It is because of the Cross and the forgiveness there wrought out that God descends to us graciously in Christ with words of peace: on the Cross righteousness and peace have kissed each other; judgement and mercy are met together. God has come and expropriated and appropriated us for his own love and fellowship (See Karl Barth, *Credo*, p. 156) He has reconciled us to himself, not imputing our trespasses unto us. The obstacle is taken out of the way which hindered and barred fellowship. We are restored to religion, genuine religion! We are restored to the place where we have to do with God in love and prayer. We have no fear. God knows all about us: he knows about our sin, our waywardness. We are hiding nothing from him. He has looked it squarely in the face and dealt with it justly. Our consciences are purged from evil and the enmity is destroyed that lurked in our souls against the Loving Father.

This act of reconciliation is also described in the New Testament as the establishing of the New Covenant with men. Just as in the Old covenant the establishing of the bond between God and his people was his *hesed* or Loving-kindness, so in the New Covenant the bond is his *Grace*, for in this new relation we receive Grace for Grace, says St. John. In the Old Testament God is represented as choosing Israel and establishing a covenant with them. Why God should choose such a weak and beggarly nation it could not be fathomed, Moses thought; it was simply referred to the Ultimate Love of God. But in Choosing his people *Jahweh* God put himself into covenant relation to them such that he freely put himself under obligation to them as it were. That obligation is represented on his side by promises and pledges which included the coming Messiah, and on the side of Israel the Law and the cultus. Within this reciprocal covenant-relationship initiated by the sheer grace of God people might call on the Lord to redeem his promises to them in times of need. In the New Covenant established once for all on the Cross God has initiated a Covenant of Grace to which, as it were, he has appended his signature in blood. God has bound himself to men through Christ in such a way that he pledges himself to save and forgive all those who put their trust in Christ. It is thus that we may claim, may I put it reverently, claim from God forgiveness and love; claim precisely because he has pledged forgiveness. In this New Covenant the great "rights" are the holy Sacraments. Every time we partake of the Lord's Supper we act within the new covenant calling upon God to redeem his pledges which he does through his Spirit. And as surely as we take the appointed pledges of bread and wine in our hands, and partake of them, so surely are we bound through them to Christ in holy communion and fellowship; we become partakers of his death and share in the blessings of the atonement; and rejoice in the reconciliation accomplished through Christ. But this does not mean that we can just take the forgiveness and Grace of God for granted. Not at all — for the Cross means precisely that we cannot! But the Cross does mean that, on the ground of the divine promise which circumscribes the Law and transcends the old covenant, God will forgive and does; that on the basis of the Cross and on that basis alone we can joyfully expect and joyfully receive the Love of God, and rejoice in the peace that passes all understanding.

This brings us to a further point. There is no forgiveness without Christ. In the last resort *he is what he does*. Christ Jesus himself is the Reconciliation between God and Man, and in Christ we are in God! It is this union with Christ made subjectively real, and really real, by the operation of the Spirit through the Word of God that the act of forgiveness is actualised in our own souls so that we are reconciled on our part too. We are joined to the Lord; we are restored to his heart and love and are transformed into his image. This means that reconciliation carries with it reformation or regeneration. "Real forgiveness", once wrote Bultmann, "condemns disobedience. Whoever thus becomes a new man through forgiveness is reborn to obedience. If any one thinks he has received forgiveness without being conscious of God's will in his own life, such forgiveness is illusory; as the parable of the unmerciful servant shows (Matt. 18:23-35). (*Jesus and the Word*, p. 211) For us to be reconciled is to love God; for his Great Love evokes in us a corresponding love; and to love is to keep his commandments. It is only when our own "egos" have been displaced by the Lord Jesus Christ ("not I but Christ", as St Paul expressed it, Galatians, 2.20), that we can love with a real and unselfish love, and so properly keep the commandments toward God and our neighbour — not otherwise — not otherwise than through the Cross and the crucifixion of self there. Such is the gateway to life; for the reverse side of the Cross is the empty tomb — and the glory of a new Life of power in communion with Christ the Son and with the Father.

And now to a final point: the fact that when God in Christ forgives us our sin, *God forgets* ! That is the astounding good news of the Gospel of the crucified and resurrected Lord Jesus Christ.

CHAPTER 15

The Resurrection of Christ

Toward the end of our thinking about Christology we have come to the Resurrection of Jesus Christ — but this was actually the point at which we began, for it is in the light of the resurrection that the Person of Christ is properly to be understood. It was the resurrection of Christ which converted the band of hesitant and doubting disciples into Apostles of Hope. It was the fact that they saw and encountered their Lord risen from the dead that sent them forth with a Gospel to preach. Before then the teaching of Jesus of Nazareth might almost be called a defeat! He had won but few disciples, and even they all forsook him and fled at the decisive moment in his life. Even Peter who had made the great confession that Jesus was the Son of God and who appeared to have reached through the Spirit knowledge of the reality of our Lord's Person wavered, and fell before the taunt of a servant girl. Still it was the miracle of the Resurrection which really and finally awakened faith in its proper and powerful form in the disciples. It was the resurrection which gave them the proper understanding of Jesus Christ, such as they have testified to. *Christ is risen! The Lord is risen*! Something unheard of and absolutely astounding had happened! And that had happened to the very Jesus out of whose mouth proceeded those wonderful words and from whose hands and lips came forth such gracious and majestic power as people had never experienced before! The combination of both and the encounter of both together in the actual Person of the Risen Lord produced an unconquerable faith that has since dynamited the whole world! The Crucified Christ has Risen from the tomb. This Risen Jesus is the very one the Jews took and crucified on the cross outside the city wall of Jerusalem at Calvary! That is the event, the fact, that bowled them over and was the "power of God" (1 Cor. 1.18) to them all.

The significance of the Resurrection does not lie simply in the wondrous event itself — great and important as that was and is. The significance lies in the conjunction of Person and Work of Christ and of his Word of power to men and women, a word of triumph and victory. It is there that we discern and experience the teaching and Person of Christ fused together in revelation with his work as nowhere else. Christ's reality is a reality-in-act: he *is* the Truth.

Now we have noted all along some of the difficulties in discussing the Person and Work of Christ — some have preferred to discuss his Person and teaching, some have laid the emphasis on his work almost exclusively. The truth is that they are rightly seen only together in their proper perspective and significance here : at the Resurrection. Hitherto the divine secret of Christ's Person was somewhat concealed, and his work was a strange often baffling work — the disciples did not understand the Cross! But now in the Resurrection the concealment is cast aside and the Transcendent Christ made himself known to the disciples in the revelation of his risen reality, when all thoughts of the Person and Work of Christ were recalled and transformed in the light and power of Resurrection. Both his Person and Work hidden in their own ways converge there at the point where the Light of Eternity burst upon them plumb down from above, like a flash of lightening manifesting everything there below. Before then men had groped about in the dark and their hopes dashed and fears ended in death, but now in a flash of blinding light such as later encountered Saul of Tarsus on the Damascus road it became indubitably clear that the Crucified Jesus Christ is actually the very Son of God, the Saviour of the world. The fact that he had risen and is Lord and God as Thomas confessed meant that the Cross was no tragic incident, but that Jesus had actually come in order to die as the Messiah and Lamb of God and to rise again from his sacrifice on the Cross triumphant in the Kingdom of God - Jesus was their Lord and their God.

Thus the fact that the Crucified Christ is Risen, that this Transcendent Lord is none other than the crucified Jesus, is the dominating and over-arching fact that gives light and meaning to everything about Jesus Christ in the Gospel. It is here that we begin to understand the facts that have been learned, the events that took place with Jesus' sojourn on earth in Judaea and Galilee. Until we also realise this, the work of Christ and his teaching will be an enigma to us, for we will not be able really to understand him. The help we are given, however, is the New Testament written under the inspiration of the Spirit of the Lord Jesus, which as Bengel once said "breathes the resurrection". Here and now we may not have to do with the Lord Jesus him without it, but because the only material we have to work upon, the New Testament, as Bengel once said, breathes the Resurrection, for it was composed view in he light of the resurrection.

The first preaching of the disciples was primarily of the Resurrection of Christ. Everybody in Jerusalem knew about Christ and the Crucifixion. The two who walked to Emmaus were astounded to meet a man who had not heard of it - even if he were but a stranger in Jerusalem, it seemed impossible that he could have been there and had not hear of it. No the whole of little Jerusalem was ringing with the news of the death of Christ — and Jerusalem, we must realise was little when we compare it to any of our cities, or to modern Jerusalem. No one could go about the city of old Jerusalem preaching and teaching as Jesus had done without the whole city knowing about it; nor could that same Person be crucified without the whole town talking about it. Then suddenly there burst upon the town like an earthquake the news that Jesus is risen from the dead!

This Jesus whom a few days ago Jews and Romans took and shamefully crucified is actually risen from the dead and they have talked with him, eaten with him and walked with him! That was the astounding fact, that would immediately throw all that Jesus did and was into the greatest religious significance — the birth, the teaching, the Cross and all. That happened to the disciples and they proceeded in new-found ardour to tell men all about it until the number that believed swelled into multitudes; and the excitable crowds that came up for the feast dispersed to their homes throughout all the world with their ears ringing with the news of the Gospel; with the miracle that a crucifixion had been transformed into a blessing!

It is just here that we begin really to understand Jesus, where the disciples did; for the resurrection immediately lights up with meaning all else that people have heard of this strange Man. Thus until the act of the Resurrection has also become a living Word of God to us, or until we realise that in the Resurrection of Christ Truth breaks out into the open, we will not understand Christ or the Word of God; far less will we understand the Atonement through the Blood of Christ the Lamb of

God who bears and bears way the sin of the world. It is in the Resurrection that Christ comes out of his *Incognito,* as it were, and we behold his transcendent glory; it is at the Resurrection that we learn the real secret of Christ's Person to be not human but divine; and therefore it is here that we see the light of the Divine breaking through every word and deed of Christ giving it that reference and orientation which constitute both as the very Act and Word of God, as *Gospel*! We cannot emphasise this too much — unless we see this Risen Christ to be the same as the Jesus Christ of whom we heard and read earlier; unless the Jesus who was always being mistaken for a Rabbi is also seen to be this Transcendent Christ, there is nothing in Jesus beyond the construction that purely human minds can put on him — that is to say, no Word of God but a word of Man. It is the Resurrection that means that Jesus Christ is to be interpreted absolutely *sub specie aeternitatis* — in the light of the Miracle of the eternal and supernatural. Thus the teachings of Jesus are no mere idealisms or ways of life; they are red-hot words which slay and make alive.

The death of Christ is no mere martyrdom but has a central place in his life; for it could not have been accidental; it must have been planned in the counsel of God and deliberately willed to take place as it did. That was how Peter proclaimed and preached it to multitudes in he Temple Courts of Jerusalem. The Person of Christ is not simply that of a at Hebrew Prophet but is the Very Son of God in actual contact with men and women, in fact within human flesh. Until we too can look at Jesus Christ candidly as the original Witnesses did — the disciples and the apostles — we do not understand the New Testament, or apprehend the Gospel which it proclaims. But to do this we have to stand beside the empty tomb — yes a tomb! It is a physical thing with which we have to do; for it was a physical resurrection; just as his birth was a physical birth, and had to do with his actual existence and life. Until we see here Humanity and Deity of the Lord Jesus in their closest act, the Gospel will be an empty story! The Resurrection of Christ is sheer unadulterated miracle. There is no sense in discussing the problem of how a man could rise from the dead — all that talk is irrelevant to the issue. The point is that it is God, the God and Father of Jesus in Christ who raised the Man Jesus from the tomb of Joseph of Arimathea. To try to explain that is to explain it away. Unless we allow ourselves to hear the Word of God in and through the Apostolic Testimony to it, it must remain trapped under the scepticism of naturalistic thought. However, it is not my purpose to discuss the credibility of the Resurrection here — that is a matter of a faith - rather it is my business to show the bearing of the Resurrection in theological significance on his Person and Work as we have discussed them hitherto.

(*The original lecture from this point is unfortunately lost*)

CHAPTER 16

The Ascension of Christ and the Second Advent

The basis of revelation for this part of our consideration of Christology is given in the witness of the disciples to the event that took place in Galilee forty days after the Resurrection. For more than a month Jesus Christ the Risen Lord tarried with his disciples and then met with them for a final time (the Greek says "took salt with them", Acts 1.4) when he opened their understanding of what he had already taught them. It was a period of remembrance, begun on the road to Emmaus in which he began from Moses and the prophets and expounded to them all the Scriptures (Luke, 24.25ff). That visit of the risen Lord to the disciples was no incidental experience of Christ for the disciples, but a calculated time of instruction to the right people — and we must think here also of the appearances of the Lord during the forty days after Easter in much the same way. Then one day Jesus announced his departure, a departure he had already spoken to them about, a departure which was to be followed by the descent of the Holy Spirit in power. Jesus drew away from them and departed visibly from them into the clouds of the heaven, and two angels appeared who announced to those men of Galilee who stood looking up toward heaven that this same Jesus whom they had watched departing from them would come again in like manner from the clouds of the heaven.

What are we to say to this? What part does this event play in our Christology? Somehow or another these passages of the New Testament have often been left out of Christological studies and relegated to other departments or to oblivion — but that we cannot do, if we are to take the resurrection of Jesus seriously. Let us to remember that what the Nicene Bishops and Theologians called "the hypostatic union of God and man" in the Lord Jesus, of the union of eternal Word of God with the humanity of the Lord Jesus, was/is eternal and never-ending. If Jesus Christ is also Man, and precisely as *Man* rose from the dead, then there must still be a proper place for our steady understanding of him in theology. Christian Theology, centred in the Lord Jesus Christ, can have a proper place only where the reality of his human nature continues. Just as there only can be revelation to us where revelation takes human form, because humanity cannot think outside of itself, so here where the Form and Reality of Christ as *God-Man* continues and where there is revelation about him and of the Eternal God through him, there theology as *Christology* must persist in its efforts to gain a clear understanding of the risen and ascended Lord Jesus, and all that he means for us in the Church and the world. Our great warrant for thinking theologically of him rests on the reality of his resurrection and his risen and ascended reality as God and Man, and on his promised gift of the Holy Spirit to guide and lead us into all truth. The ascended Lord Jesus Christ is God become Man. It was as such that he rose again from the tomb and as such that he has ascended. And it is, therefore, as Man as well as God, that we must continue to think of him, as the eternal Son of God incarnate who does not succumb to death but lives for ever at the right hand of God the Father as our Saviour and Lord. We must still have to do with him as *Jesus*, with whom we human beings can have to do in the communion and illumination of the Holy Spirit.

If the Lord Jesus Christ is still very Man as well as very God, then his relations as Man with mankind, with men and women, will continue; and indeed it is precisely in order that they might so continue that he became man and united himself eternally with our humanity. If then Christ became man and as Man really rose again from the dead, such that he is even now a risen Man as well as God incarnate, then we must have something to say about him. This "something" we have in the two articles of faith which the Apostles' Creed expresses in the words: "He ascended into heaven and sitteth is there at the right hand of the Father; from thence he shall come to judge the quick and the dead."

1. The Ascension of Jesus Christ

We cannot think here otherwise than we have been thinking of Christ all along. We are not here departing into the realm of myth but are dealing with the Continuous Living Reality of the Lord Jesus after the Resurrection. If this is not also fact, if this is not also a reality after the Grave as much as before the Grave, then we are most miserable. For that would carry with it the corollary that we who in the Church continue to stake our existence and faith on the Life and atoning death and resurrection of Christ have nothing to do with reality either. It is the continuation of the divine-human reality of Christ Jesus after his death as his disciples knew him and thought of him before and after his resurrection, that is the foundation of the Church, and the bed-rock of continuing Christian belief. The Resurrection to be sure takes us into a realm different from that occupied by Christ before the Cross, but it is yet within the same realm of revelation as that enjoyed by disciples of Jesus before and after his resurrection. And so here we have to think of and about the Lord Jesus in the same way under the same divine revelation.

What then are we given? Not very much to be sure, precisely because we step out now into the age of the Church, the age of faith and trust — and where there is no sight but where there is faith. But we are given certain facts upon which faith must proceed, and proceed we must! These facts are however of the same nature as those which preceded the resurrection. We cannot view them from any different angle than we have viewed the facts of the Person and Work of Christ, namely from the aspect of his saving work. In other words, when we address ourselves to the Ascension of Christ we must still interpret the act of Christ as deliberate and calculated with a definite purpose in view. He ascended into heaven and is enthroned at right hand of the Majesty on High. Calvin very rightly and wisely remarked that we must think of these events as speaking of the function or work of Christ rather than understand them in terms of strict space-time categories - for example "sitting at the right hand of the Father". Certainly we must never let go of the physical incarnated reality of Jesus; for the Resurrection means as we have already seen that the creation of God is not done away with, that God's original purpose is not thwarted. Rather do we have a reaffirmation of the Lord Jesus the man as he was meant to be known and believed; and with the resurrection we have the promise of a new heaven and a new earth.

Precisely because we pass here into the future it is not within our reach at all to say how much of this is metaphorical or figurative and how much literal fact — but at any rate wherever there is metaphor it stands for something even more potent than the visible facts may do. We must remember too that precisely because the Word has united himself to humanity, the conditions created for and intended for humanity must continue in eternity for man, inasmuch as he is redeemed precisely as man and by a Saviour who was human as well as divine. Or to put it into other language, because in the Lord Jesus eternity moved into time and took time seriously, we must take time seriously too and not allow it to vanish with the mists ·of mere symbol and empty theological or philosophical speculation. Time is real for eternity and therefore is not illusory; and thus even time and human relations have their place in eternity — Jesus Christ is actually risen, Christ the Man and as Man as well as God is at the right hand of God the Father Almighty! Therefore whatever else that means it means also this that these human conditions somehow have their place in the eternal purpose of God, right beside his Throne in Eternity, and point ahead to a new heaven and a new earth in God's sovereign purpose. The drama has not ended! Man does not end with his being saved; he lives for ever, just because Christ has gone before!

Leaving this question aside for the moment, we must turn to the purpose behind this relation of man to God which the Ascension of Christ guarantees to be eternal. Once again it must be said that Jesus Christ is to be functionally not metaphysically interpreted. What then is the function of the Ascension and the sitting at the right hand of the Father on High?

Fundamentally the function of the risen and ascended Lord Jesus cannot be anything other than the dominating purpose of his incarnation and life on earth: the revelation of God to mankind and the redemption of mankind. If the Ascension is really the ascension of the very Jesus Christ who came into this world, lived, taught, died and rose again, then the purpose of his coming is linked with the purpose of his ascending to the Father, in its complete fulfilment of the revelation and redemption with which he unites us to God through himself. That is surely what is now being fulfilled by Christ at the right hand of God. The fact that he is at the right hand of God means this, that the function of Christ on earth in revelation and redemption is not some transient matter but has its place at the very throne of the eternal God. Thus the function of Christ at the right hand of God is to finalise his saving and revealing work on earth and to assure us that really was and remains the very work of God; and to assure us that Christ after all really came from the very bosom of God, and is our surety at his right Hand. Christ *IS God's right hand* — that we have already considered when we discussed the cosmic significance of Christ. It is through Christ that we are created and it is through Christ that we have fellowship with God for Christ really is God manifest, and it in Christ, as St Paul tells, that all things in heaven and earth, visible and invisible realities, will be reconciled. The Ascension to the right hand of God means therefore the completion of the humiliation of Christ; the completing of the heavenly side of the ellipse which he made by descending into this vale of tears. But just because the ellipse is continuous, therefore Christ at the right hand of God continues the very work in heaven which he came here to do, extends it, and establishes its reality once and for all. Thus we may well think of the ascended Christ clothed, as it were, with the final revelation, the divine guarantee that what he had done as the incarnate Son of God on earth and in history, what he was, what he taught is secured for ever and ever, thus assuring us that what he was and taught and did on earth, was eternally of God. The saving work of the Lord Jesus Christ was and is the work of God's right hand! Thus we may think of the Ascension as a visible experience given to the disciples to assure them, as it continues to assure us, that in Christ Jesus and all that he was and did as Man, as Jesus Christ on earth, he for ever is and will be in and with God in Glory. That Christ is installed at the right hand of God means the perfect endorsement in heaven of his revealing and redeeming work on earth. It means that all that took place at the Cross and Christ's saving passion on earth is endorsed in heaven. It means that there is a perfect continuity between Jesus and God in this regard, for example, to the relations Jesus had with publicans and sinners! In Christ Jesus *we* are raised to the right hand of God, yes *we* unworthy as we are, we who are publicans and sinners and all unprofitable servants redeemed by Christ, are actually seated by the side of God in heaven in Christ - if so be that we have faith in him!

In the Old Testament dispensation God was ever 'far away' in many respects from the people of God. They did not have the revelation that we have been given in human form; they did not have the human contact with the Christ as the disciples had and as we may have through his Spirit in Christ. But in the New Testament dispensation, this ascension of Christ to the very right hand of the Divine Majesty on high means that the same relations that obtained between Christ and people on earth, intimate relations in which people might go straight to God our Father in heaven without intervention, now continues and prevails for us in heaven. We may all, sinners that we are, go to God through God himself, God-Man in Jesus Christ. There is a *MAN* in heaven today, one who knows all about us, one who suffered with us and for us, one who was tempted in all points as we are, and knows all our infirmities, trials and temptations, and who nevertheless came through them all and ascended to the very right hand of God the Father to be *our* representative before him for ever. Humanity and human relationships in and through Christ Jesus have been carried to the very seat of God and pronounced valid and glorious! That is part of the meaning of the Ascension. *Christ is our eternal High Priest in the heavens*! What Christ IS, God IS, because Christ IS God's Right Hand.

When we read in the Old Testament Scriptures about the making bare of the right hand of God, what else is that but Christ Jesus, incarnate Son of God? What else is God's Word and Act but Christ? The fact that Christ not only descended but ascended doubly perfects the guarantee that God is none other than just he whom we have come to know in the face of Jesus Christ! There is nothing at God's right hand which is not Christ! There is no work, no Word, no Will, no Judgement of God other than the act and word and will and judgement of the Lord Jesus Christ. There are no dark spots in God which lie hidden him and uncovered by the His Self-revelation of Christ. Christ *IS* God; and what Christ *IS*, God *IS*! What God *IS*, Christ *IS*! That is the way we are to understand the humiliation or descent of Christ together with the exaltation or ascent of Christ. At both ends, in his descent and his ascent, we have the perfect unshakable guarantee and revelation that God is really who he is to us in Jesus Christ and ever is in himself. There is nothing in God which is not like Christ, and indeed which is not Christ; for Christ *is* God's right hand; he *is* God in Act as well as in Word. The Ascension means therefore that the act of Christ actually is the very omnipotent action of God — and that there is no other power or "potence" in God which is not and is not revealed in Christ. Christ himself IS the "omni-potence" of God; the right hand of the Father! So far then for the purpose of the Lord God's Self-revelation in Christ.

The Ascension must also be understood in terms of the *redemption* through Christ. Karl Barth has pointed out (see, *Credo*, p. 110.) that we are to think here again of the *triplex munus*, that is, of Christ as "Prophet, Priest, and King". He writes: "The three offices of Christ differentiated by the older Dogmatics run into each other at this place so as to be almost indistinguishable. The Prophet (for what is the resurrection but the decisive act of Jesus Christ's prophecy?) announces the Priest (Who appears for Man before God, for God before man) in order to proclaim Him as such, *King*." If we can take for the moment the Teaching of Christ as interpreted in the light of the Resurrection as the Prophetic Work of Christ, and the Humiliation and the Cross and the Resurrection as the Priestly Work of Christ, then we may take the Ascension of Christ to be at the right hand of the Father on High as the office of Christ's Kingship, his Royal Priesthood. The Ascension means that in the work of redemption Christ is also King and assumes his Place as such in the midst of the Church or the assembly of the Redeemed. He is himself the King of the Kingdom, and as the King and Lord of heaven and earth is fulfilling the purpose of his redemption for the world. Christ Jesus crucified and risen is on the Throne — of that the Christian must never doubt. Jesus, yes, he Jesus, is now at the right hand of God holding the reins of the world in his hands, the hands that bore the imprint of the nails hammered into them on the cross.

We may not now understand all that happens and can happen in the world of today offers; it is black — and when has it been blacker than this very moment? (i.e. 1939) — but of this we are assured by the Ascension that the Lord Jesus Christ is reigning over the kingdoms and nations of the world and working out his redeeming purpose for redemption. He Reigns, he is King and Lord, and all things are made by him to work together for good to them that love the Lord and are called according to his purpose (Romans 8.28). The fact that it is Jesus of Nazareth, Jesus who suffered under Pontius Pilate, Jesus who was nailed to the Cross at Golgotha, who reigns there, the fact that his Ascension guarantees to us what his Incarnation revealed, that *God is like Christ*, and that *Christ is God* in his actuality among men, means that the hands which rule and guide the wheels of providence are in the hands that have been pierced and scarred at Calvary!

The Ruler and King of the Universe is none other than the Man who suffered on the Cross and descended to the uttermost depths in order to raise his redeemed people to the Highest. And having descended to the lowest he has now ascended to the highest that he might have with him those for whom he died rose again. Meantime as the enthroned Jesus of Bethlehem and Calvary, Christ is working his purposes out toward that final end. The means that the ascended and enthroned Lord Jesus uses for his work of redemption the Church on earth and in history, which as "the Body of Christ" throughout the centuries in its testimony and word, is as it were the visible `incarnation' of Christ on earth in lieu of his very Self, just as the Bible is, so to speak, the audible `incarnation' of his word in lieu of his living voice. It is through the Church in this age that Christ the King is fulfilling his purpose to actualise his redeeming purpose for all mankind, by renewing them and raising them to the very footstool of God, the Lord and Creator.

However, in order that they might be so raised, in order that they might be transformed in the power of the resurrection, they must meet the Man of the Cross; the One who still is the Crucified One though risen from the dead. And so at his ascension the Lord Jesus Christ departs, that is to say, he withdraws himself as the Risen One, for people may not know him enthroned at the right hand of God, who have not known him as the Christ who suffered and died for them. People may not now know him except as the Saviour of pardoned sinners proclaimed to all mankind through the Gospel, that through believing in him they may be saved and receive the quickening power of the Spirit, the very Spirit of Holiness by whom Jesus Christ himself had been raised from the dead.

This we must note, then, in the Ascension of Christ: that Christ removed himself from us in his visible form, having ascended to the right Hand of God in the heavens. That means of course that he is near us in a way that he never was before; that he is now on the throne triumphant over sin and evil. But it also means the removal of his "visible presence as Man" in order that people may know him, really know him as their Saviour and Lord. And for that reason he sends the Holy Spirit, his other Self as it were, his very own Presence mediated through the Spirit, even though he as the Risen Jesus is not visibly, physically present! That we must take seriously too, in order to understand the function of Christ in the Ascension.

The Ascension of Christ meant the end of direct revelation through the immediate incarnate presence of Jesus — there was one exception, that of St Paul who spoke of his experience as a kind of abortion, an event out of due time. But apart from that event on the Damascus Road, Christ does not now appear to people (normally at any rate) as he did to St Paul; he has really ascended on High! And so, let it be said that the time of the New Testament revelation is closed — closed at least till he comes again when knowing of Christ Jesus through faith will give way to sight! We are thus now living *Zwischen die Zeiten,* as Barth expressed it, "between the times", between the Ascension and the Second Advent of Christ. It is between these times that the Church has its work — that is to say, in an interim period! The Church as we know it on earth and in history is an interim affair! As such it is the company of pardoned sinners who are still sinners though called to be saints! This time in which the Church lives is a time of reprieve, a *Galgenfrist* or *Gnadenzeit* as our German speaking brethren call it. It is the day of Grace; the time granted in the forbearance of God to the world for repentance.

Just as before the Cross, as the Apostle said, God as it were "winked at" the sins that were past and did not mete out to the world the just judgement on sin, so after the Cross God winks at the sins of the world for a time in his gracious forbearance that they may still have time to repent: that is why the preaching of the Kingdom of God must ever be: "Repent for the Kingdom of God is at hand"! That must be our preaching in this age of Grace, for the Kingdom of God is coming; Christ the King now at the right hand of God will come to judge the quick and the dead! And then the Kingdom of God will come in apocalyptic power and glory and put an end to this "day of Grace", to this time of divine forbearance. Then no Hitlers will be able to rampage about with a loose rein. Meantime, however, the Devil still goes about like a roaring lion seeking whom he may devour. And meantime evil is allowed a "loose string", as it were, in that people everywhere may have the opportunity to repent and face up to the question of the Man on the Cross. However, the time will come just because Christ is the Right Hand of God, just because as he said all judgement had been committed unto him, when he will reprove and convict the world in righteousness and judgement! Until then the mission and work of Christ is that which Christ carries out through the Church which is his "Body" on earth to which he has committed the proclamation of the Gospel, and into whose mouth has been put the very Word of Christ, the Word of God. And so, in between the times, Christ has withdrawn himself visibly from men and women just in order that in this time of repentance they might be held by Christ at arm's length, so to speak, and given space and time to repent and decide for him; and decide for him again and again. Throughout their persistent disobedience Christ appeals to people - but that could not be the case were he to confront men and women everywhere now directly with the Majesty of his risen Glory; for then his very Advent Presence would decide things finally there and then once for all. Then the refusal of the Gospel message and the rejection Lord Jesus, the Lamb of God who came to away the sins of the world, would mean death and final judgement. The departure of Jesus Christ visibly from us, therefore, is thus the patience of his Grace. He has gone "away" to give the world time to think him over, time for decision; time to face up to the proclamation of the Gospel, the urgent message of the crucified Christ, before they meet him as the King in his risen power and Holiness.

It is to this end we are all called as Christians constrained in the life of Christ — constrained to be ambassadors, and knowing the terror of the Lord, to persuade men, as Paul said! It is our calling as Christians, as believers in Christ, to go forth into all the world and preach the Gospel to every creature in this age of Grace in order that all men may be confronted with the Christ and trust him and place their hope in him. For it is only in committing ourselves to Christ, and only if we suffer with Christ that we shall reign with him; it is only if we meet the Crucified Messiah here and now that we may meet him again in joy as the Glorious King! This is the dominating passion of Christ — that *all* people, men, women and children, may get to know him in love and mercy. It was for this reason that he came into the world, when in Judaea and Jerusalem and the zeal of God's House had eaten him up, as the Gospel record reports, in the days of his life on earth. He came to give his life a ransom for many, to minister the Gospel and not to be ministered unto. As Christians, as members of Christ's Body the Church, we may through union with him take on the same master-passion of the Crucified and Risen Lord, and make our own the same mind and purpose of the Christ who came to earth, the preaching of the Gospel that all men may repent and believe. "Believe on the Lord Jesus Christ and you shall be saved"! That is the urgent message of the Christian evangel, knowing that Christ is not the propitiation for our sins only but for the sins of the *whole* world. And this work, done truly, as the Apostles and disciples did it, is always done under the apprehension that the Kingdom of God draws nigh. That Christ is about to leave the Throne and descend to earth, to judge evil and exalt good. Unless the Church's preaching of the Gospel is realised to be the preaching of this interim period it will not have the proper urgency that it ought to have; it would not have behind it the constraint of the love of the crucified, risen and ascended Christ for the peoples and nations of the earth. We need to recapture the urgency of that Gospel commission again today — the urgency to evangelise the World!

2. The Lord Jesus will come again

He will come again, as the angels announced to the disciples, in like manner! He who ascended through the clouds of the heaven will return in glory in fulfilment of all his saving and redeeming life and work.; just as he was seen by the disciples to depart from them, so he will be seen again — that is the message of the second Advent! The second Advent means that the same Jesus who was born of Mary at Bethlehem, who was slain on the Cross, who rose bodily from the dead, will come back to us again in the same way as he was seen by the Disciples to ascend into heaven, that is, as the crucified and risen Lord. Yes, it is precisely Jesus of Nazareth exalted to the right hand of the Father who shall return — the Risen Jesus who is also the Lord Christ. Again here all our previous discussion about time and eternity, their relation to human conditions and those that transcend these, must all be recalled here; for it is the very same Jesus Christ who will return, the Christ who is Man, and who is Lord and King. Just as we thought of the Ascension in terms of the work of Christ so must we think here of the Return of Christ in relation to the same work of revelation and redemption, only this time bringing human history to its final consummation in a great act of crisis in which all time will be gathered up and be changed. The Coming of the King means that Kingdom of God will come and the interim time of the visible Church will cease — the time when we live "in the body of this death", as St. Paul called the present life on earth.

Here and now we still live in an evil time, the kingdom of darkness though we are not of it, having been redeemed from it. But the coming of Christ the King will translate us out of this kingdom into that of the Eternal Kingdom of God; in which there will be a new heaven and a new earth — and in which all the kingdoms of the earth will pass away, and Time or *Chronos* itself will pass away. (Rev. 10:6)

The Creed speaks of this coming of Christ as his coming to Judge the living and the dead. We may think of this in terms of the self-impartation of God and the self-assertion of God; that is to say, in terms of the redemption of God through the bestowal of himself in holy love and of the judgement of God through his holy self-affirmation, or the revelation of the Holiness of God before the earth, when at the end of time God appears to put away evil for ever. We have to think here of the final reaction of God, on the basis of the Cross, against sin. This is so because it is Christ who comes, the King from the right Hand of the Majesty on High, the one to whom has been committed all power, even all judgement, as is symbolised by his Ascension to the very *Throne* of God.

This self-bestowal and self-assertion of Christ which will take place in a final way at Christ's second coming will work differently with the people who have trusted the Crucified and risen Christ and with the people who have refused to surrender to the Cross - rather in accordance with Jesus' teaching as we read of it in the 25th Chapter of St Matthew's Gospel. But to both, believers and unbelievers, it will mean the consummation of their experience and relations with God. Just because Eternity has come into time into our human contingent world characterised by fallen time, just because even though Christ's bodily presence hid from the world, he works in and among men, women and children through the Eternal Spirit, the whole of this world defeated by the death and resurrection of Christ will be gathered up into crisis, into eschatological crisis in which there will be brought about a final settlement of all times! When Eternity enters time, Eternity with which there is no past, present, future, it must travel in and through time and gather it all up into a great catastrophic crisis in which time will pass away in its fallen condition, but judged, and slain, as it were, and a *new time* will be born in the Kingdom of God which has already invaded this present evil time in the presence of the Holy Spirit in the hearts of the believers, and who is as such the earnest of our inheritance, the pledge and *Arabbon* of our future life.

The discussion of this leads us into the realm of eschatology which we cannot properly discuss here. However we may think briefly of the relation of the Second Advent Christ, who will come in Person and power, to those who believe in the Lord Jesus Christ as their Saviour, and to those who refuse to believe in him.

a) *The relation of the coming of Christ to the faithful.*

This must be thought of in terms of revelation and redemption or in terms of the Lord's full self-bestowal and self-affirmation as the Saviour of the world. It is the final revelation of God's Love and Holiness in the Advent of Christ which completes the incarnate revelation, and indeed the redemption accomplished in Christ Jesus. That will not take place "until the consummation of all times that God has spoken of by his holy prophets" (χρόνων ἀποκατάστασις τῶν παντῶν, Acts 3.21), a consummation which the New Testament speaks of only in Apocalyptic terms and, as it were, with bated breath, but which will mean the finalisation of God's self-revelation in the Lord Jesus Christ, and of our own appropriation and experience of his salvation.

The consummation of faith does not lie completely within human knowledge and experience here and now. This is where we trespass on eschatology or the fulfilment of our hope in Christ which transcends earthly existence in the form we know it here and now. That future experience of the Christian hope, as far as we learn of it in the New Testament revelation, points transcendentally to a heavenly life and a resurrection or spiritual bodily existence with the Risen Jesus Christ. But nevertheless although that is in the future, and can therefore be spoken of only in broken apocalyptic figures or terms, yet those terms or figures must not be used in such a way as to destroy or invalidate the reality which they are meant to convey. The future reality of which they speak is continuous with the work of Christ on earth, with our knowledge and experience of him here and now to-day.

The coming again of the Lord Jesus Christ risen, triumphant and transcendent, means the end of faith in the form in which we have it now — for we shall see Christ himself face to face, as he is, and become like him. The coming of Christ will thus be a personal one in which we will be changed and the new life begotten in us through the Holy Spirit will be manifested in its glory and power as the Glory of Christ himself was only manifested at his resurrection from the dead. Christ Jesus to whom we are now united in the Spirit will come and consummate that union with his very Presence. But this revelation of Christ involves his self-assertion. You remember that in discussing the significance of his atoning life and death as the remission of our sins, we held to the fact that the forgiveness of sin here and now, real as it is in Christ, did not necessarily mean for us the removal here and now of penalties incurred by our sin in the enmeshment of sinners in this world of persons and nature.

But the return or coming of Christ again will mean the final judgment and doing away of our sin. It will means the self-assertion of the Holiness and Deity of Christ against all evil whatsoever, against all the evil effects of forgiven sin in penalty, disease, consequences etc. It means the actualisation of the final victory of God's love and grace over sin and guilt achieved at the Cross; for it means that sin which has been cancelled there is finally judged and put out of the way. The coming of Christ to the believer thus not only means the self-bestowal of God in complete love and revelation consummating the believer's union with Christ, but in that self-bestowal will mean the self-assertion of Christ against this body of sin which as yet is not redeemed. This old man of ours which we carry about with us every day, says St. Paul, like a corpse tied to us, is still here and it must be severed from us. Our independent selfish personalities which have been crucified with Christ in our surrender to him must be dealt with in radical fashion. That is called the final judgement for we must all appear before the throne of God. There, however, the believer has nothing to fear from this judgement, for it is the act of the tender hand of God separating us from the evil consequences of our sins and finally preparing us for eternal life in fellowship with himself. That may occur through death and resurrection of the body, Paul points out, or it may occur through a transformation of the living who meet the advent Christ. At all events believing people who have put their trust in Jesus Christ as their Saviour and Lord, will have nothing to fear at the final judgement for the coming of Christ is and will be the vindication of believers and the defeat of all that is against them in the way of evil and sin in this world. Thus what apprehend to Christ who carried our humanity and our flesh to the cross will happen to us in the mercy of God. We cannot think of this as a long purgation as the Roman Catholics do; for we are already forgiven and there is no sacrifice for sin apart from the Cross — the atonement of Christ avails completely for us all now and for ever. At death and resurrection or when we meet the advent Christ as King we will be transformed "in the twinkling of an eye", as Paul puts it, into the likeness of Christ Jesus. We are fully and finally reconciled and our adoption as sons of God in which we partake now gain through the indwelling of the Holy Spirit is perfectly consummated in every way — and we shall live for ever with God in glory.

b) *The relation of the Advent Christ to the faithless.*

This is commonly called "the last judgement"; the coming of Christ to judge "the quick and the dead", to judge sin and the sinners who finally resist him and who persist in their resistance — that is the sin against the Holy Spirit of which our Lord spoke. It involves again the self-revelation of God and the self-assertion of God. That is, both of these merge in the final self-revelation or self-affirmation of God in Christ Jesus toward recalcitrant sinners. When the Holy Lord God bestows his presence to the sinner who is yet unforgiven, he or she is judged and damned. With the Second Coming of Christ the day of Grace is at an end — and the life and mission of the Church whose charter is the evangelisation of the world in this day and generation will be consummated. With the final coming of Christ the time for people's decision is at an end; and it is God's time for decision when all nations and peoples will be called before him. Then the final self-revelation God in the Lord Jesus Christ will mean the Apocalypse of the Wrath of God; that is the resistance of God which his Holiness as Holiness cannot but take against unrepentant sinners. This a dreadful reality, one which we can speak about only with bated breath and hesitation. It is just because the Kingdom of God *is* coming but when we do not know, just because there is a doom approaching all those who refuse to believe the Gospel and take up the Cross to which Jesus calls us all, the message or proclamation of which that Christ calls us all to gird up our loins and preach: "Repent for the Kingdom of God is at hand!" Therefore let us gird up our strength, throw ourselves wholeheartedly into the mission of Christ, and preach the Gospel while it is yet day, for the night comes when no man can work.